The CROWDED Desert

The CROWDED Desert

The Kalahari Gemsbok National Park

Wilf Nussey

WILLIAM WATERMAN PUBLICATIONS

For Doreen

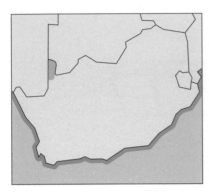

William Waterman Publications
A Division of William Waterman Publications
(Pty) Ltd
PO Box 5091
Rivonia 2128
ISBN 0-9583751-4-3
© Wilf Nussey 1993
First Published 1993
Book design: Photoprint
Typesetting and Reproduction: Photoprint
Cover design by Peter Stuckey
Printed and bound by CTP Book Printers,
Cape Town

Frontispiece: The Kalahari Gemsbok National
Park is aptly named after its commonest and
most distinctive large antelope, the gemsbok or
oryx gazella whose straight horns and black-
masked white faces are unmistakeable.
Anthony Bannister – ABPL.

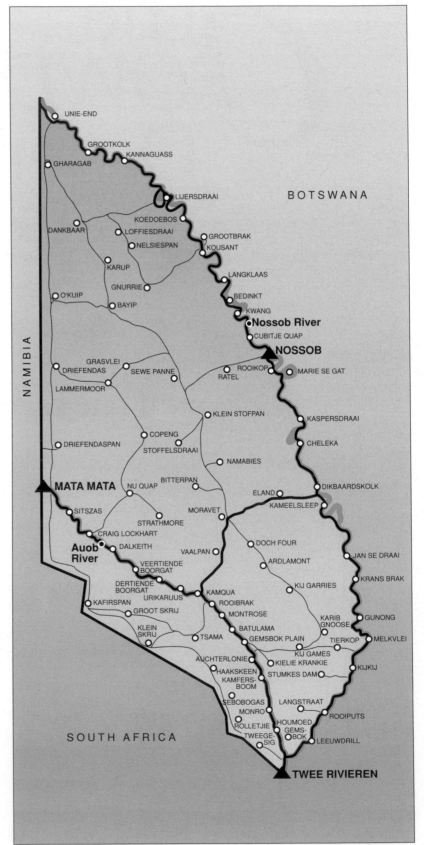

Contents

Introduction

The long, lonely lines of dunes in the south-west Kalahari – a motionless sea of sand.
Anthony Bannister – ABPL.

*i*ts impact on the senses is so striking; it is so alien, that it stamps an indelible impression on the memory.

White, blinding sunlight floods down from an infinite dome of clean cobalt sky. The horizon for the full 360 degrees all around is low, flat and bare. Long monotonous vistas of sand stained bold red, pink and grey stretch endlessly, speckled with lonely, haggard trees.

Its barrenness is deceptive. Suddenly life appears with startling clarity – a single animal, a herd, or a flock of birds. The silence is overpowering, until abruptly there is a bird call, the far-away yap of a jackal, or the snort of a buck.

The contrast of colour and emptiness; of beauty and severity; of desolation and life, is powerful and disturbing.

This is the enigmatic world of the remote Kalahari Gemsbok National Park (KGNP), the largest game reserve in Southern Africa.

Covering more than 36 000 square kilometres of a distant corner of the Kalahari Desert, an area shared by South Africa and Botswana, it is a place that challenges the emotions to the extreme.

Underlying its stark scenic drama is the constant awareness that this *is* the legendary Kalahari Thirstland. The vast expanse of flat sandy plateau has lured many adventurers to their deaths by heat and thirst. The only people who have learned to live in complete harmony with its harshness are the Bushmen (San).

The name *Kalahari* is derived from the SeTswana word *Kgalagadi* which has been given several interpretations, the likeliest being 'the land that has dried up' or 'the dry land'.

And yet it sustains a remarkable abundance of life. In the Kalahari Gemsbok National Park fifty-eight species of mammals have been recorded, fifty-five species of reptiles and more than 260 species of birds. It vegetation looks meagre, especially in very dry times, but scores of plant species have been recorded. It has many kinds of insects, spiders, scorpions and other invertebrates but just how many is not yet known – research is still incomplete.

The other South African reserves can boast a greater range of fauna and flora, or more varied environments, or both. This park, however, exists specifically to preserve a segment of the extraordinary Kalahari Desert and fills an exclusive place in the catalogue of conservation. Although it is so stunningly different, it is aesthetically and scientifically on a par with such renowned parks as the Kruger National Park, Namibia's Etosha and Zimbabwe's Hwange.

Unique is a word devalued by over-use but it is a justified description of this park for several reasons.

First, it is an international game park – not one park but two, straddling about 250 kilometres of border between two countries, South Africa and Botswana. It is run as an integrated conservation area. On the South African side is the 10 000 square-kilometre Kalahari Gemsbok National Park and on the Botswana side the 26 000 square-kilometre Gemsbok National Park, including the small Mabuasehube game reserve. The entire 36 200 square-kilometre area (which for convenience will be called the KGNP) is one of the biggest game reserves in the world.

It is a model of international co-operation in conservation. Administration of the KGNP is the responsibility of South Africa's National Parks Board of Trustees and is carried out by the park's warden in collaboration with Botswana rangers. Poachers caught in Botswana, for example, appear before a Botswana court and those caught in the South African sector are dealt with by a South African court.

Tourists travelling along the park's Nossob River find themselves moving willy-nilly from country to country because the road meanders back and forth across the border, the middle of the riverbed.

That there is no fence is a pragmatic recognition that wildlife is contained not by political boundaries but by physical barriers.

Second, unlike any other reserve – certainly in Africa – it is a largely self-contained ecological unit that needs very little management.

Third, all living things in it, plant and animal, share a remarkable ability to survive severe aridity and some have evolved extreme physical adaptations to retain moisture.

The KGNP owes its birth to concern by local settlers in the early 1900s about the growing slaughter of wild animals and to the initiative of the then Minister of Lands, Mr Piet Grobler – the same man whose determination finally consolidated and gave parliamentary protection to the famed Kruger Park.

The British government followed his lead by proclaiming an adjacent park in the then Bechuanaland Protectorate which, after it became independent as Botswana, expanded the area to its present size.

It lies in the south-western corner of the Kalahari Desert, spanning the northernmost tip of the Cape Province and the south-western

Right: The wind-rippled desert sand is the 'newspaper' of the Park, a chronicle of the movements of many creatures that stays until the wind sweeps its pages clean again. These tracks and tail mark are probably those of lizards.
Anthony Bannister – ABPL.

Far Right: The black-breasted snake eagle with its mesmerising yellow stare earns its name by feeding largely on snakes.
Lorna Stanton – ABPL.

Flowers appear magically in the desert soon after rain showers, bringing splashes of colour to the uniformity.
Left: Striga Gesnerioides.
Right: Cleome Angustifolia.
National Parks Board.

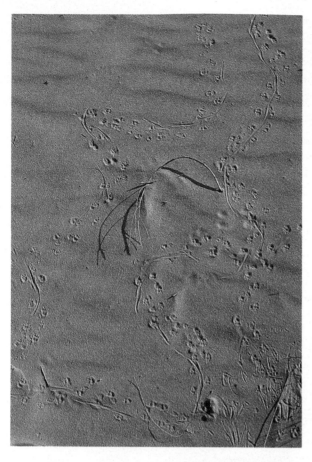

point of Botswana – an irregular slab of territory whose western boundary is the straight-line north-south border of Namibia and which extends for roughly 200 kilometres at its deepest and widest points. It is a small part of the entire desert, which covers two-thirds of Botswana and reaches into Namibia as well as South Africa.

The park has had mixed fortunes, having experienced poaching, opposition by settlers who lusted for its land, and neglect until after World War II. But its existence was never seriously challenged, probably because it was so remote. Few people had ever heard of it and it cost taxpayers nothing. Furthermore, because of the astonishing dedication of a singular Huguenot family, it was protected and nurtured for generations.

They are the Le Riche family, whose history is so intertwined with the park's since it was established on 3 July 1931, that they have become inseparable. Every park chief since then has been a Le Riche as control was passed on by the National Parks Board from brother to brother; to son to brother, down to the present warden, Elias le Riche.

The first Le Riche, Johannes, tackled this forbidding, virtually trackless wilderness with one assistant and a donkey-cart. That he endured at all is a tribute to his doggedness.

Given the much greater size of the park today and the greatly increased responsibilities, Warden Elias le Riche seems not very better off: to help him he has only three rangers and fifteen assistant rangers among a total staff of seventy-three including administrative, technical and tourist officers. Kruger, by comparison, has nearly 4 000 personnel, though there the burden of management, research and tourism is far greater.

He is, however, able to draw on the large staff of experts and on the equipment and the expanding store of scientific knowledge of the National Parks Board, which in the past ten to fifteen years, has been giving more and more attention to this lonely, neglected ward.

So have the public. The misconception that the KGNP can be visited only in muscular four-wheel drive is steadily fading as more people go there in small cars – albeit with some care, especially on the last several hundred kilometres of bone-rattling dirt road to the park's gate. Now there is the alternative of flying in and hiring transport in the park.

In 1954 a dribble of 515 tourists came. In 1988 there were 31 000 – close to its maximum annual capacity, and in 1991-92 the numbers dropped to 17 823 The low rate is not because only the South African sector is routinely open to visitors (the rest being a closed wildlife refuge) or because it has about 500 kilometres of road making a mere 0,8 per cent of the entire park accessible, or because of its fierce summer heat and knifing winter cold.

By far the commonest buck in the Park is the legendary springbok, which once migrated in the millions. These grazing peacefully on a river bank present a typically Kalahari scene.
Anthony Bannister – ABPL.

It is because, in spite of the desert's apparent imperviousness, its ecosystem is delicate and finely balanced.

This is not a true desert by the popular concept of a barren, waterless wasteland where little life can be sustained. The Kalahari gets an average of between 150 mm and 500 mm of rain a year, the fall diminishing from north-east to south-west.

It is actually a semi-arid savannah; grassland sprinkled with shrub and trees which in the south-west, including the KGNP, gives way to a huge region of long parallel rows of bright-red, sinuous sand dunes rising some fifteen metres above the valleys or 'streets' between them.

It gained its menacing reputation because it is a world of formidable extremes. Rainfall is so erratic that in some years parts of, and sometimes the whole of, the Kalahari get no rain at all. In other years it is drenched – so heavily that a Botswana government official once boasted that he used a canoe where normally his truck raised dust.

Temperatures are equally extreme. The lowest night temperature recorded in the KGNP was –11,3°C. The highest day temperature was 42°C and that was in the shade. In the sun (and at midday there is little else) the temperature rises much higher: on the surface of the sand it reaches 70°C but can be more than 20°C lower in the shade of a bush. It can vary by as much as 30°C in twenty-four hours.

It is the effect of these radical fluctuations that makes the Kalahari and thus the KGNP so special. Heat and drought have wonderfully

focused the overriding attention of the animals on water which is often hidden – moisture in the ground and the air, in stalks, leaves and fruit, and in flesh and intestines.

The pyramid of life is elegantly revealed here. Many creatures are able to survive for long periods, some indefinitely, without drinking while they can ingest moisture from their food. Moisture absorbed by plants from earth or air is sufficient for the insects and birds and animals which feed upon the plants. They in turn contain enough moisture to sustain the other insects and birds and animals which eat them.

When the desert becomes too dry, as it often does, all creatures must take special action to survive.

One of the experts at this is the animal after which the park was named – the gemsbok or Southern African oryx, *Oryx gazella gazella*. It epitomises the challenge of the Kalahari.

Gemsbok are strikingly impressive buck with their black and white masked faces, burly bodies and long straight horns that lions treat with great discretion. Their most distinctive characteristics, however, are invisible.

They are highly selective feeders that both browse and graze and they concentrate on vegetation with a high moisture content, especially in dry times.

Their digestive systems extract and store more moisture from their food than those of perhaps any other animal.

They have a remarkable ability to allow their body temperatures to rise well above the ambient temperature, even above levels fatal to most animals, to avoid having to cool off by sweating, which wastes moisture. Most astonishing of all, in extreme heat they can cool down the flow of hot blood from their hearts to their heads to prevent their brains from cooking.

Several other species have similar or identical mechanisms but none is as efficient a water-conserver as the superbly specialised gemsbok.

For many creatures, particularly the larger animals such as eland, gemsbok, wildebeest, hartebeest and springbok, the ultimate response to shortages of food and water is migration.

It is this pattern of behaviour that gives special importance to the KGNP. To understand it, it should be seen against the desert background.

The regular ravages of drought on their habitats oblige them to trek sporadically in search of fresh forage, sometimes for long distances.

There are several different migration patterns within the whole Kalahari Desert. In the south-west, where the park lies, animals tend to move anti-clockwise, travelling slowly north-east in the summer in a large loose circle and returning south-west in the winter.

Entering its sandbank nest, a swallow-tailed bee-eater shows why it has that name.
Joan Ryder – ABPL.

Far Right: If the fork-tailed drongo perched on the branch looks bemused and weary, it is because the huge chick whose voracious appetite she is trying to satisfy is not her own but a cuckoo.
Clem Haagner – ABPL.

The small-spotted genet – seen here unusually in full daylight – is a night hunter of small animals, birds and insects and in camps becomes so bold it wanders among people in search of scraps.
Clem Haagner – ABPL.

Extreme climatic conditions cause extreme patterns of animal migration. When food and water are abundant they breed prolifically. If a harsh period follows and they have consumed all the available food and water, or the air becomes so dry that the vegetation loses all its moisture, they are forced to move.

Such conditions caused immense migrations in the past before the animals began to be blocked by settlers, farms and fencing and the depredations of hunters. In those times animals moved freely in an area stretching more than 1 000 kilometres from the Okavango Swamps south to the Orange River and even beyond, and to the Atlantic shore in the west.

Springbok migrations were the largest of all the land animals. Less than a century ago people were witness to teeming herds of them trekking south and west – literally scores of millions on the move, close-packed, passing for days, eating and drinking the land bare, sweeping livestock and even lions before them, and leaving a path of devastation behind. Settlers shot them by the thousand, at first for meat and for the sport, and then in desperation to try to protect their grazing, livestock and water. Eventually starvation took its toll and left behind small pockets of springbok.

Treks of such tragic magnitude are a thing of the past but there are still periodic migrations in the Kalahari equalled in size only by those in East Africa's Serengeti Plains.

Ordinarily the park holds some 3 000 to 4 000 eland, the largest of all antelope with a weight of up to 900 kilograms, 2 000 to 3 000 wildebeest and the same number of hartebeest, about 25 000 springbok, nearly 10 000 gemsbok and some 500 kudu – in addition to about fifty leopards, the same number of cheetah and some 100-150 lions.

Migrations swell this buck population up to fifty times. In 1979 and 1985 the KGNP experienced huge treks of as many as 150 000 blue wildebeest, 15 000 eland and 6 000 hartebeest.

Park Warden Elias le Riche recalls that when he was a small boy travelling with his father, who was then the warden, they came across a moving herd of 15 000 springbok, ten kilometres deep. 'We stood still for one and a half hours until the last buck went past.' Three years later his father found another herd which took three days to pass by.

In 1979 an aerial survey revealed an estimated 130 000 blue wildebeest on the move in the park inside an area of just over 2 000 square kilometres: 269 herds of up to 750 animals. The figure could have been as high as 170 000.

In the 1984/85 rain season falls were so weak and scattered that throughout the Kalahari forage was severely depleted and surface water in the natural pans dried up. Moisture-rich tubers and fruits that animals usually resort to, failed drastically.

In 1985 Warden le Riche and his rangers watched about 150 000 wildebeest, 15 000 eland and the 6 000 hartebeest in addition to flocks of ostriches stream in from the north-east. Despite the elands' extraordinary capacity to survive for long periods without water, they were so thirsty they forgot their fear of man and drank water from a plastic jug held by a photographer, Lorna Stanton.

The wildebeest literally piled up at the park's waterholes, trampling each other to reach the life-giving fluid, draining the supply, and dying in large numbers. They emptied the drinking places so fast that the wind-driven borehole pumps could not cope, putting other animals in danger, and the park staff had to hurriedly install temporary power pumps to suck out more water.

Most of the wildebeest and hartebeest went right through the park southwards, leaving a trail of carcasses. Lions were so stuffed with food they simply lazed alongside their latest kills and ignored easy meat.

The eland travelled west to the border fence between the park and Namibia, which turned them south. Of that entire stretch of border, park officials wrote: '... the soil was trampled to snuff. Over the whole distance the hoofprints of the animals could be seen lying across each other, like the prints of cattle in a kraal'.

Just south of the park the surviving eland turned east and vanished back into the depths of Botswana.

Exactly how many trekking animals died is not known but on the park's few roads alone the rangers counted the jawbones of 1 600 wildebeest. The toll was certainly many thousands more.

The irony of the 1985 trek was that the animals had plenty of forage available. But it was bone dry – so dry grass crumbled to the touch – and they could not gain moisture from it or digest it without water.

Such migrations would take a more devastating toll and seriously endanger the survival of the trekking species were the park not so large thanks to its international structure. It is that alone which makes it a viable ecological unit.

The Botswana side consists of some dunes but mostly savannah with a good cover of scrub and trees by Kalahari standards, into which animals move when rain generates fresh food there. The South African side is sparsely covered dune country creased by two usually dry rivers, the Auob and the Nossob, to which the animals have been coming since time immemorial for forage and moisture when the land to the north and east is sere and bare.

Neither part could exist without the other.

So naturally does the KGNP's life ebb and flow between the two, that Warden le Riche and his rangers need hardly ever interfere. The culling of animals – essential in Kruger and some other parks to keep populations within the limits their habitats can sustain – has never been done here. Nature does its own culling, winnowing the weak from the strong more effectively than man can.

Wildlife management in the KGNP essentially involves keeping its more than 100 boreholes and windpumps in good repair, maintaining the fence along the Namibian border which is electrified to prevent game breaking through, regularly patrolling for poachers, keeping a count of the larger animals wherever possible, and sometimes shepherding back lions that have wandered into neighbouring farms – a chore not without a degree of excitement.

The boreholes, from which water is pumped into fibreglass tanks (it resists corrosion better than iron or cement) and from there into shallow drinking troughs or 'cribs', are the subject of much debate among National Parks Board (NPB) conservationists.

Purists argue that there should be none because animals were migrating to the Auob and Nossob valleys long before the first boreholes were drilled in the early part of this century, and their existence interferes with a natural cycle. Others say the boreholes attract permanent populations of animals that damage the surrounding environment by constant use.

The counter-argument is that boreholes are necessary not merely to attract wildlife to the tourist sector of the KGNP, but also because the Namibia border fence, farming and other human activities now prevent that wildlife from migrating further in search of food and water.

There is general agreement that the boreholes that produce water so brack or salty that animals cannot drink it, should be closed. As to the fate of the rest, hopefully scientific research will come up with a compromise.

Research is one thing the KGNP needs much more of. It offers huge scope for scientific research of all kinds but little has been done, compared to other parks, because of its remoteness.

From the outset the park has had so few staff they have had their hands full simply running it. They could do little more than record their personal observations and experiences. Administration leaves Warden le Riche little time to use his graduate skills in zoology and botany.

The first scientific report was made in 1954, its twenty-third year, by A M Brynard, later Director of the National Parks Board. One of his main conclusions was that far more investigation was necessary under many disciplines.

This view was echoed in 1983 when the NPB held a symposium on the KGNP's ecosystem although, by then, information was being garnered on many basics such as its geology, soils, water resources, fauna, flora, food and climate.

A great deal of information was gathered by professional research officers appointed to the KGNP from 1972, the first being Dr Michael 'Gus' Mills who studied predator-prey relationships and large herbivore ecology and who also specialised in his studies in hyena behaviour.

Now the park is at last receiving the attention it deserves. An increasing stream of scientific pilgrims from many universities and institutions study such intriguing esoterica as parasites in the blood of raptors, tenebrionid beetles, the metabolism of antlions, vegetation dynamics and leopard behaviour.

One man who has visited the KGNP many times over the years is the Chairman of the NPB, Dr Fritz Eloff, retired Professor of Zoology at the University of Pretoria, who has intimately studied the activities of the renowned Kalahari lions.

At the 1983 symposium he said:

There are few areas in the world which contain so many exciting components as the Kalahari ecosystem: the historical and alas diminishing migratory movements of its animals, its remarkable sand dunes, its survival problems, its underground plant food, its underground animal community, its remarkable micro-ecosystems, its primitive territorial man ... This is how we must regard the Kalahari: one ecosystem, one giant organism, the parts of which compete with each other but also live together in harmony.

His definition is as valid for the ordinary wildlife enthusiast as it is for the specialised scientist. The KGNP is an entirely captivating, often intimidating, but always challenging, experience. It offers a rare view of nature stripped to the basics of survival by a unique and demanding environment.

One of the many alkaline pans sprinkling the desert, this one with an access road to a wind-pump and waterhole at its edge.
Anthony Bannister – ABPL.

CHAPTER ONE

Past, Present ...

*t*he history of the Kalahari, the unique desert-yet-not-a-desert of which the KGNP is a small part, can in fact be traced to pre-history. The Kalahari Gemsbok National Park, today, is itself a very small remnant of a vast true desert that more than 200 million years ago covered most of the ancient supercontinent of Gondwanaland before it began its infinitely slow division into what are today Africa, South America, Antarctica, Australia, India and Madagascar.

After the separation of the land masses, in the last 100 million years, powerful geological and climatic forces slowly smoothed the jagged face of the young continent of Africa, grinding down the rock into pebbles, gravel and sand. Successive ages of ice, drenching tropical rains and intense aridity continued the erosion.

In a huge, shallow depression in the continent's south, enormous volumes of sand were gathered by a wind process that lasted more than sixty million years and was completed only a few million years ago. Rivers, lakes and wind dumped the sand in deposits up to several hundred metres deep and randomly sculpted it into the plains, dunes and pans we see today, pierced here and there by rocky outcrops.

Thus was created what many geologists believe to be the largest single expanse of sand on earth, the Kalahari Sand Beds, an irregularly shaped area stretching northward from near the Orange River in South Africa, virtually covering Botswana, reaching into Zimbabwe and Namibia and extending through Angola and Zambia into Zaire, the Congo and Gabon.

Today much of the ancient parent desert is invisible, scoured away by water or overgrown with vegetation as the climate has changed and the earth's crust has shifted and settled.

The modern Kalahari Desert lies mainly in Botswana, blanketing about two-thirds of its 582 000 square kilometres and extending west into the eastern edge of Namibia, east into Zimbabwe and south into the northern part of South Africa's Cape Province.

The dunes that are so characteristic of the KGNP are found in several other parts of the Kalahari. There are two more large dunefields

13

in north-western and eastern Botswana that overlap into the neighbouring states. The dunes lie in rippling rows that may stretch for hundreds of kilometres, more or less parallel but sometimes meeting in confusing overlaps of sand. Elsewhere they are white or cream in colour but in the KGNP they are in the red range of the spectrum from pale pink to bright vermilion because of the minutely thin coating of iron oxide on the sand grains.

In two places in the park, unfortunately inaccessible to visitors, there are 'irregular' dunefields whose creation is a mystery – roughly circular blotches of paler dunes like volcanic bubblings in a solidified sea. Roughly a kilometre in diameter, they stand conspicuously out of the linear dunes and the sand within them is heaped into a completely haphazard jumble of crests and troughs. Geologists deduce that they, like the other dunes, are aeolian – that is, formed by the winds – but have no idea how or why they occur.

The Kalahari dunes no longer move, unlike the sickle-shaped 'walking' or barchan dunes on the gravel plains in the Namib Desert a few hundred kilometres east, on the Atlantic coast. Those in the KGNP are fossil dunes, formed by winds many thousands and possibly millions of years ago, that are now static.

Their size – roughly between ten metres and twenty metres high and spaced about one to two kilometres apart – and volume of sand indicate prehistoric gales of almighty power. There is no accurate way of gauging that force but one pointer to it is the gigantic dunes at Tsossus Vlei in the Namib. The largest rise to 300 metres and today only the top metre or two of their crests is moved by the wind.

Scientists have calculated that to have piled the sand to that height, the wind velocity must have been in the region of 1 200 kilometres an hour. It would have been considerably less in the Kalahari but still phenomenally strong by modern standards.

Underneath the Kalahari sand are the Karoo Beds, ancient sedimentary rock formations which further south in the Cape, where they are exposed, have yielded the world's richest crop of prehistoric reptile fossils including some of the transitionary stages between reptile and mammal.

The concealing carpet of sand makes geological investigation of the Kalahari extremely difficult and for many years it was largely hypothetical until the discovery of alluvial diamonds generated intensive prospecting, including the drilling of many boreholes to pinpoint and define the kimberlite pipes from which they came.

Botswana now has three rich diamond mines, one of them the second largest in the world, and prospecting continues but the overall geological research is far from complete.

Hopefully it will one day resolve the mystery of what happened to the rivers. The Auob, the Nossob, and the Molopo into which these two rivers run on their way to the Orange River, were obviously once very much larger than they are now as their width and depth reveal. In places the Nossob's bed is more than a kilometre wide. The same holds for other dry rivers in the desert.

German researchers, in the days when Namibia was German South West Africa, believed that the Okavango and Kuando/Chobe rivers rising in Angola once fed water to the Kalahari rivers via the complex network of waterways that is now the Okavango Swamps/Chobe/Zambezi system – possibly through Lake Ngami which has dried up within recent history. Water might also have come via the drainage network that now ends in the huge, sometimes full, Etosha Pan in the north of Namibia, they surmised.

Another theory is that the water came from that system to the Limpopo and into an enormous lake, almost an inland sea, in the middle of the Kalahari which in turn fed the Orange through the Molopo while the Auob and Nossob gathered their waters from the Namibia catchment area.

Certainly there is evidence for all these postulations ... but why did the rivers dry up?

Two things clearly happened. One was the successive climatic phases of thousands of years which alternatively drenched and desiccated the region. In the wet periods the rivers flowed full and strong and scoured out deep beds. In the dry periods like the present one, their dwindling flow was unable to carry away the silt and dumped it, gradually clogging their beds. Windblown sand filled them further. This is what has happened to the Nossob River between Kaspersdraai and Union's End.

The other, geologists have discovered, was shifts in the earth's crust. These tectonic movements, as they are called, caused the land surface to rise in two places, one in the north-east of present-day Botswana and one in the south-west. So slight that they are unnoticeable to the untrained eye, the low watersheds are nevertheless high enough to stop the flow of water through the Kalahari to the Orange River. The rivers choked and died.

Man, it is now known, has been part of the Kalahari scene for a very long time. Archaeology is continually uncovering new evidence that enriches the saga of his activities and alters old theories. Early, Middle and Late Stone Age hand axes, scrapers and other artefacts dating back possibly more than 200 000 years have been found and ongoing studies of this treasure-house of pre-history indicate a considerable traffic of various peoples in the Kalahari during the past 3 000 or so years.

It was a very slow traffic: the gradual influx over generations of black peoples from the north and east and the movements of the original inhabitants overland, in later centuries, by visiting traders and perhaps slavers, as evidenced by the discovery of cowrie shells and glass beads – currencies of those times. Wetter conditions made the desert more attractive and accessible than it is now.

Before the coming of the black peoples the Kalahari was the domain of the San people – the Bushmen and their forebears. There are no Bushmen left in the KGNP today and only some 60 000 in Botswana and Namibia, very few of whom still live in the wild.

How long they have been there is difficult to state with certainty. Science is still investigating; perhaps it is for tens of thousands of years; perhaps much longer or less. The Kalahari was certainly not their only habitat; Bushmen lived all over Southern Africa in all kinds of environments.

People of the Bakgalagadi tribe were probably the first blacks to drift into the present-day Kalahari Desert from the north. After them came a number of Batswana tribes, now the dominant population of Botswana.

The several different ethnic groups appear to have co-existed although the Bakgalagadi enslaved Bushmen and were themselves made serfs by the Tswanas. Only the Bushmen lived by hunting and were in harmony with their desert environment; the others mainly farmed livestock and raised some crops, which closed off most of the desert to them. Wildlife therefore survived and thrived in its vastnesses – until the advent of organised ranching, fences and guns.

The first white man known to have seen the Kalahari came there in 1760. He was Jacobus Coetse Janze, a Dutchman from the Cape who coined the name *Kameeldoornboom* for the tree that giraffes like to feed on, the camelthorn. Who first penetrated as far as what was to become the KGNP is not known but the first whites to reach the nearby Kuruman River, which runs into the Molopo from the east, were commissioners P J Truter and Dr W Somerville sent by the British colonial administration in Cape Town to buy cattle from the black tribes in the north.

On the way they met William Edwards and Jan Kok of the London Missionary Society and travelled together to what is now the small town of Kuruman.

Edwards and Kok tried unsuccessfully to start a mission at Kuruman. Later when the mission was established, it became for ever associated with two of Africa's most redoubtable characters, Dr Robert Moffat and the man who married his daughter Mary, the renowned Dr David Livingstone.

The history of the KGNP is synonymous with that of the Le Riche family, rugged people of Huguenot stock who are to the park what Colonel James Stevenson-Hamilton was to the Kruger National Park: midwife, mentor, protector and moulder of its character. Since its inception in 1931 there has always been a Le Riche in charge of the park – four so far from two generations.

The Northern Cape was wild and hazardous country in the last century, the homes of Namas, Griquas and other peoples, elusive Bushmen, Batswana tribes, a few intrepid missionaries, hunters and traders, and rogues escaping justice like Upington's notorious Scotty Smith. Distances were great, water was scarce and it was hot except in mid-winter when the temperature fell below zero at night.

Into this land there came in the early 1880s the first Le Riche, Christoffel. Like many other settlers of Cape Dutch and Huguenot descent, he had quit the beautiful Cape Peninsula to shake off British colonial rule and seek his fortune in the vast African hinterland. After a sojourn in the Orange Free State he moved to the diamond-mining town of Kimberley from where he made long trading treks as far afield as the north of South West Africa, which Germany occupied in 1884.

It was on these trips that he was captivated by the Kalahari, and also by trading prospects among the San people settled along the South West African border.

With his wife Martie and two small children he moved again, this time in wagons loaded with trade goods to the hamlet of Rietfontein on the South West Africa border about fifty kilometres south of Twee Rivieren, where the Rhenish Church had opened a mission station.

There the Le Riche family finally settled, prospered from their trading post and bought land. Among their three sons and two daughters were Johannes, born in 1899, and Josef, born in 1904.

The South African Anglo-Boer War came and went. Father Christoffel stayed at his trading post and under the cover of his licence as a trader supplied arms and ammunition brought through South West Africa to the Boer forces – once narrowly escaping a British firing squad in the process thanks to fast talking by Martie.

The dust of that war had hardly settled before another loomed: World War I. Suddenly the neighbouring German colonisers just across the border became the potential enemy.

Foreseeing the prospect of conflict with South West Africa, the South African government quickly had a number of boreholes drilled along the Auob River to supply its troops with water should they invade by that route.

Guards were hired to look after the boreholes, mainly poorer people from the local community. Each was allowed to settle next to his borehole with his family and keep livestock to supplement their meagre pay.

In the event, the successful South African invasion of South West Africa went by other routes and the Auob was never used. The half-forgotten borehole guards stayed on and used mud and wattle or the local calcrete stone to build small houses and sheep and goat pens, some of which can still be seen on the east bank of the Auob.

After the war the whole of what is now the KGNP was carved up into farms by the Scottish surveyor Roger 'Malkop' Jackson who left his mark by giving curious Scottish names to the boreholes there.

Six of the farms of between 10 000 and 13 000 hectares were bought but not occupied by whites before the government decided that the region should rather be settled by Coloured people. The British authorities had already settled small groups of Coloureds on the Nossob River's east bank in Bechuanaland (Botswana) between Rooiputs and its confluence with the Auob. The ruins of an old house still remain at Rooiputs.

Another sizeable Coloured community lived in the Mier settlement area south and west of the confluence of the Nossob and Auob.

With the passing of the years Christoffel became a pillar of the local community and the owner of several farms. He closed down his trading business in 1917 to settle on the farm Saulstraat. His sons also farmed and his daughter Lulu married Willie Rossouw who came from Montagu in the Cape. They settled on their farm Loubos (colloquial for Leeubos – lion bush), where she started a school that was the precursor of the present one at Askham.

Another well-known personality in the Northern Cape's Gordonia district at that time was Pieter 'Mof' de Villiers who, as inspector of lands based at Upington, came to know the desert so intimately he was known as the 'king of the Kalahari'. These two men – Rossouw and De Villiers – are the true fathers of the KGNP.

In the late 1920s some farmers in the region were becoming deeply disturbed by the growing impact of hunting on the wildlife which had always been an integral part of their surroundings.

The Great Depression was collapsing economies worldwide and South Africa was no exception. The people of the Northern Cape, where farming was at best a precarious business, felt the impact profoundly. Many had to hunt to live – white and Coloured alike – while the black people hunted as they always had done.

Most of the settlers on the Nossob bank and in the Mier area were full-time hunters anyway, their 'farming' consisting of a few scraggly goats. They shot not only to eat but for the market in biltong and hides.

The slaughter was fast becoming an annual massacre. Willie Rossouw and Piet de Villiers decided to do something about it. Both were friends of the Minister of Land, Piet Grobler, one of the three fathers of the Kruger National Park and the driving force behind the National Parks Act which was passed in 1926. Rossouw and De Villiers decided to play upon the Minister's well-known soft spot for

Flowers of the duiweltjies plat-doring provide a carpet of colour in the desert.
Clem Haagner – ABPL.

conservation and invited him on a hunting trip (one of the main reasons for conservation was and still is to sustain hunting).

They set out on a winter's day from Rossouw's Loubos farm not far south of the Auob-Nossob confluence and deliberately took him along the Nossob, knowing game was scarce and that the presence of the Coloured 'farmers' on the Bechuanaland side was highly visible.

Their plot could not have worked better. Minister Grobler, a genial fellow who enjoyed the sociability of camping in the bush, sat in glum silence next to the fire that first night, gazing into the coals. Rossouw and De Villiers guessed what was bothering him and pushed the needle deeper: not to worry, they told him, there would be better luck tomorrow with more game and good hunting – hopefully.

Grobler growled that he had better things to think about and went to bed. It seems he spent much of the night pondering. The three men were drinking coffee early the next day to dull the edge of the wintry chill when Grobler announced that he intended to make the area between the Auob and Nossob rivers up to the South West African border a national park.

There was a problem, however: it had already been proclaimed a settlement area for Coloured people. No, said Rossouw and De Villiers, who had worked all this out beforehand, the problem was not unresolvable – the government could buy the land south of the proposed park and west to the border and use that for the settlers instead, a total of about 450 000 hectares including Rossouw's farm Loubos.

Minister Grobler thought this an excellent idea but insisted that the leaders of the Coloured community be consulted first. Meetings were held for which they came from as far away as the Bastergebiet in South West Africa and the Coloureds accepted the exchange; the new settlement was on better farmland than the harsh duneveld between the rivers. The deal was sweetened when the government also agreed to open for settlement a nature reserve adjoining the nearby Kuruman River.

Someone eventually remembered that there were still people guarding the string of boreholes in the Auob River. They had been there so long now they were virtually settlers. They were offered land beside the Kuruman River and accepted with alacrity. When the boreholes were inspected after they had gone, all their tall windpumps had vanished – the guards had dismantled the lot and taken them to their new farms.

All but a few of the farms that had been sold between the Auob and Nossob were bought back by the government and on 31 July 1931 the Kalahari Gemsbok National Park was created by a state proclamation. Four years later a row of farms on the Auob's southern bank was bought and added so that both sides of the river were protected, and also the farm Twee Rivieren, which brought the rivers' confluence into the park. This left a jagged boundary that was later straightened by a give-and-take of land between the government and neighbouring farmers.

Now the country had a new national park at the end of hundreds of kilometres of bone-rattling road in the middle of a nowhere that the locals regarded as their hunting ground by right – and nobody to look after it.

The brand new National Parks Board with only five years' experience, no capital, no income and very little subsidy from the state because of the Depression, might understandably have despaired over what to do about this distant addition to their responsibilities.

They sought around for a custodian to the park and, no doubt with prompting from Rossouw and De Villiers, settled on Rossouw's brother-in-law, farmer Johannes le Riche. It speaks much of the effect of the Depression that he accepted the NPB's offer of £7.10s. a month to take charge – not an unreasonably low salary in 1931 but not much to shoulder authority in 13 000 square kilometres of desert.

The NPB generously gave him assistance: one ranger constable, Gert Jannewarie, horses, a cart and donkeys. Johannes found a man who was prepared to work for £6 a month plus one springbok and one gemsbok and another who would have worked for even less, but the NPB could afford neither.

Johannes and his wife Bettie and their family of nine, including two pre-school children, made their home at Gemsbok Plain in a mud-and-wattle house abandoned by a borehole guard. Their company was Jannewarie, his family and a few servants.

The problems of turning the new park into a practicable reserve would have intimidated a modern professional with the best of facilities and assistance. Antelope were few and very shy, fleeing at the sight of man after all the years of being hunted. The hunters laughed off the law and came and went as they pleased, especially those whites with cars who used the Auob and Nossob as bundu highways, knowing this ill-equipped ranger had scant hope of catching them with horses and a donkey-cart. Without staff there was no way of setting up control posts at Mata Mata and Union's End where the rivers entered from South West Africa.

Water was a critical problem. Years of searing drought had left riverbeds and pans barren and although there were sixteen boreholes and three good wells in the Auob, the windpumps had vanished with

Johannes le Riche, first ranger and warden of the Park and his wife, Bettie.
National Parks Board

the guards. The NPB could afford only two windpumps. The Nossob had only four waterpoints: two wells dug in the south by Coloured settlers, a very brack borehole at Kijkij and a well at Union's End with a hand pump.

To patrol his territory, Johannes had to travel south down the Auob to the confluence with the Nossob, then north up the Nossob to Union's End, due south along the South West African border through heavy sandveld and dunes to Mata Mata, and finally down the Auob again to Gemsbok Plain. This 650-kilometre journey took about a fortnight and for 250 kilometres of it there was no water at all, obliging them to carry enough for men and animals in drums on the cart.

Communication with the outside world was daunting. There were no telephones or radios and messages had to be sent by horseman. Fetching the post at Askham was a week-long ordeal of over 200 kilometres. Upington, the nearest centre of government and civilisation, was 800 kilometres to the south and the trip there and back took two weeks.

Whether Johannes had any misgivings is not on record but he was a rawhide man born and raised in this world and knew as much about it as any of the hunters. He could not catch the motorised poachers unless he came upon them unawares but they were not the main threat to the park's wildlife. That came from the people living on the Bechuanaland side of the Nossob – the so-called 'farmers' who lived by hunting. They had all but wiped out game on their side and raided routinely across the river border.

So he and Jannewarie concentrated on patrolling the Nossob, with quick results. The easy life of poaching with impunity abruptly became an expensive risk for the poachers, who were fined £15 or £20 for every animal they shot by a conservation-minded magistrate at Upington and had their rifles confiscated.

This made the KGNP the first national park in the Cape Province to generate revenue. No tourists came to the park then, only the transients travelling between South West Africa and South Africa, and there were no real roads for them anyway and no proper camps – just rudimentary camping places for those prepared to risk the park's highly inquisitive and aggressive lions.

Johannes' dedication to his work (which then, like now, was largely chasing poachers, maintaining water sources and observing wildlife) earned him high praise from a three-man commission who visited the KGNP in 1933. It was the last visit he had from headquarters.

The next year the weather went berserk. The skies darkened and massive thunderclouds dumped huge loads of rainwater in and around the park. Floodwaters roared down the Auob and the Nossob for the first time this century. Johannes and Jannewarie watched this

Joep le Riche, Johannes' brother and successor, whose 'temporary' appointment lasted thirty-six years.
National Parks Board

astonishing scene from Gemsbok Plain where they were virtually trapped, their usual riverbed route closed by the muddy torrent and the desert too sodden to travel. It went on for weeks.

Both men were struck down by probably the last thing either expected in the usually arid Kalahari – malaria. An urgent message was sent and Johannes' brother Josef rushed, if that is the word, by ox-wagon to fetch him back to the family farm Saulstraat for treatment.

There Johannes died. Gert Jannewarie died soon afterwards, at Gemsbok Plain.

This left the NPB in the extraordinary position of having a national park without staff. Several times they turned to Josef, would he please take over his brother's task? He thought over the offer for some time. He was a busy farmer. Finally he agreed to do it temporarily to give the board time to find a permanent ranger.

The park hooked him too. This 'temporary' ranger retired thirty-six years later after achieving fame throughout South Africa's world of conservation and passing his ward on to his sons.

That year, 1934, was a watershed one for Josef, universally known by his nickname Joep. He started his temporary career at the munificent salary of £7 a month with the promise that it would rise by ten shillings a year to £10, presumably the board's bait to keep him on the job.

He hired a Coloured named Gert Mouton as his right-hand man. Gert became one of the park's great characters and went through many tribulations with Joep until he retired to a farm just south of Twee Rivieren.

On 10 July in Upington Joep married Cecilia 'Cillie' Steenkamp and took her home. She came from Kakamas, the Dutch Reformed Church settlement on the Orange River downstream from Upington, and was thus attuned to the ferocious Northern Cape desert climate. It would nonetheless have been interesting to know her reaction when she first saw her married home.

It was the wattle-and-daub 'hartbeeshuisie' on top of the east bank of the Auob at Gemsbok Plain surrounded by a desolation of stone and sand relieved slightly by bush fringes of the river.

It had a living-room, bedroom and a stone lean-to kitchen built on the outside. The roof was thatch and the walls and floors were of clay. The household's water was heated in an old soap boiler over a fire of cowdung and wood.

The future was hardly bright. The NPB was so strapped for cash that the KGNP's annual operating budget was about £100 and when Joep asked to buy a corrugated-iron reservoir for £2.5s. the board refused because they did not have the money.

They did, however, agree that Joep could have a car to tackle the problem of the free-shooting transients through the park. This was no flush of generosity because they put up the price of £200 on condition he paid it back in monthly instalments, with interest.

With it Joep bought a spoked-wheel Ford in Upington, something of a novelty even then. Having bought it he had to get it home, which was a problem because in that climatically remarkable year the rains struck again, once more flooding the rivers and turning the veld into a sandy morass.

The drive back to the confluence of the two rivers took him two days, a pleasant change from the tedious trips by cart or wagon. There he found his first obstacle: his home was in the terrain between the rivers but he could not drive the Ford through the Nossob's waters. Nor, if he managed to get across, could he drive straight over the dunes to Gemsbok Plain, never having used a car in the desert before.

Joep continued driving north following the firmer ground on the Nossob's east bank for about twenty kilometres until he came to a settlement of Coloured people at Leeuwdril, one of the communities of 'farmers' who lived largely by poaching in the park. Although they were opponents in a way, they respected him and helped load his car on one of their wagons drawn by twenty donkeys, then hauled the wagon across the Nossob through water about 1,2 metres deep.

On the west bank Joep waved them goodbye and turned south back to the confluence from where he followed the Auob's east bank to Gemsbok Plain. It was the kind of journey that became routine for him.

The car made an immediate difference by putting Joep on an equal basis with the transients. He travelled the riverbeds and used his authority to stop cars on the roads and search them. He caught people with whole springbok, fresh venison, half-dried biltong, complete hides and rawhide strips in the boots and backseats. A medium-sized but hard and wiry man, he brooked no nonsense and dealt firmly with the truculent.

In a very short time word spread that the park was no longer a happy hunting ground for anyone with a car and a rifle. Fines were steep and the conservationist magistrate at Upington imposed them liberally. Motorised poaching did not stop but it reduced considerably and became surreptitious.

The South African Police expanded Joep's anti-poaching abilities by giving the KGNP four camels from their desert patrol unit. With these evil-mannered but long-range animals Joep was able to extend his own patrols well beyond the range of his horses and donkeys and step up the pressure on the poachers.

In 1935 Joep and Cillie's first son was born at Gemsbok Plain – Christoffel 'Stoffel' le Riche, destined to take over the reins from his father.

Years ago camels were used to patrol the Park but were outmoded by four-wheel drive vehicles. They are still used by the Botswana Police in the south of the country near the Park.
National Parks Board

In the spring of the same year the Kalahari revealed another ferocious side to its character. Because of the extraordinary rainfall of the previous year, about three times greater than the average, the veld burgeoned with an abundance of plant life not seen for decades. The hot sun after the rains quickly dried it out and bolts of summer lightning set it on fire, causing widespread devastation. There was nothing Joep and his small staff could do about it.

The 1934 floods had also drowned the boreholes, covering them for weeks and clogging them with silt. Cleaning them out was tedious, backbreaking labour; first the steel piping had to be lifted out and unscrewed section by three-metre section with a block and tackle attached to the windpump derrick. Then a heavy steel sand-bailer or grab was dropped into the hole on the end of a rope and hauled back up with its load by a team of donkeys.

Joep and Gert resignedly set about the task, starting with the 109-metre deep Kleinskrij borehole. They slaved and sweated to lift the pipe sections and then came the sand bailing, for which they needed a team of donkeys from Gemsbok Plain about thirty kilometres away.

While they waited, said Gert, they might as well lower the bailer into the hole. Joep demurred, it was very heavy. No problem, Gert said, he would act as anchor like the end man in a tug-of-war game to take the weight while Joep paid the rope out hand by hand over the block and tackle to lower the bailer into the hole.

Joep was hesitant but surrendered his doubts when Gert knotted the loose end of the 120-metre rope around his waist and walked away from the borehole to stretch it to its full length.

Gert dug his heels into the sand, leaned back to tauten the rope and signalled that he was ready. Joep struggled to lift the bailer and lower it with both hands, then released his grip on it for a moment to seize the rope, expecting Gert to hold its weight.

The jerk made Gert take a step forward and lose his balance. Suddenly the rope was rigid and Gert took another and longer step and then he was running, frantically trying to regain his balance and dig his heels in.

Joep grabbed at the racing rope. Somehow his trouser leg had been caught in the tackle and ripped open from ankle to stern. By now Gert was racing straight towards the derrick with huge kangaroo strides, his eyes like saucers. Halfway towards it the bailer's acceleration took him clean off his feet. He fell flat and sped closer in a spray of sand, leaving bits of clothing on passing bushes.

Joep tried again and again to seize the rope to slow Gert but it stripped skin from his hands. He could never have stopped the plunging bailer.

Fortunately, the rope was eleven metres longer than the hole was deep. Gert was skating swiftly towards a fatal collision with the derrick when the bailer hit bottom, the rope abruptly went slack and he skidded to a stop a few metres from the hole.

In the silence with the adrenalin singing in their ears the two men looked at each other in shocked wonder – they were covered in sand, minus sizeable areas of skin and their clothes were torn – but otherwise they were intact. Gert watched Joep nervously, fearing an outburst of anger, but Joep said nothing. After several minutes Gert spoke: 'Boss,' he said tentatively, 'I think we must give up this work, it's not going to pay.'

The year 1938 was another milestone. Following South Africa's lead, the British colonial authorities in Bechuanaland proclaimed a twenty-five-mile strip of land along the Nossob River between the South African and South West African borders as a game reserve and gave jurisdiction over it to the NPB.

This was the first major breakthrough against poaching from the Bechuanaland side. Some eighty-four 'farmer' families there agreed to move to the Mier settlement area south of the park.

Now that he was responsible for enforcing the law on both sides of the border, Joep had to define it so that he could determine whether poachers should go before Bechuanaland or South African courts. Previously, the riverbed was adequate and any poacher lucky enough to reach the Bechuanaland bank was safe.

He marked off the entire 270-kilometre border with creosoted wooden posts sunk into the ground at long intervals with their tops sticking out a half metre or so. His surveying was not perfect and some of the poles were about fifty metres further into Bechuanaland than they should have been, thus inadvertently relieving the British protectorate of a few hundred square metres of land. On the posts he stencilled the letters BPGR for Bechuanaland Protectorate Game Reserve.

Some of the posts are still there but Elias le Riche, the present warden, has replaced the rest with concrete markers painted white and carrying the letters RSA and RB on opposite sides, for Republic of South Africa and Republic of Botswana. These are in their proper places.

Thirty-four years later, in 1972, the independent Botswana government made a further important stride by adding another 26 000 square kilometres to the reserve on their side to make the whole park on both sides a total of 36 000 square kilometres. They run it with the help of the NPB and they have created hunting concession areas on the park's borders within Botswana – giving another small degree of protection although hunting permits there are extremely cheap, as little as fifty cents for the harmless bat-eared fox.

In Joep's early years the NPB bought out the few remaining white-owned farms within the KGNP boundaries – several of them only after Joep threatened to buy them himself. The addition of the farm Twee Rivieren south of the park brought the confluence of the two rivers into it.

In 1938, on the recommendation of Piet 'Mof' de Villiers, the NPB built a corrugated-iron house at the confluence, Samevloeiing, and Joep moved his family and headquarters there. It was slightly larger with two rooms and a kitchen but far from ideal – the iron roof and walls made it like an oven in summer and an icebox in winter. Samevloeiing, however, was a more convenient base both for patrolling and for the monitoring of travellers on the two riverbeds.

That year the Le Riches were graced with a visit by an NPB commission headed by its Vice-President, J F Ludorf, and charged with investigating the state of the park. The worthy commissioners had to stay a night in Joep's new home.

That night the Kalahari sided with him. It rained non-stop. Water streamed, trickled and dripped through holes in the roof. So much came in that the commissioners had to move about all night seeking dry places as fresh leaks drove them from their blankets.

By morning they had had enough. They resolved that a proper house be built a few kilometres further south of Twee Rivieren. It was built by an Upington builder of cement-and-sand bricks made by Joep, had three bedrooms, a living and dining-room and a kitchen with pantry, and cost £50.

Having solved the drip problem, the commissioners made a flock of other recommendations for the park's improvement. Some were major: close the Nossob River border crossing into South West Africa (which was eventually done in 1945), hire more ranger constables, get more camels, sink more boreholes.

The police provided more camels, beefing up the anti-poaching patrols considerably and Joep hired more men to supplement the small staff complement that consisted of himself, Gert Mouton, constable Jan Jannewarie at the Union's End post and Ranger Piet Moller, son of Giel Moller, who sold the park the Twee Rivieren farm, at the Mata Mata post.

Boreholes, however, were not a simple matter to address. Even today there is controversy about them.

Purists argue that permanent waterholes in the Kalahari are artificial – abnormal in an environment where migration is the norm and most animals are not water-dependent. Waterholes create concentrations of animals that damage the environment by over-usage, they say.

While this is true, it is equally true that the ability of migratory animals to reach fresh grazing or water has been drastically curtailed by human development. If they are to survive, water must be provided albeit to a limited extent.

Stoffel le Riche succeeded his father Joep, but died early of heart failure.
National Parks Board

The Ludorf Commission reported that in a severe drought a few years before their visit thousands of animals died of thirst in migrations that went as far south as Upington. Their mass movement depopulated the KGNP. In any case, they said, water was needed only in the hot, dry summer months between October and February, when it would prevent depopulation of the park.

Subsequent research has shown that local, smaller migrations in search of new grazing are dictated by local rainshowers, not water availability, and that there are other causes for the mass migrations of springbok, eland and hartebeest. Only the wildebeest have to drink every two or three days and therefore must find water.

At the NPB's behest, Joep drilled thirteen boreholes in a year between 66 metres and 133 metres deep. Most of the cost and effort were wasted; four were dry, five gave water so salty it was undrinkable, two yielded under 700 litres an hour and only two had a strong supply of drinkable water.

Elias le Riche, the present warden, maintained the family tradition by taking over from his elder brother Stoffel.
National Parks Board

This is a permanent problem in the KGNP, whose copious underground water appears to come from a large artesian basin just to the north-west in Namibia. Unfortunately, much of it is very saline.

Water fit for human consumption should contain no more than 0,5 per cent of dissolved salts. Water with a salt content between 0,5 per cent and 1,8 per cent is classified as hypersaline. Sea water contains about 3,5 per cent.

Some of the waterpoints in the park have more dissolved salts than the sea, especially in the cribs next to the reservoirs where concentration by evaporation is high. The higher the salt content, the more quickly it concentrates.

Of the more than 100 boreholes in the KGNP (the number varies with closures and new drillings) forty-six per cent of the reservoir tanks and sixty-two per cent of the cribs in the riverbeds have water

which is considered too salty for animals by agricultural standards, and the same goes for thirty-eight per cent of the tanks and fifty-five per cent of the cribs on the duneveld between the rivers. The park's best water is from the Auob River boreholes.

Wild animals and birds can cope with saltier water than can humans and some domestic animals can drink very saline water, having special glands or other bodily devices for voiding it. The water also contains many of the trace minerals their bodies need.

Twee Rivieren camp's water seems extraordinarily soft, making it very difficult to rinse off soap. It is an illusion – the water is potable but to make it more so it is chemically treated before it is piped into the camp.

The Nossob camp presented a special water problem. Many holes were drilled, one of them to the extraordinary depth of 372 metres, and all yielded undrinkably salty water. So for six years staff and visitors drank precious runoff rainwater collected in tanks from roofs and gutters and perforce had to use the brack water for everything else and thereby developed a taste for saline tea and coffee. The mineral content of the borehole water was so high that pipes and kettles quickly clogged up.

And then Warden Stoffel le Riche, Joep's son and successor, found strong indications of water at Kwang twenty kilometres north of the camp, using the time-honoured divining technique of a forked stick held between his hands.

Two boreholes there of seventy metres and seventy-six metres yielded a bountiful supply of beautifully fresh water. A diesel pump was placed on the strongest and a buried pipeline was laid to take the water to the camp, where visitors enjoy it at the cost to the park of R1 per kilolitre.

Boreholes opened the way for tourists. The road between Nossob camp and Union's End stayed closed to them until 1964, after holes had been drilled and water found, because it was considered too dangerous to let people in there without waterpoints they could turn to in an emergency.

Near every roadside waterpoint is a small, rather cryptic signpost with a number – thirty-six metres or eighty-two metres or seventy metres and so on. Each gives the depth of the nearby waterhole. Many visitors do not realise this.

'I caught a man speeding once,' chuckled Warden Elias le Riche, 'and he said "I wish you people would make up your minds – here you say the limit's thirty-six and then it's eighty-two and then it's seventy and so on." I had to let him go.'

The anti-borehole purists are justified in another of their criticisms: that the multi-vaned windpumps with their lattice-steel derricks, their adjacent fibreglass tanks (chosen because the salt corrodes both steel and concrete) and the cement-and-stone cribs are a scar on the desert's natural beauty.

The ugliness will be largely removed over the coming years by a device initiated in the Kruger National Park, the solar-powered pump. There they have not been so successful because inquisitive elephants tend to ruin them so they have to be strongly fenced, again causing an unnatural scar on the landscape.

But there are no elephants in the KGNP and more sunshine than in any other park. The first two solar pumps were installed in the mid-1980s and have worked well. More will follow. One can be seen at Rooiputs. Eventually the fibreglass reservoirs near the pumps will also be removed and water will be fed directly into the cribs.

In 1939 World War II broke out and the nation-wide impounding of private firearms brought blessed relief from poaching. The following year Elias Albertus Nel le Riche was born in the new family home at Twee Rivieren.

The park was still a wild and woolly place then with none but the most primitive facilities for visitors, who, because of wartime petrol restrictions, were reduced to nothing anyway. As it was, distance and bad roads were an ordeal few people liked to endure.

Elias remembers his first long trip in the park as a small boy, to Union's End and back with his father by wagon. It was a five-metre-long rubber-tyred vehicle drawn by fourteen donkeys and loaded with water-filled oil drums plus half-drum troughs for the animals to drink from, in addition to all their own camping gear. The journey took two weeks.

Later his father Joep acquired a Chevrolet Imp – one of the first cars in South Africa with a 'bakkie' or truck back – to replace his ageing Ford. Even in the new vehicle travelling to Upington took two days with an overnight camp, compared to four or five hours now.

Elias le Riche, in somewhat younger days, with a poacher and the evidence. Bushmen 'poachers' were not punished severely because hunting was their way of life.
National Parks Board

Elias le Riche with hides and traps found in the Park.
National Parks Board

With the end of the war came the end of petrol rationing, the return of private firearms, voluminous sales to the public of surplus army rifles, and a huge resurgence of poaching.

Desperately under-manned and ill-equipped to cope with the flood of joyous poachers making up for five lost years, and determined to fulfil his responsibilities on both the South African and Bechuanaland sides, Joep wrote to the District Commissioner at Tsabong seeking his help:

Peace for man meant war on animals. On one occasion I saw 153 springbok carcasses at a poacher camp ... They cut out only the fillets and abandoned the carcasses. I can assure you that they did not hunt for food, but in order to sell the biltong at 3s.6d. or 4s. a pound ... They are still hunting illegally. It is extremely difficult to catch somebody in the Kalahari with its thousands of sand dunes. You can imagine how we are fighting with our backs against the wall for the protection and preservation of our game ... The possibility that all our wildlife can be wiped out is greater than we realise, and therefore I appeal to you for your assistance. The time when we could afford our game to be killed for money is long past ... Now is the time to co-operate and conserve what is left.

Peacetime helped to balance the struggle with a bonus on the rangers' side – four-wheel-drive vehicles. They began with ex-army jeeps and since then the KGNP staff and those in all other parks have had the means to go almost anywhere, nowadays in such powerful mechanical beasts as Land Rovers and Landcruisers with support from light aircraft.

With help from the Bechuanaland side and the backing of the courts on both sides, Joep began to get the upper hand and poaching diminished steadily. It will never stop entirely but it no longer threatens the KGNP's existence.

The flush of money, cars and fuel after the war and a public urge to forget its horrors brought visitors to national parks in quickly rising numbers.

By 1950 three tourist huts had been built and were in use at Twee Rivieren – the only indoor accommodation in the KGNP – and in that year the park earned £1 288.112s.9d. from tourism. Foreseeing the prospects, the NPB opened a camping ground at Mata Mata in 1952, and enlarged the Twee Rivieren campground and built another two rooms there in 1955, giving it five altogether with enclosed verandahs. Petrol and oil went on sale and by 1957 Twee Rivieren could accommodate twenty people and Mata Mata twelve in huts.

Today Twee Rivieren has 120 beds plus camping accommodation for thirty families, Nossob sixty beds plus twenty families and Mata Mata twenty beds plus twenty families. At an average of five people per family, that means the park can take a maximum of 550 visitors on any one night.

No records were kept of the numbers of visitors before 1954, partly because the personnel were preoccupied with other tasks and partly because it was difficult to distinguish between tourists and transients. In that year there were 515.

The KGNP had very little publicity or promotion but word of mouth spread quickly that this was a place for real nature-lovers, not casual holidaymakers, who if they were prepared to rough it a little and suffer heat and cold could find extraordinary rewards.

A small shop selling basic necessities was started at Twee Rivieren in 1959. The next year the tourist flow reached 4 853. In 1962 the park obtained its own road-grader which enabled Joep and his men to extend the distance for tourist traffic, including the dune road in 1966 linking the Auob and Nossob rivers between Kamqua and Kameelsleep.

The Nossob camp was opened in 1964/65 (officially in 1966) and in 1970 all three camps were equipped with electricity generators. In the 1971/72 year the KGNP attracted 11 000 visitors. The total rose to 14 794 four years later, to 26 348 in 1987 and to about 27 000 in 1990 in spite of South Africa's soaring petrol prices.

The park's gross income averages about R1,5 million a year, which covers running costs but is not enough to finance development, which has continued apace. In 1956/57 the South West African border was resurveyed because the original 1946 beacons were buried by sand, and thirty kilometres north of Mata Mata were fenced. Fencing of the entire border was completed in 1966. In 1962/63 a fence was erected between the park and the Mier settlement area south of it, with wild animals on the outside being driven through the last gap just before it was closed.

This has left only the Botswana side unfenced, as it should be because of the ebb and flow of migrating animals – the bloodstream of the park.

Nearly two decades later a patrol road was cleared along the full length of the South West Africa side and the fence was electrified. This was done to keep predators inside the park and away from farmers' livestock on the outside. Some lions had become adept at digging under the old fence, killing on the far side and then dragging their prey back with them. The electric charge also protected predators from poisoned bait traps set for them on the other side.

There were also changes to the people who looked after the park. In 1958 Piet Moller of Mata Mata left and Stoffel, Elias' elder brother, promptly abandoned his agricultural studies in Pretoria to take the job. He was in such enthusiastic haste that he ignored his father Joep's warnings and set off for Mata Mata from Twee Rivieren at night.

Next morning Joep could not contact him by radio and went in search. He found Stoffel sitting disconsolately at the roadside, unable to travel or to use his radio because his Land Rover had been badly damaged by hitting a gemsbok.

In 1963 Elias, fresh from the University of Pretoria with a BSc in Zoology and Botany, applied for and got the job of ranger at Nossob camp, making the KGNP almost a family affair. Two years later Elias married Antoinette 'Doempie' Smith, a girl with a golden smile he met while she was studying teaching at Pretoria and who hails from a part of South Africa diametrically opposite to the arid Kalahari – the lush, misty montane forests and streams of Tzaneen in the Eastern Transvaal.

When Joep retired to Upington in 1970 after his long and eventful stint as the park's head, he was succeeded by son Stoffel. Ten years later fate stepped in when Stoffel died of a heart attack, predeceasing his retired father by eight years.

Elias became warden and carries on the family tradition. It may continue beyond him: he has a son studying veterinary medicine at Onderstepoort and another still at school.

Elias commands what must be the smallest conservation staff relative to size and importance of any park in South Africa: one ranger each at Twee Rivieren, Mata Mata and Nossob, plus a research officer at Nossob.

Supporting them is a staff of nearly seventy including assistants and tourist officers and, at Twee Rivieren, a camp manager and a caterer. Many of those jobs are done by wives, who might be driven to distraction with nothing to do. Rangers' wives are tourist officers at Mata Mata and Nossob and Doempie le Riche is the park's administrative officer.

Scientific interest in the park lagged behind public interest in the post-war years. The first scientific report on this pristine desert environment was made in 1956 by A M Brynard, who later became Director of the NPB. It was necessarily a broad overview because of the broad scope of the subject and the scarcity of earlier research, but it got true scientific investigation under way.

In 1957 a large group of scientists from the University of Pretoria, University of the Witwatersrand, Wits Medical School, Transvaal Museum, Department of Agriculture and the Pest Research Laboratory descended upon the KGNP to decide what research needed to be done.

This was followed by a botanical survey by Dr O Leistner and the creation of a small but thus far impressively productive research laboratory funded by the Rembrandt Organisation, sited first at Twee Rivieren and now at Nossob camp.

There research officer Mike Knight studied herbivore and carnivore movement patterns, which involves putting radio collars on springbok, hartebeest, wildebeest, gemsbok, lion, leopard and cheetah and tracking them daily from a light plane fitted with special antennae. Before him the laboratory was used by the first research officer appointed to the KGNP by the NPB, Dr 'Gus' Mills, who arrived in 1969. He investigated the larger predators and their relationship with their prey and made a special study of spotted and brown hyenas, on which he has become a leading authority.

Other research in the KGNP focuses on a wide range of subjects including its archaeology, geology, soils, vegetation, butterflies, rodents, antlions, beetles and reptiles. One project examines the effect of rainfall and waterpoints on animal movements including migrations, another looks at bird and animal adaptations to the peculiar environment, yet another studies the haemotology and biochemistry of certain antelope.

One of the longest studies is of lions by Professor F C Eloff, zoologist and Chairman of the NPB. For many years he spent up to weeks at a time following lions about the park on wheels and on foot, recording their behaviour, diet, day and night activities, mating, playing and hunting – often getting too close to them for comfort.

A man who has held or holds many scientific, cultural and sporting offices in South Africa, Professor Eloff has written some two-score scientific papers, most alone, among which the KGNP and his work on lions figure prominently.

His name is inscribed as the unveiler of a plaque on a cairn at Gemsbok Plain commemorating the park's fiftieth anniversary. Standing on the pebbly flats atop the east bank, the short cairn is the only prominence for kilometres around and is much favoured as a perch by passing raptors.

In October 1984, at a symposium in Pretoria, forty-eight scientists delivered papers on various aspects of the KGNP. They yielded a sizeable volume of new information about this part of the Kalahari, much of it very basic, but the note that rang loudest was that this was only the beginning, there was much to be done.

Fellow citizens meet in the Kalahari: the late Mr Blackie Swart, South Africa's first president and a very tall man at over two metres, poses with one of his shorter countrymen, an unnamed Bushman, in the Park.
National Parks Board

'This symposium shows clearly how little is known of the functioning of this extensive system,' remarked Dr Anthony Hall-Martin, head of southern parks for the NPB and the world's foremost expert on elephants.

As a scientist himself, Elias is involved in research – specifically a project to monitor leopards and wildcats – but the flow of people and paperwork through his office leaves him little time. He tries to escape from it at least twice a month by going on a two or three-day patrol with ranger sergeants Willem de Waal and 'Vet Piet' Kleinman.

Once a week he pilots himself on routine inspection flights in the park's Cessna 260, covering a different area each time, and once a fortnight he makes a four and a half-hour flight around the park's entire perimeter of about 1 500 kilometres. On top of that, he flies in aerial surveys and other game control operations, occasionally flies to Upington in emergencies with people or equipment, and has to travel regularly to the NPB headquarters in Pretoria.

His home is his fortress and retreat, a cool and comfortable house in the private staff village at Twee Rivieren filled with Le Riche and Kalahari memorabilia and always, it seems, with his or someone else's children.

More than anyone alive today, he can survey the nearly one million hectares of desert reserve surrounding him with satisfaction.

The original concept of the KGNP was indeed that of Piet de Villiers and Willie Rossouw more than sixty years ago and Minister Grobler and the previous Bechuanaland and present Botswana governments breathed life into it.

But the dedicated day-to-day care that raised the park from feeble infancy to the lusty, lovely creature it is today was undoubtedly the work of the Le Riches.

A typical Park scene: a living frieze of blue wildebeest marching along a riverbed with the backdrop of fossil dune behind them.
Anthony Bannister – ABPL.

... and Future

*t*he traffic of South Africans to their national parks is growing swiftly as they become more appreciative of their environment in this conservation era, as they seek escape from urban tensions and as the demise of apartheid has opened the doors for black and Coloured people.

The Kruger National Park is in such demand that it has reached the maximum level of development possible without serious loss of quality, is booked out for up to a year ahead and cannot cope with more people.

Other national parks have to help take the load and new ones have been created recently on the West Coast, in the Karoo, and elsewhere. Existing parks, national and provincial, large and small, have to brace themselves for a rush of humanity in the coming decade.

The KGNP has begun to taste the tide. Its tourist flow is being swelled by its own growing reputation and the overflow from Kruger.

To some people it might appear that the KGNP is the answer to Kruger's prayer. Here is a park nearly twice the size yet it receives less than a tenth of Kruger's maximum capacity of about half a million a year. Why not double the KGNP's tourist capacity, or more?

Not even the Kruger's conservationists would suggest that. The size of the KGNP's surface area is wholly misleading.

In the first place the two-thirds chunk of it in Botswana is not yet open to visitors. At present it is strictly a wilderness area to which the Botswana authorities reluctantly permit entry only for exceptional reasons – and then only with four-wheel-drive vehicles and full survival equipment.

It is vital that the Botswana side be retained primarily as an undisturbed animal reservoir and a passage area for migrations. Its use for tourism is a decision that lies with the government of Botswana and that can be made only after a thorough study of the effect on the environment.

Secondly, the scope for expansion of the KGNP's existing three camps is severely limited by the restraints of water, costs and (odd though it might seem) space.

Third, and most important, the Kalahari ecosystem is highly sensitive to intrusive influences including people traffic. As a random example, in the comparatively lush Kruger endowed with greater resilience by its more generous climate, water, vegetation and diversity of life, each additional visitor might impact on a few square metres of territory. In the KGNP each would impact on a square kilometre.

Hard and indestructible though it looks, the environment would suffer serious damage were more camps and roads built at random. The KGNP has a sparse large animal population except very sporadically in times of migration, and the territorial creatures among them perforce need large territories. Too many camps and roads would disrupt them, driving many further afield and out of reach.

Too many people would ruin one of the KGNP's great characteristics: it has so few visitors now that when one stops to look at a lion or leopard or simply a hawk in a tree, there is no instant traffic jam of rubbernecks.

And yet, somehow, this magnificently lonely park *must* take in more visitors if it is to survive financially. Like all parks, it will have to pay its own way in the future because the government cannot go on subsidising them; it needs the money for political and economic priorities.

So, after much study, the National Parks Board has decided in principle that when and if funds become available, the KGNP's accommodation will be increased.

Various plans have been mooted but none has been put into effect yet. They include four new camps that are very simple in character: two-bed huts with couches that can be converted into two more beds, a small shop and no restaurant or other frills. If such a camp had to accommodate a busload of visitors their meals could be prepared at Twee Rivieren's restaurant and sent along with them.

A logical site for one such camp is beside the Auob River near Grootskrij, roughly halfway between Twee Rivieren and Mata Mata. It is interesting country, a little too distant from either base to be savoured fully before one has to leave to be back before the gates close.

Other potential sites, because they have sweet water, are Kannaguass, Stoffelsdraai and Kij Games. The last two are at present inaccessible to visitors.

Kannaguass is in the far north of the park, two waterpoints south of Union's End. It would make more accessible a remote area that is now so far from Nossob that one has hardly arrived there before it is time to turn back.

Stoffelsdraai, named after Stoffel le Riche, is a waterpoint in the depths of the dunes almost on a line between Nossob and Mata Mata. It is much loved by patrolling rangers and visiting scientists, who would be sad to see it go public.

Kij Games is also on a patrol road in the dunes but much further south, almost due north of Twee Rivieren and west of the Melkvlei waterpoint on the Nossob River.

The future plans include a 'bush' or 'adventure' camp, something like Kruger Park's wilderness trails, near each of the new chalet camps. Their keynote will be simplicity – tents, open fires and an ablution block.

Each is intended to hold no more than about twenty people and one ranger to take them on walks so they can experience the Kalahari with all their senses.

Other ideas are for a very exclusive wilderness camp at Kij Garries and (which is certain to draw heavy opposition from the purists) a special camp for the four-wheel-drive brigade – who will be allowed to go so far but no further.

If any of this comes about, it will only be after some expansion of Twee Rivieren and the refurbishing, but not expansion, of the Nossob and Mata Mata camps.

And that will be that, say the ecologists, especially Elias le Riche, who knows the park and its limitations better than anyone. It would be the most expansion this sensitive area could survive without damage.

There is no doubt the flow of visitors will swell. One of the main deterrents to going to the KGNP is the rough roads. But the one from Upington has already been tarred for eighty kilometres and its completion, plus the tarring of the road from Hotazel, are on the agenda, subject to finances.

One proposal likely to generate a storm of controversy is the tarring of the 500 kilometres or so of roads in the park itself. When the tarring of main roads in the Kruger Park began many years ago an uproar echoed around South Africa and it drew sneers from conservationists in other African states who dismissed Kruger as an oversized zoo.

The critics were wrong. Any loss of wilderness authenticity in Kruger has been more than offset by the benefits. There is no dust, therefore the roadside bush is clean and does not put off browsers and grazers, moisture run-off from the tar generates growth that attracts animals, maintenance time and costs are much reduced, and the comfort of visitors is considerably improved.

The KGNP is a somewhat different proposition. It has only three roads and they are as intimately a part of the park's character as its dunes and trees and dazzling heat. Their very crudeness is an indicator of how precarious is man's presence here and the smell of dust is the desert's special perfume.

The roads are also the desert's diary, a daily log of life. Every day they are swept by wind or traffic and then become a record of what has passed in the previous twenty-four hours – in the tracks of animals, birds, reptiles and insects.

Much has been learned about animal behaviour by reading spoor in the KGNP's vast, clean sands, including the fine dust of the roads. Here a shallow depression cornered by four pug marks shows where a leopard paused during a stalk and lay on its stomach. There a flurry of scraped hoofmarks reveals where two springbok rams jousted. A double row of saucer-sized paw prints at the road's edge, first evenly spaced and then bunched and deeper and blurred, tells that a lion was ambling along when it spotted a buck and charged.

Much of this will be reduced or disappear if the roads are tarred, but there are persuasive advantages. So powder-fine is the desert dust, especially in the clayey riverbeds, it billows in clouds from the wheels of the slowest of vehicles. A light breeze can make it unpleasant to be on the roads, with dust obscuring the view and getting in everywhere – with harmful effects on binoculars and cameras.

Tarring would stop that because the roads are the major dust source. Little comes from the desert itself, where the surface is better consolidated and not churned up by tyres.

In places the dust is so thick and deep, cars become stuck and have to be rescued by rangers. Elsewhere the roads are bone-shakingly rutted. In wet weather the dust transforms into a stewy mud and the riverbed clay becomes as slick as ice, leading to close encounters with roadside banks, or simply bogging vehicles down. Tarring would make travel easy in any weather and leave the roadside vegetation its natural colour instead of the present drab grey.

Elias le Riche and the NPB have thought about tarring for a long time, quailing at the mental vision of hot black ribbons snaking through river and dune, jarring terribly with the park's character and scenery. However, a technical breakthrough has persuaded them it can be done: the roads can be surfaced in almost exactly the same colour as the dust.

Hard surfaced roads will inevitably increase the flow of visitors and with them the park's revenue. When that day comes it will place a heavy onus on the shoulders of the NPB's decision-makers: balancing the need for money against the needs of nature.

The temptation is always there to build more huts, open more camps, cram in more people, raise more cash. The finite capacity of this park, however, must be carefully and permanently defined. The desert ecology is extremely sensitive and the balance they must find is a needlepoint one.

The delicate little bat-eared fox is one of the Kalahari's most intriguing characters with its masked face, huge ears, slender legs and bushy tail. Once accused by farmers of killing lambs, it lives on small animals and insects.
Hein von Horsten – ABPL.

In Botswana the park faces change from another threat: livestock. Both its population and its economy are expanding and the economic base – that which involves and benefits most people most directly – is cattle. Ranching is a deeply ingrained tradition and beef is one of Botswana's main exports.

Using modern borehole drilling technology, the cattlemen are moving their stock ever deeper into the Kalahari Desert by tapping its sizeable underground water reserves.

Livestock and wild animals cannot easily share the desert's limited resources, and in the view of many Batswana people, the wild animals must go. Ranching will approach steadily closer to the park on the Botswana side and is inexorably reducing the area of desert open to free movement by wild animals.

The natural movement by migrating animals is already severely restricted by fences erected to prevent buffalo meeting cattle and supposedly spreading foot-and-mouth disease – a method of prevention rejected outright by many experts.

Encroaching cattle herds will restrict migrations in and out of the park, forcing its administrators to resort more and more to artificial management methods to retain a viable animal population.

The Botswana and South African sections of the park are heavily interdependent. Neither could survive adequately without the other. Fortunately, the conservation authorities on both sides appear sufficiently aware of this to make the park's future look safe.

CHAPTER TWO

The Tales of the Names

The stark beauty of contrasting colours in the desert is stunning – brilliantly blue sky, cotton-white clouds, red and tan sand, green trees.
Nigel Dennis – ABPL.

*N*ames are the footprints of history, telltale signs of the past often obscured by fading memories. In their own way they can be as rewarding as an archaeological dig and give revealing glimpses into the lives and times of forgotten people.

The KGNP is no exception. It has a curious mixture of place names in several languages along the Nossob and Auob rivers – and in the unpeopled expanse of sand dunes – that are the clues to a lonely pageant. None of the happenings they record was of any particular importance and indeed some names were plucked at random from the minds of the givers. Others are cryptically descriptive, born of incidents of drama or humour, or reflect the unrelenting challenge of staying alive in the desert.

Together they form an absorbing picture of what life was like in the south-western Kalahari when it was a wild and empty world and the home of few and very durable people.

Some of the names on the KGNP map are self-explanatory, like Gemsbok Plain – obviously bestowed by someone who came across many gemsbok there. The origins of others, like Urikaruus, are lost. Those described here were chosen for their historical or curiosity value or simply as examples of how names originate. Most are found on the tourist maps and some only on more detailed maps which can be seen in camp offices.

One of the oddest features of the KGNP is the collection of Scottish names in the south in terrain so incongruously different to the wet, cold world of heath and hills whence they came.

Behind their mystery lies one of that band of wandering Scots who filtered into the remotest corners of the world in the days when most of the map was British Imperial red.

He was Roger Jackson, nicknamed 'Malkop' (Crackpot) by the predominantly Afrikaans-speaking peoples of the Northern Cape. A land-surveyor by trade, he happened to be in the vicinity of the small hamlet of Rietfontein when the Great War began in 1914.

Rietfontein lies south-west of Twee Rivieren and right on the border between what were then the Union of South Africa and the German *Schutzgebiet* or protectorate of South West Africa. Not surprisingly, when war was declared 10 000 kilometres away in Europe, tension grew on this remote frontier between the far-flung representatives of the Great Powers.

With so few people scattered through such arid emptiness there was no immediate or great confrontation. But zealous opponents on both sides carried the flag on impromptu across-the-border raids that did more to inflate their self-esteem than deflate the enemy.

One such enthusiast on the South African side was a captain with the paradoxically Teutonic name of Stumpke who gallantly, if somewhat foolishly, led a small force into German territory near Rietfontein. What he thought he would achieve is a mystery because before him lay a vast, almost empty expanse of sun-blasted desert and plains.

His lieutenant was Roger 'Malkop' Jackson, who had enlisted for King and Country.

Unbeknown to Stumpke, a force of the very efficient *Schutztruppe* – protectorate troops – was encamped on a farm not far from the border. They saw him before he saw them. Stumpke was strutting about studying the lie of the land when a German sharpshooter felled him with a fatal shot in the stomach.

Jackson fell flat at the sound of the shot but the keen-eyed Germans had spotted him. He was readying himself to fire back when a bullet ploughed through his hair and grazed his scalp, momentarily stunning him. After a few more accurate German shots the British force scampered back to the border and relative safety.

Whether it was the bullet so close to his brains that gave Jackson his 'Malkop' nickname, or his other activities, is unknown.

The government hired him later to survey and beacon off farms in the extreme northern corner of the Cape that years later was proclaimed the KGNP.

It was during this task that, possibly feeling homesick, he imposed such discordant names as Strathmore, in the dunes, and along the Auob River's bank Craig Lockhart, Dalkeith, Montrose, Auchterlonie and Munro – not Monro. This last is incorrect on current maps and was very likely the one name Jackson gave for a specific reason, after a policeman, Munro, was literally caught napping in the Kuruman River by German raiders and shot.

He did give an Afrikaans name to one place, a pan in the north of the KGNP well off the tourist paths. He was busy surveying a farm there when his water supply began to run very low. There was barely enough for him and his crew, none for his horses and oxen. It was a time of severe drought and even the tsamma melons, the emergency moisture ration for all animals and humans in the desert, had run out. The next water source was a very long distance away and his animals were suffering.

He was at the remote pan when he saw massive cumulus clouds build in the sky and soon there came thunder and lightning and then the downpour. He yelled at his men to spread out tarpaulins and they caught enough water for men and beasts. In five minutes the downpour was over; by sheer luck he was in the right place at the right time.

He named the pan Dankbaar – 'Grateful'.

Two of the more intriguing oddities among the KGNP names are Grootskrij and Kleinskrij, the fourth and fifth waterpoints in the Auob south of Mata Mata, rather primly renamed 13th Borehole and 14th Borehole, counting from Twee Rivieren.

The reason for the primness is their slight indelicacy. 'Skrij' is the polite, rather antiquated Afrikaans euphemism for 'skittery' or, in the older spelling, 'skitterij' – which means diarrhoea.

It appears that a surveyor, probably Jackson, arrived at these places in his ox-wagon and camped overnight. His oxen grazed on tsamma melons and drank the brackish water – and promptly emptied their bowels. Hence the no-frills names which served as a warning to any who followed after.

It is not known what became of Jackson. He left two legacies: the collection of curious names and the small heaps of stones that can be seen in riverbeds – boundary markers for the farms he surveyed.

Afrikaans names were given by the first white settlers who moved into these parts and also by the Nama people whose second language was, and still is, Afrikaans. Some were inspired by local features or their association with individuals.

Rooibrak or 'Red Brack' is for the red stone and brack water at this waterpoint. Rooiputs or 'Red Well' is for the red sand there. Melkvlei, 'Milk Hollow', refers to the white chalk banks of the river. Kransbrak or 'Cliff Brack' is for the miniature cliffs or 'kranse' and again the salty water. At Rooikop there is a prominent red dune now topped by a beacon. Kamferboom is named after a World War I borehole guard named Kamfer.

A meeting between man and lion gave Leeuwdril its unusual name. 'Leeuw' is lion, still spelt the old Afrikaans way with a *w*, and 'dril' means to shiver.

Long ago a tough desert-dweller named Matthys paused there and climbed up a sand dune to kill his boredom. It did. As he came over the crest he found himself face to face with a lion. They stared at each other in much surprise. Matthys had left his gun with his other gear down in the riverbed. He was shivering with fright but boldly crossed his arms and faced the lion, having no option because had he run, it would have pounced on him.

'I said to it,' he recounted afterwards, 'If I had my gun I would shoot you.'

The lion eyed him for a few more moments then turned and stalked away. Matthys stopped shivering but the name records his fright for ever – 'Lion Shiver'.

Jan se Draai means, loosely translated, 'Where Jan Turned' and is a short version of its older name Jan se Draai se Gat, 'The Hole Where Jan Turned'. Evidently it marks the well where Jan, a Nama, thought better of it and came home from a trek into the Kalahari. Similarly, Kaspersdraai was named for a man named Kasper who turned back.

In Afrikaans a giraffe is a 'kameelperd' – a word not very different from the little-used English name 'cameleopard'. It was colloquially shortened to 'kameel' and that is the origin of the name Kameelsleep – 'Giraffe Drag'. It is where the last giraffe known to inhabit the area was shot in the late 1800s and dragged across the bed of the Nossob River to the Bechuanaland (now Botswana) side.

Another Nama farmer-hunter of the old days named Matthys (probably a different one, the name was common) was renowned for his thick mass of beard. His memory is preserved for ever at Dikbaardskolk – 'Thick Beard's Hole'.

The origin of the name Lijersdraai in the north near Union's End is uncertain. Some old hands contend the 'lijer' means a baby's nappy ('luier' in modern Afrikaans) because a nearby pan is shaped like one. Others hold it means 'lyer' or 'sufferer' and that this was as far as some travellers got before suffering forced them to turn for home. The second seems the likeliest – it seems improbable that nappies were much used in those days.

Grootkolk, the last waterpoint before Union's End (where vultures are often found because they like the sweet water), is a tenuous link with another war, the bloody rebellion against German rule by the Nama people in the southern part of South West Africa.

It began in 1904 when Namas under one of their senior chiefs, Hendrik Witbooi, rose in revolt and slaughtered hundreds of settlers and their wives and children and ambushed unsuspecting German officials and *Schutztruppe*. It ended four years later in the depths of the Kalahari inside Bechuanaland.

Hendrik Witbooi died in the war, a grim contest between excellent marksmen in broiling heat, and the Nama leadership shifted to another chief and outstanding guerrilla fighter, Simon Koper.

The growing *Schutztruppe* force with better equipment, supplies and transport began to close in on the elusive Koper, determined to crush him finally and for ever. They drove him and his few hundred remaining followers steadily south-east.

Koper took to the bed of the Nossob River, crossed the border into South Africa and, in the vicinity of Grootkolk, led his whole

The caracal – unmistakeable with its red fur, short tail and large, long-tipped ears – is a superb hunting machine. Weighing about fifteen kilograms, it is so fast it can flush birds and pluck them from the air, and so strong it can kill a springbok.
Clem Haagner – ABPL.

The porcupine is active by night but occasionally emerges on cool days, like this one displaying its spiky defences while it feeds on wild cucumbers.
Anthony Bannister – ABPL.

party east straight into Bechuanaland and the Kalahari – territory the Namas knew well but the Germans did not.

Two researchers have scoured the dusty papers in German archives for the story of this long-forgotten Kalahari conflict, a desert drama in the same mould as the French Foreign Legion exploits. They are author Hannes Kloppers and Wulf Haacke, herpetologist at the Transvaal Museum in Pretoria who was born in South West Africa close to where the drama began. Their versions differ slightly and this is a distillation of both.

The pursuing Germans knew very well that to catch Koper they would have to intrude into South Africa and British territory. They did not hesitate – their presence was unlikely to be reported until they were long gone.

Realising it would be disastrous to enter the Kalahari Thirstland on horseback without knowledge of its scarce watering places, they decided to use camels.

Near Gochas in South West Africa Hauptmann (Captain) Friedrich von Erckert of the *Schutztruppe* assembled baggage camels and trained them to become accustomed to riders.

On 4 March 1908, he received orders to move across the border to Geinab – the German name for present-day Grootkolk. Seven days later two *Schutztruppe* groups met there under his command.

They numbered twenty-three officers, 373 riflemen, 130 supporting troops drawn from South West Africa's indigenous population and four medics. They had four machine guns manned by men of an artillery unit but no cannon. They formed a formidable force for those days, a small army.

For transport of men and supplies they had 710 camels – probably the largest number of these animals ever assembled in Southern Africa.

Grootkolk became briefly a bustling military outpost complete with a heliograph station, observation post in a big camelthorn tree to pass messages back into home territory, entrenchments and a small gun battery on a nearby prominence.

On 11 March, and the next day, they rested and filled their containers with water for the coming foray into unknown Thirstland.

Koper and his Namas had no need of such a load. Born Kalahari dwellers, they knew where to look for water and could easily subsist on the tsamma melons, the wild fruit that sustains so much life.

The Germans also knew about tsammas but could not depend on them. The fruit constipates people unused to them and can swell the joints of draught animals.

The German expedition set forth eastwards into the Bechuanaland Protectorate at dusk on the second day, 12 March, to travel in the cool of night and stopped when the moon set at 1.25 a.m.

German Schutztruppe *in the Kalahari. Their pursuit after the fleeing Nama tribe was relentless.* Namibia Archives.

Next morning they moved forward another five kilometres to a pan which historians cannot identify with certainty but believe to be Dimpo, then known as Rempu or Limpo. There they built a heliograph tower with logs.

Leaving behind a team of signallers they moved thirteen kilometres more that night and rested the next day while more water was fetched from Grootkolk. The heat, as usual in March, was ferocious. In the evening they continued to Molentsana Pan, site of an abandoned settlement.

There Hauptmann von Erckert made a bad mistake. He chose to make a night reconnaissance himself and became lost. He fired a flare to summon help and find his way.

Simon Koper saw the flare. It was a complete giveaway. At first light he left, pushing further east into the Kalahari.

On 15 March, sensing they were close, the Germans left the men of their ambulance corps at Molentsana and went on. They found the fresh tracks of Bushmen scouting for the Namas and sent their own scouts ahead. Shots were heard but the Bushmen escaped.

That evening the *Schutztruppe* came across a Nama camp that had been abandoned earlier the same day. Soon after this a message came back from their senior scout, a Lieutenant Geibel, saying the fleeing Nama group was fourteen to sixteen kilometres north-east of Molentsana near a pan named Seatsub, today known as Sitachwe.

By the time the Hauptmann received this news his scouts had approached to within two or three kilometres of the Namas. It was clear the decisive moment was near. The Namas had obviously decided to make their stand – hard and angry men who used good rifles with great skill.

Hauptmann von Erckert stopped his force thirty-five minutes after midnight on the morning of 16 March and gave his battle orders at 2 a.m. His plan was to surround the Namas and defeat them once and for all in a dawn attack.

The Germans deployed in the dark and the fight began at 05.15 a.m. Crawling forward to get closer to the enemy, Von Erckert came rather too close – right into a small group of entrenched Namas. He was killed by one of the first shots of the battle. Hauptmann Grüner took command.

The German attack wobbled. Attempting to close the circle around the Namas, a weak point developed in their line, a lieutenant and nine men were killed and twenty-five Namas slipped through.

At 06.30 a.m. Hauptmann Grüner ordered a bayonet charge to try to overwhelm the enemy. Faced by the horror of cold steel, the Nama force broke up and fled into the Kalahari.

The German pursuit stopped at 07.30. When they had calmed down and recovered their breath they made the gloomy count: fifty-eight Namas and thirteen Germans dead. Twenty Germans wounded. How many Namas were wounded is unknown because they were carried away by the fugitives.

Hauptmann Grüner decided not to continue the pursuit because the Kalahari was vast, the fugitives were scattered and water was running short. The ambulance corps came up from Molentsane to treat the injured, two of whom died later on the trek back to Grootkolk.

Koper's wife was one of the few Namas captured. Another was a man named Eliesar and for him, the killing was not yet ended. Eliesar was believed by the Germans to have murdered a Scot in South West Africa during the uprising, a man named Duncan who had married a woman of Nama descent. One of the German scouts was also a Duncan – a son of the murdered man. When he saw Eliesar was a prisoner, he shot him dead.

The *Schutztruppe* had penetrated about eighty kilometres into Botswana and now had to make the long trek back, weary and battle-worn.

They made it without great difficulty because they were able to catch rain in tarpaulins and were met on the way by supply camels from Grootkolk bringing enough water to give each man 2,5 litres.

The battle was decisive insofar as it finally dispersed the Namas as an effective fighting force but it did not destroy them. The rest were absorbed into the somnolent life of Bechuanaland, where other Namas had long lived.

Koper appealed to the British government for asylum. The British let him make his home at Lokgwabe, a dismally remote spot not far north of the KGNP, where he became known as Cooper.

And far from displaying indignation at the German invasion, they passed on to him an annual remittance of £60 paid by Germany on condition he stayed out of South West Africa.

Koper/Cooper died in 1913 but his descendants and those of many of his followers still live in the western Kalahari. No reminder remains at Grootkolk of the long-ago German presence, only the sweet water and the name 'Big Hole', because this is where they dug a large well for their camp.

The location of the battlefield where so many died has been forgotten. Neither Kloppers nor Haacke have been able to find it using old German official records, letters and diaries.

The most recent name in the park is for a waterpoint near Nossob camp, and as the individuals concerned are still extant, they shall remain unidentified.

The man hired to drill the borehole there started the job and then hit the bottle so hard it flattened him. Without his direction his labourers could not carry on and work ground to a halt. After some

Wattled starlings gather cockily at a waterhole.
Nigel Dennis – ABPL.

The glossy starling's iridescent blue and its bright yellow eye contrast strikingly. This one is surfacing from a bath.
Paul Funston – ABPL.

A pair of red-eyed bulbuls and a weaver (centre) at a waterhole.
Anthony Bannister – ABPL.

days of this, his exasperated wife Marie rolled up her sleeves, chivvied the men into action and supervised the rest of the drilling herself. Her determination and her husband's binge are thus immortalised in the name Marie se Gat – 'Marie's Hole'.

A considerable number of the park's place names – too many to detail here – are in the Nama or Bushman languages or are corruptions of these. While the meanings are clear it is not always known how they came about although, like the Afrikaners, the Namas and Bushmen tended to be forthrightly earthy in choosing their words.

The meanings given here come from Ranger Sergeant Karel 'Vet Piet' Kleinman, or 'Littleman', who has lived and worked in the KGNP for many years on and off and says his real name is Kruiper (but he was misnamed when given his first identity document). The nickname of Vet Piet – 'Fat Piet' – was tagged on him when his mother worked in Warden Joep le Riche's kitchen because he refused to eat bread unless it was liberally spread with fat drippings from roasting meat.

The two most obvious indigenous names in the KGNP are Auob and Nossob. Auob means bitter river because its water was brackish and Nossob dry river because it flows so seldom or, according to a dictionary of Hottentot words, difficult river because it flows with difficulty.

The origin of Mata Mata, name of the small camp on the Auob at the Namibia border, is not certain. In SeTswana, the language of Botswana, it means 'run' according to Vet Piet but in Nama *Ma* is 'mother' and *Ta* is 'father'.

Sitzas, its closest waterpoint, is Nama for 'come and taste', an invitation to test if water is fresh. Kijkij on the Nossob means 'Big Big' but why it is called this, is a mystery. Possibly it refers to the breadth of the river there and the strength of the water supply. Kij Games and Kij Garries, both in the dunes between the rivers, mean respectively 'Big Pride of Lions' and 'Big Scoop' – in this case, of water, says Vet Piet.

The dictionary, compiled by pioneering academics, contains another and less prosaic translation of Kij Garries. 'Kij' is 'big' and 'garrie', their source states, means 'anthrax' – thus Big Anthrax.

It records a tragedy. Wandering people of the Koranna tribe turned up there and their cattle grazed and died. Rescuing something from this appalling loss (because cattle represented almost all the wealth of these semi-nomadic folk), the people ate the cattle and many of them died too.

The tongue-twisting Cubitje Quap, made more so when correctly spoken with a click at the beginning, is 'Antbear Pan' and actually refers to a pan full of antbear holes close to the waterpoint north of Nossob camp.

Further north is the sweet-water drinking place Kannaguass or 'Place of the Camelthorn', 'kanna' being the Nama name for the tree.

Among the names off the beaten track is O'Kuip, the 'O' indicating 'bitter'. But Vet Piet cannot identify the 'Kuip'. Bayip means the ram of a sheep and Nu Quap, also with a click, is 'Black Street' – the term for the long hollows between dunes covered with dark scrub.

Namabies is a brown female ostrich, Karib Gnoose the small or pinkie finger and Karup, north of Bayip, is for the contents of the tsamma melon.

Gharagab is for pans of brack water, Sebobogas means 'Blue Bush Pan' after the vegetation there and Garakap is the name of a long-gone headman.

Twee Ndabas Pan on the park's southern border is a misnomer, Vet Piet believes, because 'ndaba' is a Zulu word for a meeting or debate and no Zulus ever came this way. He thinks it is a distortion by alien tongues of Nama Cam, 'Two Faces', the Nama term for two pans close to each other.

An account of names could go on forever. These are merely a taste to give something of the distinctive flavour of the KGNP.

CHAPTER THREE

Ecology

An army of gemsbok thunders across a Kalahari riverbed beneath a forest of spear-like horns.
Clem Haagner – ABPL.

Seen from a light plane flying a few hundred feet above it, the KGNP is a russet ocean suddenly turned solid. Its twisting sand dunes snake to distant horizons in long parallel swells above wide troughs as if they were heaving towards some faraway shore when they were stilled.

Travelling the single road in the park that crosses the dunes gives the same impression: the constant up and down motion through the troughs and over the rounded crests is akin to riding deep-sea swells in a trawler.

This ocean is broken by stretches of rippled sand plains, islets of pale pans and the winding grey ribbons of two dry riverbeds, the Nossob curving south-south-east to the park's entrance and main camp at Twee Rivieren, and the Auob leading south-east to its confluence with the Nossob a few kilometres north of the camp.

These three – the sandveld of dunes and plains, the pans and the riverbeds – are the only kinds of surface terrain in the KGNP and play interlocking roles in its cycles of climate and animal behaviour.

The long, long dunes, which sometimes converge and cross like waves in a turbulent sea, lift ten to twenty metres above the troughs and are ridges of a mantle of sand between three and a half and thirty-five metres deep, blanketing a bed of sandstone, calcrete and conglomerate. They are alab dunes, so called because they are lined in the direction of the winds that shaped them, and were created in a dry period two million to seven million years ago when gales blew them into roughly their present forms but probably as high as fifty metres.

Their striking redness shading from pinks through orange almost to crimson comes from the minutely thin coating on every sand grain of iron oxide leached out of the earth millions of years ago by slow geological and climatic processes.

The bounty of the sand is that it quickly absorbs and holds precious rainfall, saving it from evaporation and giving life to an abundant growth of edible grasses, flowers, shrubs and trees that in good seasons clad the countryside in a multi-coloured patchwork of white-gold grasses and brilliant flowers. It is also so good an insulator that when its surface is a roasting 70°C, the temperature a few centimetres beneath the surface can be 15°C lower – making it possible for a whole mini-world of small creatures to live there in their own micro-ecosystems.

The pans are still being explored by scientists but most are believed to be the relics of ancient watercourses that drained the region until wind covered it with sand. They are of no particular shape or size and are scattered all over the Kalahari Desert.

The pans' contribution to life is that they have more kinds of soil than the sand area, they accumulate rainwater, they sustain a more varied and denser growth of plants, and they concentrate chemicals needed by animals, including salt.

Both the Auob and the Nossob are sometimes described as 'fossil' rivers because their flow has diminished vastly since the time when they sliced southwards through the sands from their catchment areas in present-day Namibia, emptying their water into the Molopo River which in turn used to feed the great Orange River. Very occasionally – at intervals of anything between ten and thirty years – they flow like cornucopias and carry in gifts of silt, detritus and even fish. Their water sometimes still reaches the Molopo but now filters away into the desert sands that block it from the Orange.

The Nossob enters the KGNP at Union's End, the most northerly point accessible to visitors, and twists tortuously for about 250 kilometres along a bed that narrows from more than a kilometre there to as little as 100 metres in the south between steep limestone banks.

The Auob enters further south at Mata Mata and flows for about 120 kilometres between limestone banks that reach a depth of about forty metres near Twee Rivieren.

The rivers are the KGNP's most important physical asset. The soils on their banks and in their beds are richer in nutrients than any other part of the park, they support different and more nutritious vegetation than the sandveld including many large trees, they hold open water for long periods after rain falls in the park or upstream of it, and they offer sustenance and shelter for a very wide range of wildlife, large and small.

The rivers are still very much the subject of research but a generally accepted estimate is that some ninety per cent of the park's fauna can be found in or very close to them. Many animals, especially the bigger buck, move commonly between the rivers and the surrounding dunes and plains, but the rivers are where they concentrate.

The rivers are also the KGNP's main highways – except in those rare years when water makes them impassable. The road from Twee Rivieren to Mata Mata camp follows the Auob River and for most of the distance runs in its bed. Similarly, the road to Nossob camp and beyond it to Union's End, where there is only a lonely picnic place, clings to the Nossob's bed.

It is here in the riverbeds that, during the course of the seasons, virtually every kind of animal and bird in the park can be seen, especially between March and May and again in August and October if reasonable rain has fallen in the first period. Even the fleet and dainty steenbok, a determined sandveld resident that can go indefinitely without water, sometimes ventures into the riverbeds.

And they can be seen with breathtaking clarity, not just because they tend to accumulate in the narrow strips of land between the river banks, but because the air is so clean, the desert view is so uncluttered and the wildlife is so uncaring about vehicles.

Medium to large creatures can be discerned from kilometres distant. Small ones like suricates and ground squirrels go exuberantly about their business a few metres from onlookers. Eagles, hawks and other raptors will perch and search undisturbed as close as thirty metres to a car before launching themselves at their prey, and will often return to the same perch to eat it. Jackals are sometimes rather shy, usually not: we followed a few paces behind one for over half a kilometre in broad daylight while it went its way, sometimes pausing to sniff, often recrossing the road, totally ignoring the car.

The purity of environment and the proximity of its inhabitants make the park a paradise for the serious observer as well as a delight to the casual visitor. Its kaleidoscopic pageant of wildlife can be examined in an ideally untrammelled natural habitat. And the more one observes the inhabitants, the clearer becomes the single characteristic common to all of them, from insect to antelope: the naked intensity of their daily struggle for survival. It is a force that oddly unifies them even in competition.

Chief Research Officer Dr P T van der Walt wrote:

The KGNP has a special attraction for the nature-lover who values the roles played by every living thing and gives particular attention to them. There is an organised interaction between a wide variety of plants and animals in an unspoilt and often harsh environment. In what appears to be simple surroundings, the tourist will discover rich and complex animal and plant life.

Of the big animals much sought after by visitors to other parks only the lion, leopard and cheetah are found here – no elephant (except once when two wandered down from the north), no buffalo (except one lost wanderer once), no hippo or crocodile of course. This difference is more than adequately compensated by the KGNP's own very special flavour, by such buck as the gemsbok and springbok found only in the arid western parts of Southern Africa, and by the visibility of animal behaviour.

It is not possible to describe in detail the complete variety of wildlife because that would take volumes. Instead what follows is a cross-section of examples to whet the appetite for this extraordinary reserve and hopefully help those willing to challenge distance, primitive roads and some expense, to visit it.

The Grazers and Browsers

The true king of the Kalahari is not the lion, but the **gemsbok** – although it is often killed by the lion – the animal best designed by evolution to live in dry country. Gemsbok continue to survive easily long after lions have been driven away by thirst and hunger.

The march of population and progress has confined the Southern African gemsbok mainly to the Kalahari and Namib deserts extending north into Southern Angola and south into the Northern Cape.

Well over a metre high at the shoulder, it is a handsome animal with its deep-chested body crowned by a V of long straight horns tapering to sharp points. Its coloration seems of little use as camouflage for it makes the gemsbok stand out against its own background: black and white face, grey coat, black spine and tail and black side stripes running from front to back above its white belly.

It is a formidable fighter with lightning-fast reflexes in spite of its bulk of up to 240 kilograms.

Hunters whose dogs have cornered wounded gemsbok have seen them back into thorn bush for protection from the rear, lower their heads and with eye-dazzling speed transfix dogs approaching too close. One man threw stones at a trapped gemsbok to distract its attention. It easily batted them away with its horns. A ranger trying to catch a big gemsbok bull in his Land Rover saw it suddenly stop. He stopped too. It lowered its horns parallel to the ground and with vicious thrusts punctured all four of his tyres.

In the KGNP gemsbok are a main item on the lion's diet, which is not unduly serious for the gemsbok because there are relatively few lion. They too treat the gazelle with respect and seldom dare to single-handedly tackle a full-grown adult.

The speciality that makes the gemsbok king is its astonishing defence mechanism against extreme heat and drought.

Being big, it already has a relatively small surface area exposed to the sun's heat – relative, that is, to the volume of its body. Because of that it has what scientists call 'thermal inertia': it gains or loses heat by radiation and conduction more slowly than smaller animals.

A gemsbok captured in full gallop, with all four feet off the ground, shows the muscled chest and neck which give the thrust of its horns such power.
Nigel Dennis – ABPL.

A classic Kalahari scene: black, white and grey gemsbok against the backdrop of grass and dune.
Anthony Bannister – ABPL.

Its most important adaptation is to let its body temperature fluctuate through an exceptionally wide range.

This was demonstrated in pioneering research by Professor Richard Taylor of Harvard University. In controlled experiments he found that when it has enough water to drink the gemsbok, like any other hoofed animal of the desert, keeps its temperature steady at about 39°C by sweating.

But thirst immediately separates it from most other animals. Deprived of water, it lets its body temperature vary more than 7°C between temperatures representing the cool of night and the heat of day – from 33,9°C to 41°C. Its low night temperature and its high thermal inertia enable it to absorb a large amount of heat in the day and then shed it again by radiation when night returns – without sweating, so its body retains what water it has.

But desert temperatures often rise higher than that, so Professor Taylor subjected the gemsbok to 45°C . Astonishingly, the animal's own temperature rose well above 45°C and stayed there for hours – in spite of the fact that a body temperature of 42°C does fatal damage to the brain of most mammals. Still, it did not sweat.

The gemsbok is actually able to save water by losing heat to the already hot surrounding air. How does it let its body become so heated without killing itself? By using a device developed over millions of years of evolution – a very special blood-cooling system situated just beneath its brain.

Here hot blood being taken to the brain by the carotid artery flows through the carotid rete, a network of small, fine blood vessels. These lie close to veins taking used blood back to the heart from the sinuses in the nose, where it has already been cooled several degrees by the gemsbok's breathing through its nostrils.

Thus hot blood on the way to the brain loses heat to the cooled blood going back to the heart and arrives at its destination at a temperatures the brain can tolerate without harm to the vital neural centres.

The carotid rete is not unique to the gemsbok – some other buck and sheep also have it – and its ability to let its temperature fluctuate is shared by the eland. But none other combines these attributes with such remarkable efficiency.

The gemsbok has several additional ways of combating moisture loss. It can slow its metabolic rate considerably. When it needs to, it breathes slower and deeper to avoid moisture in its breath while still getting all the oxygen it requires. Its digestive system extracts considerably more moisture from its food than most other animals can, producing concentrated urine and drier droppings. It both grazes and browses and is very selective in its feeding, choosing plants with high moisture content. It feeds by night when grass absorbs much moisture from the air, as well as by day.

In dry times when most vegetation contains little water the gemsbok depends heavily on two unusual Kalahari ground plants that are staples for a great many other animals, including carnivores and birds, and also for people. They are the tsamma melon and the gemsbok cucumber whose content is about ninety per cent water. It is also a great digger for tubers, bulbs and roots when grass is scarce – in short, a highly versatile animal.

Gemsbok are commonly seen anywhere in the KGNP, singly or in small groups and sometimes in herds of thirty or more. They often gather to drink at waterholes but, paradoxically, leave the water in dry periods because their non-dependence on it frees them to seek food where they wish.

The bulls are determinedly territorial and stake out for themselves patches of desert anything from four square kilometres to ten square kilometres. There they stay most of their time, gathering up private harems from passing groups of cows. They do not appear to mind young bulls sharing their territories provided they behave themselves and do not seduce the cows, but will fight off any competing bulls that intrude.

They mark their territories with small beacons of odorous dung at prominent boundary points, by anointing shrubbery with scent from cheek glands, by pawing the ground to leave scent from foot glands, and by beating up inoffensive bushes with their horns to demonstrate to would-be intruders what their fate will be if they dare to cross the line.

When cows give birth they hide their calves by day for up to six weeks, at the end of which the youngsters join the herds.

Having a territory has distinct advantages for a bull quite apart from containing its harem, as Mr Michael Knight, who did research at Nossob, points out.

The bull gets to know his territory as well as a suburbanite knows his own backyard. It knows the other animals there, the paths they follow, where the food is and the quickest way in and out. Familiarity is security: if a lion comes after it, the bull has a better chance of escaping its intentions. Once a bull leaves its territory it becomes much more vulnerable to predators.

The elegant **springbok**, which has the pleasantly rhythmic scientific name of *Antidorcas marsupialis*, is the most famed of South Africa's antelope and justifiably the national symbol. It once roamed the great dry Southern African savannah in millions but is now confined in the wild to roughly the same regions as the gemsbok, although an increasing number of farmers in the Orange Free State, Karoo, Namaqualand and Western Transvaal maintain sizeable herds.

They are to the KGNP what the impala are to the African bushveld – the buck bourgeoisie, a strolling larder for many hunters, and a constant source of entertainment.

Standing about seventy-five centimetres high at the shoulder, springbok are beautiful, long-necked antelope which always appear freshly groomed in the sunshine. A broad dark brown stripe separates the light brown from the clean white of their underparts. Symmetric lyre-shaped horns perch in front of slim pointed ears. The rather superior expression of its white face, striped with red from eyes to mouth, is often spoilt by a sideways motion of its jaws as if it is chewing gum – in fact it is cud.

But the idiosyncrasy for which the springbok is most famous is its 'pronking' or stotting. When a herd becomes alarmed they will start moving at a fast, high-stepping trot with heads held erect and alert. This can break into a sprint exceeding eighty kilometres an hour, with leaps of two metres or more that carry them several times their own length, legs outstretched.

Many will pronk, both rams and ewes. It is a spectacular sight. They arch their backs, lower their heads, hold their legs stiffly straight beneath them and effortlessly bounce high in the air, landing repeatedly on pointed toes with a precision and grace ballerinas must envy. It seems impossible that the force of their forty-kilogram bodies does not snap their slender limbs.

At the same time they hoist their signal flags. Tall crests of snow-white hair fan out from pouches along the lower part of their spines. There are few things so thrilling in nature as the sight of a rippling stream of springbok with scores of erect fans constantly bouncing up above the herd as if gravity were a plaything. It is small wonder these antelope captured the imagination of the early explorers when they were discovered centuries ago.

The spinal pouches, about ten centimetres long and unseen until they perform, are the reason for the *marsupialis* in their taxonomic name – not any ability to carry their young as kangaroos do. The crests go up when the springbok are alarmed but as often as not they will pronk and flourish the flags for no apparent reason except the fun of it.

Over many years of observation Dr 'Gus' Mills who has done voluminous pathfinding research in the KGNP, found that springbok, together with gemsbok and red hartebeest, have the paradoxical habit of gathering in the riverbeds, which have copious borehole water-points the year round, 'during the rains, when it would be expected that their need for water would be lowest.

'Then, as conditions dry out, they disperse into the dunes, most of them into areas in Botswana where there is no water. Moreover, in dry years fewer of these animals come into the riverbeds than in wet years.'

One reason is that, like gemsbok and also the hartebeest, springbok need little water. As long as their food contains at least ten to fif-

A herd of springbok browsing through a river bed makes a striking pattern of black, white and brown.
Clem Haagner – ABPL.

One of the springbok's peculiarities is its ability to bounce about the veld on four rigidly extended legs as if on coil springs – hence its name. Sometimes it bounces with head down and a flag of white hair erect on its rump – 'pronking'.
Richard du Toit – ABPL.

teen per cent moisture they survive. They are catholic feeders and their movement is dictated by food more than by water. Their small mouths enable them to graze new growth at ground level.

Again like gemsbok, springbok can breed at any time of the year. The ewes' readiness is determined by their physical condition, which is determined by their nutrition, so most lambs are born when there is enough green food available, which in the KGNP is usually about February or March.

The principal advantage for the species of the mass lambing is that each calf is much less vulnerable to the local predators, who can eat only so many, in a large crowd than on its own.

According to Dr Mills, it is this species' survival device which led to the gigantic springbok population migrations of the last century. He found that in particularly good climatic conditions a springbok can become pregnant at six months and again at just over a year.

The mothers hide the lambs in undergrowth for the first few days when they are wobbly on their feet and highly vulnerable. At this stage, it is believed, the lambs have no body smell, making it difficult for predators to find them except by stumbling right on them. Within a few weeks they run with the rest of the herd.

Herds as large as several hundred can be seen moving about in the cooler hours of the mornings and evenings, delicately nibbling grass and flowers and leaves, suddenly lifting their heads to gaze about them, their white, black-tipped tails flicking metronomically.

The younger ones playfully lunge at each other or skitter about in bubbling bursts of *joie de vivre*. Young rams lock horns – rumps high and forelegs spread – in tests of the strength and skill they will later need to compete for dominance of a territory.

They pay little attention to visitors only twenty or thirty paces away but sometimes, as if to demonstrate their contempt, the whole herd will turn their white backsides and exclamation mark tails towards one.

In the heat of day most of a springbok herd, which might be mixed, or all males or all females, or young or adult, will rest in open patches of riverbed. In hot weather they like to lie down with heads or tails towards the sun to expose as little of themselves as possible to its radiation, forefeet tucked cat-like under their chests, meditatively chewing their cuds, small gardens of bright brown bodies and curled horns against the dun sand. A few stand to keep an eye on the world around.

All along the Auob and Nossob riverbeds, most of the year, are solitary springbok spaced like haphazardly placed milestones. They are the territorial males, the biggest and strongest and the prime breeders.

What looks like a collection of heads is a herd of springbok lying in long grass in the midday heat. Leigh Voigt.

Springbok fight fiercely when defending their territories. This victorious ram has its horns locked around its opponent's neck. Clem Haagner – ABPL.

Instead of venturing out to find mates the territorial ram waits for a group of females to pass through its territory and tries to detain the whole lot. Posturing with head stretched far forward, horns flat back and tail sticking out behind, it tries to shepherd and coax the potential harem into staying.

In response the females sometimes pronk, bouncing around on the tips of gathered toes with spinal crests up but now with heads erect like belles at a ball.

As often as not the females will decide that better prospects lie ahead and stalk right through the territory. The male can do nothing. He cannot follow into the next territory without fighting its ruler. In the end the rams all seem to gather enough ewes to fulfil their mission. It is not without risk because when they are alone the rams are a favourite prey of predators, especially leopards.

One curiosity about springbok, according to Park Warden Elias le Riche, is that when they go on trek it is usually into the wind, presumably because of the smells and promises it carries.

The massive **eland**, between ten and twenty times the size of the springbok, fills a quite separate niche in the natural order and is always on trek.

These biggest of all African antelope were once widespread in Southern Africa as far south as the Southern Cape coast, as evidenced by the many farms, rivers, mountains and other places named after them, though they were never in large numbers. Jan van Riebeeck recorded their presence in the Cape Peninsula more than three centuries ago and their name, eland, which is Dutch for elk, was given to them because the bemused settlers could not think of anything better.

Now they occur in the wild in South Africa only in the far Northern Cape and in the Transvaal's Kruger Park, though they are gradually coming back to their old regions as farmers and private game ranchers reintegrate them.

In Russia, eland bred from animals originally brought from Southern Africa are being farmed experimentally, like cattle, and some ranches in South Africa are trying to do the same. One of the problems of marketing them, however, is transporting them.

They live in complete compatibility with cattle because they are browsers, they can be easily tamed and the cows produce extremely rich milk. They have another endearing quality that, for them, is a distinct disadvantage: they taste very good.

That was why they were decimated in large areas and might have gone the way of the equally tasty dodo had not they been reasonably safe in the arid fastnesses of the hinterland. Their tender venison made them a favourite food and they were an easy mark for hunters; they are not as fast as other antelope and tend to run in straight lines

Eland – like this herd galloping across the sands – are the largest of the antelope and are well adapted to desert life. They appear periodically in the Park, usually in the north.
Anthony Bannister – ABPL.

without jinking. 'You get a lot of meat with one bullet,' as one KGNP ranger exasperated by poachers put it.

Taurotragus oryx oryx, the Southern African sub-species of the eland, weighs about 450 kilograms for cows and 700 kilograms for bulls (although much heavier bulls have been recorded) and is a statuesque animal up to two metres high at the shoulder.

The bulls are markedly larger than the cows and their twisted horns are considerably thicker, though shorter. Both have floppy tufted dewlaps beneath their thick necks, short manes and fawny bodies that blend well into the desert background. Their large gentle eyes peer at one across broad, dark muzzles.

There are usually several thousand in the KGNP, mainly in the north and in the duneveld. Sometimes their numbers suddenly jump fivefold or more. This is because their main roaming ground is the depths of the Kalahari, including that large portion of the KGNP on the Botswana side. Like gemsbok, springbok and red hartebeest, they can go indefinitely without fresh water while the leaves, pods, twigs, flowers, fruit and the occasional grass they eat contain enough moisture. And they too have the strange facility of saving water by allowing body temperature to fluctuate.

It happens every now and then, however, that the moisture content of their food drops below the bottom line, or that conditions have been so favourable that they have produced more calves than usual and there is not enough food for all. Then they go on long treks and arrive in the Auob and Nossob river areas in tens of thousands – an awe-inspiring spectacle of herds of several hundred of the

great beasts with heads held high moving at a steady trot that carries them 100 kilometres in twelve hours.

They have great strength. An adult eland will stroll up to a two-metre-high fence, gather its hindquarters in a slight crouch, and then sail right over the fence from a standing jump. Using their thick straight horns they stretch up into trees and snap off wrist-thick branches to get otherwise unreachable leaves.

Fights between bulls are sometimes fatal. The fights are for dominance, to establish the pecking order in a herd because, unlike all of the other buck in the KGNP, the eland bull is not territorial. He holds no ground and is constantly on the move with the herd because such large animals consume food quickly and they constantly have to seek more.

The dominant bull's 'territory' is in effect the proximity of its harem and it defends it vigorously. When any of its cows are on heat it drives off young bulls with warning displays of its horns and will fiercely attack full-grown bulls who intrude, even goring them to death.

Eland calves find their feet within a few hours of birth. The mothers hide them for a short time before leaving them to look after themselves, when they join nursery herds.

In the KGNP eland tend to be a bonus for visitors because they are not common in the riverbeds, seeming to prefer the dunes and being so independent of water.

Hardly more common is the **red hartebeest**, last of the large KGNP buck who are not bound to water. There are not many in the park at any given time – seldom more than 2 000 to 3 000 – but hartebeest also move at will following the rains to graze and browse the new moisture-rich growth and large herds may suddenly turn up.

Lone hartebeest can sometimes be seen plodding the riverbeds with herds of springbok or wildebeest, perhaps less for the company than for the protection of a crowd. They are very fast runners and if an approach by lion, wild dog or other hunters puts the group to flight, they will outrun the rest.

More than a metre high at the shoulder and weighing between about 100 and 150 kilograms, the hartebeest is easy to distinguish with the high hump on its shoulders, oddly back-twisted and ribbed horns, bold russet body and long lugubrious face. It also appears to be wearing thigh-high black stockings like a Moulin Rouge dancer.

Once almost as widely distributed as the eland but driven even further north since the times of Van Riebeeck, *Alcelaphus buselaphus* are now returning to their former fields under the protection of caring farmers and wildlife organisations.

It is firmly entrenched in the Afrikaans language in the name *hart-beeshuisie* – 'hartebeest house' – for the flimsy one-room structures

Red hartebeest with their oddly-curved horns mounted on top of their heads are among the fastest of all buck. These two bulls duelled over territorial rights in the breeding season. The duel ended only when one collapsed from fatigue among the rocks on the river bank. The winner stood by for a long time, ready to fight to the death if his opponent rose again.
Clem Haagner – ABPL.

of wattle and daub or sticks and reeds commonly erected by pioneering hunters and settlers centuries ago. Legend has it that a fleeing hartebeest galloped straight through one of these as if it was not there.

In the Kalahari they gather in small herds, some of bachelors, others of cows and youngsters dominated by adult bulls holding their territories against all comers, as do gemsbok and springbok. Sometimes under environmental pressures such as lack of rain and consequent shortage of grass, their staple food, the herds will drift together in migrations numbering thousands.

Their young are born in spring and early summer and are hidden by their mothers until, a few days later, they can walk with the herd. They can run surprisingly fast after a few weeks but those unable to stay with the herd in full flight fall prone to the ground and lie still to avoid pursuers.

The last of the KGNP's five large buck is an oddity in the desert – the **blue wildebeest** or brindled gnu, *Connochaetes taurinus*. This deceptively ungainly animal with its grey-blue hide, hump-backed body and Roman nose set on an oversized, bearded head is commonly associated with the African bushveld and savannah where water is never too distant.

Here in the Kalahari – waterless for most of the time and with

In a dangerous world, one of the blue wildebeest's built-in defences is the ability of babies to run within half an hour of being born. This newborn youngster has struggled to its feet with its mother's encouragement (above), is able to wobble after her within some fifteen minutes (top right), and stands with more confidence by the time she rejoins the herd (bottom right).
Anthony Bannister – ABPL.

permanent drinking places only in the KGNP's rivers – they seem distinctly out of place, bumbling actors on the wrong stage.

They are the animals least adapted to aridity, needing water every two or three days, preferring it fresh and unsalty, and being eaters only of grass – and mainly short grass at that. Yet wildebeest wander far and fast throughout the Kalahari, sometimes in outsize herds streaming across dunes and plains like swarms of ants.

As a species the wildebeest is a superb survivor; as an individual, not. They are adept at following rainstorms to drink from puddles and graze on the moist green grass. When conditions are right they breed in great numbers. When conditions are wrong they trek in large herds which transform into huge migrations.

And they die in tens of thousands when they cannot find enough water and grazing. On one trek the toll was estimated by conservationists at 80 000. Despite this, sufficient numbers, the strongest, reach water and grazing to live on and ensure that their kind multiplies again.

Because of its permanent waterholes the KGNP has a resident population of wildebeest and they can be seen at any time of the year, sometimes in quite big herds, at other times in small groups when the rest have been lured as far as 200 kilometres away into the sandveld by thunderstorms promising succulent grazing.

At irregular intervals that might span a decade or more, the average resident population of 2 000 to 3 000 is dramatically swelled by refugees from drought in the deeper desert. In 1985 roughly 150 000 emaciated, famished, thirsty wildebeest poured in, overwhelmed the waterholes and perished in piles around them before the survivors plodded on, temporarily refreshed, to seek new pasturage.

Once described as 'a horse designed by a committee', the wildebeest is not as oafish as its oddly disproportionate body, floppy fringes of hair, handlebar horns, long face and coltish movements might suggest. It is a fast, alert and reasonably large animal with the bulls standing one and a half metres at the shoulder and weighing a not inconsiderable 250 kilograms (the cows weigh rather less).

If wildebeest could be given a human attribute it would be an amiable gregariousness. Singly and in small groups they mingle easily with other buck, which seem to tolerate them with a sigh. Usually they gather in family herds from a few dozen to several hundred strong, rising sometimes to thousands – bulls, cows, youngsters all together.

Only when the cows' breeding time comes is there any sign of aggression, and even then it is tempered by tolerance. Wildebeest too are territorial and mark off their ground with foot and cheek glands, droppings and malevolent glares.

In the season they, too, frantically gather up harems of ready and able cows, but with a difference: a bull might hold his territory on his own, or he might share it and the harem with two or three other bulls – a buddy system that works because they all help to keep the harem at home and hold seducers at bay in head-butting battles.

In this time the unlucky bachelors join together in club herds to mope disappointedly outside the territories, which also happen to occupy the choicest grazing.

Literally within minutes of being born a wildebeest calf can stand on wobbling legs and within half an hour it can run – its best defence. Comical they might be, but the wildebeest tribe are survivors in a hard world.

Several other kinds of buck appear in the KGNP permanently or temporarily. It has about 500 **kudu**, *Tragelaphus strepsiceros*, the ubiquitous antelope favoured by many people as the most beautiful of all with their shapely striped bodies, great eyes and ears, the bull's long spiral horns and their lissom grace of movement.

Widespread in Namibia, Botswana and the northern parts of South Africa, where they persist in considerable numbers in spite of hunting and development, kudu generally appear in the KGNP in small groups and are usually seen in the early and late hours of sunshine when the air is cooler and they emerge to wander and feed.

They eat just about anything including crops, flowers and vegetables and will jump with ease over two-metre fences to get at them, which is one reason why they so often find themselves gazing into the gun barrels of irate farmers.

Two other buck common in the KGNP are the stocky common **duiker**, *Sylvicapra grimmia*, possibly the most widespread antelope in Africa, and the dainty **steenbok**, *Raphicerus campestris*, equally tall at about half a metre but much lighter and longer-legged.

Neither appears as often as other buck because they seldom come into the riverbeds from the dunes and plains. They can best be seen beside the dune road linking the two rivers or along the northern end of the road to Union's End where it runs between broad grassy plains, the duiker greyish and round-backed, the steenbok slim of build and fawn in colour.

The rams of both the duiker and steenbok live alone in their territories except during breeding seasons when they pair with females, and they never gather in herds. Quite shy creatures, they are usually seen running away from the intruder – the duiker with the distinctive bounds which give it its Afrikaans name meaning 'diver', and the steenbok in a flat jinking run with short leaps.

Every few years a lucky tourist in the KGNP will see one or several most peculiar springbok in a herd – bigger and bright red with pale instead of black side stripes and quite different facial markings.

They are not springbok but **impala**, *Aepyceros melampus*, mistaken at first sight from a distance only because impala are the last

thing one expects to find here. They come only in good rain years when the desert can sustain travellers but why they come and where from are not certain. It could be from the Lake Ngami region of Botswana some 500 kilometres to the north, where impala are fairly common.

Sometimes only one or two impala are seen and once a herd of twenty-seven was seen roaming with the springbok. After short visits they vanish as mysteriously as they appeared.

The Hunters

Probably nowhere else in Africa can carnivorous animals be as easily observed as in the KGNP.

Here the terrain is so uncluttered that activities ordinarily screened by bush often take place in full view, and most animals are so engrossed by the pressures of living they pay little heed to watchers.

There is an added blessing: because of the park's limited tourist capacity the watchers seldom have the irritation of being crowded by scores of other vehicles loaded with onlookers, which is becoming the bane of the Kruger National Park.

There are nineteen species of carnivores in the KGNP ranging from the jet black and pure white striped polecat weighing in at less than a kilogram to the big black-maned lion weighing more than 230 kilograms.

Some, like the striped polecat, are seldom seen because they are out and about only at night. Others function by day, and some at any time. But there is always the chance, day or night, of coming across even the rarities because their activities are so changeable.

The beautiful bat-eared fox, for example, is a night-time rover almost everywhere else in South Africa, partly because it used to be ruthlessly and pointlessly hunted. In the KGNP this small hunter with the huge dish ears and tiny black legs beneath a voluptuous fur coat, wanders happily by day in cooler weather, sometimes in groups of up to six.

The African wildcat is also a hunter in the dark but is often seen streaking across riverbed or sandveld, black heels flickering, pausing to frown back at intruders.

Wild dogs might be nowhere in the park and then suddenly one morning there they will be, patchwork coats glossy in the sun as they lope along a riverbed.

Watching carnivores in particular takes patience. Ask the rangers where they might be, go there, and wait. There is no guarantee; nothing might appear for a week and then on a single day lions, leopards, cheetahs, foxes, jackals, badgers and others can be seen. And then it takes more patience; a leopard may sleep all day on a branch, legs dangling, before it condescends to move.

All the KGNP carnivores have one characteristic in common: they can live indefinitely without water provided they can find enough prey because about two-thirds of the animals they eat are made up of fluids. They also lick dew from plants and will eat tsamma melons and other water-rich fruits. They save energy by resting in shade or in burrows during the heat of day.

The principal attraction for many people is the **Kalahari lion**, *Panthera leo*. Some people hold that it is a bigger lion than those of the South African bushveld, not necessarily a sub-species, but different. Others say it is exactly the same and merely looks bigger because of the wide open landscape. The debate goes on.

Certainly it looks lighter in colour than, say, the lions of Kruger, and cleaner, and the gold ruffs and black manes of the big males seem longer and thicker. They are handsome arrogant cats blessed (or cursed, according to one's nerves) with inordinate curiosity.

Elsewhere the traditional safeguard against lions when camping in the bundu is to keep a hearty fire going all night. Not here. 'Kalahari lions are very inquisitive,' says Elias le Riche speaking from the experience of countless bundu camps. 'If you want to attract them you light a fire.'

All lions are lazy layabouts that spend most of their time sleeping

A steenbok peers at the intruder through curtains of lush grass following good rains.
Richard du Toit – ABPL.

in the sun, according to many authorities. The Kalahari lion also loves to loaf, but has to work hard for the privilege.

Both Professor Fritz Eloff, NPB chairman and doyen of lion researchers, and Dr Gus Mills report that these lions – there are about 150 in the KGNP – travel extraordinary distances to find and catch their prey.

Professor Eloff, who has spent many weeks following lions through the desert to observe their behaviour, records one instance when a lioness covered 41,2 kilometres one night – travelling as far as twenty kilometres from the cub it was feeding – in search of food. It tried and failed eight times to kill. The next night it hunted for twenty-two kilometres and the night after that twenty-four kilometres, at last killing and eating two small animals and feeding on a carcass from which it chased two spotted hyena.

Then it returned to the hungry cub, to find it gone. It had been killed, partly eaten and buried by a jackal.

It is commonplace for Kalahari lions to travel far. Three lions caught outside the park in farmland were released ninety-two kilometres inside it and promptly headed back. Three days later they were found on the move 137 kilometres away. Again they were caught and freed at the same place. Six days later they arrived back in the farmland where they were first captured, 192 kilometres distant. They had covered a total of 205 kilometres in nine days.

This unusual mobility is enforced by the environment: the relative paucity of medium and large prey animals except during migrations, and the increased difficulty of catching them in the open terrain with little cover.

Kruger Park scientists logged about fifteen kills per lion per year. In the KGNP the rate is about forty-seven animals a year, Professor Eloff states. The reason is simply that in Kruger there are more and greater concentrations of medium to large animals; in the KGNP lions are obliged to kill more often to subsist on a wide variety of small as well as large animals to meet their intake averaging 7,2 kilograms a day for a lion and 4,7 kilograms for a lioness.

Dr Mills analysed 370 lion kills in the KGNP over eight years. The results are revealing: thirty-seven per cent of their prey were wildebeest, 32,4 per cent gemsbok, thirteen per cent springbok and seven per cent hartebeest – in each species mostly adults. The rest included ostriches, antbears, and, of all things, porcupines.

The range of diet is actually much wider and the lions involved must have killed many more than 370 animals, but of course lions leave little or no trace of their smaller prey. Professor Eloff says that when the bigger animals are scarce, lions will eat anything that comes their way – springbok, bat-eared foxes, jackals, whatever.

A lion cub sprawled over its sleeping mother in search of milk. They are born with spots and retain them through adolescence.
Nigel Dennis – ABPL.

Kalahari lions are genetically the same as those found elsewhere in Southern Africa but the males appear to have darker and thicker manes. It is not known what this fine specimen found so interesting up a tree.
Clem Haagner – ABPL.

But porcupines? Yet another veld tradition is that only young, foolish or devastatingly hungry predators will tackle a porcupine because even if it succeeds in killing and eating this toothsome rodent, it will finish the meal with paws and jaws like pincushions. Elsewhere this condition has often been seen to be fatal.

Not so often in the KGNP, apparently. Lions (and also leopards, which are more adroit at it) flip porcupines over to reach their vulnerable stomachs and end up filled with quills. Yet this does not appear to bother them unduly and they seldom suffer serious harm. Pieces of quill have been found in their scats.

Senior Sergeant Willem de Waal, one of the more experienced rangers in the KGNP, attributes this to the desert climate. It is so dry, he says, that infection is uncommon and after a time scar tissue forms around the quills and they drop out.

These resourceful lions have been known to break open and eat the contents of ostrich eggs (though with some reluctance), happily eat carrion when they find it and steal the prey of other animals.

One fascinated watcher saw a big and hungry black-maned lion circling a large camelthorn tree in the Nossob riverbed, staring up. About ten metres high in the tree hung a dead springbok, obviously freshly killed by a leopard the previous night.

In spite of its size, this lion abandoned the tradition that its species is not supposed to climb very high in trees and scrambled into the lower fork then precariously climbed the branch to the springbok.

There it picked up the carcass 'like a rag doll', climbed back to the fork and jumped to the ground. It ate the whole springbok.

Like all lions, those of the Kalahari are gregarious and gather in prides headed by the dominant male. They occupy loosely defined territories that in the desert tend to be larger than usual – roughly 1 200 square kilometres – because of the scarcity of prey and the distance across which they have to hunt.

Professor Eloff describes 'a beautiful sight' in the KGNP: 'Two lions were sitting on a high dune; it was raining softly and the lions were licking each other, quenching their thirst with droplets of rainwater.'

Their desert life is not all beauty, however. More than two-thirds of their cubs die before they are a year old – compared to between half and two-thirds of cubs elsewhere.

The main cause appears to be starvation. If the mother cannot find enough to eat, she cannot provide milk and the cubs either die of hunger or are so weakened they fall victim to disease. Many, like the one taken by a jackal, are killed by other predators because the mothers have to leave them for long periods to hunt.

Sometimes their mothers, unable to cope, simply abandon them. Sometimes male lions taking up with their mothers kill them and have

A superb example of a leopard in peak condition. Although not in profusion in the Park, they can be found by looking into trees where they like to lie up in the heat of day.
Hein von Horsten – ABPL.

been known to eat them. Until a lion is a full adult it gets the short end of the stick: lionesses in a pride generally make the kills, the males eat first, then the lionesses and finally the cubs get what is left.

They have to be very tough to survive. Their desert life is natural selection at its most uncompromising.

Unlike the lion the **leopard**, *Panthera pardus*, is a loner. Both males and females have their own hunting ranges and intruders must beware. When a female is ready to mate, however, the male makes an exception and condescends to allow her to enter his territory of some 400 square kilometres, temporarily.

There are between fifty and 100 leopards in the KGNP, predominantly in and near the riverbeds because that is where most of their prey are concentrated. Being night hunters they are not very easy to find and one must know where to look: in large trees with thick limbs, in the deep shade under bushes, in cool crevices of the shallow calcrete cliffs.

Once discovered they are not likely to move in the heat of day unless approached too closely, when they will slide away to remoter shelter, sleek and supple cats whose every fluid movement exudes power and grace.

Leopards are spread across more of Africa than any other big cat, living in all kinds of habitats from dense forest to the Kalahari,

though not in extreme desert like the Namib. They are able to do this because they can catch and eat an enormous variety of prey from mice to buck twice their own size, and they grow to as large as ninety kilograms and more than two metres from nose to tail tip.

Here their favourite food is the commonest of the buck, the springbok, which forms about sixty five per cent of their diet according to Dr Mills. But they are highly opportunistic hunters and will seize anything edible in their path be it wildcat or rat or grouse or antbear or ground squirrel or fox. Leopards are known to have a predilection for canines and quite often take jackal. When they kill porcupine they carefully pull out the quills with their teeth before eating them.

Just how catholic are the tastes of a leopard was demonstrated by an incident in the KGNP recorded by Dr Mills. Travelling on the Nossob River road he and his wife saw two cheetah at the Rooiputs waterhole. One was limping and the other had a badly injured face.

Next morning the badly injured cheetah was found hanging high in the fork of a nearby tree – killed and placed there by a leopard. A little of it had been eaten.

Dr J du P Bothma of the University of Pretoria has studied the KGNP leopard by putting to ingenious use the age-old technique of 'reading the desert sands'. In this, trackers find the spoor of a leopard by day, when it is resting, and follow it until they come upon the cat and flush it from its resting place. They note the place and go home. Next morning they return to it and by following the spoor further, the trackers, experts at this business, can decipher exactly what the leopard did during its night.

Smooth body impressions in the red dune sand under a tree will mark the place where it was resting when they flushed it. Wide-spaced pad marks will show where it strolled in a zigzag up the side of a dune apparently to scan the locality from the top, for their night vision like their noses is exceptionally keen. Gouges in the sand are where it sprayed to mark its territorial boundary and then raked the ground with its hind paws to spread the scent. Long scratches down tree trunks reveal where it sharpened its claws or again marked a boundary.

They can tell where it crouched low to stalk a prey by the smooth patches between its pad marks where its belly scraped or it paused. The story of the final furious charge is told by the deep ruts left by the launching thrust of its hindquarters and the imprints of all four feet bunched close, extended claws leaving holes, where it touched down in bounds of four or five metres for distances up to 100 metres.

They will stick to the spoor until once more they flush the leopard, which once more will flow away for anything up to a thousand metres until it finds a fresh place to rest away from the pestering attentions of people. And the whole process will be repeated. It can go on for days.

Secretive though the leopard is, therefore, the researchers can plot its nocturnal prowls as thoroughly as a detective can follow the tracks of a tram.

They have found that it will travel an average of fourteen kilometres a night but more if prey is sparse. The maximum recorded, says Dr Bothma, is thirty-three kilometres. A male kills every third night and a female twice in that time. It will haul the dead prey two or three kilometres to eat it and drag it into a tree only if scavengers are about. Small victims are consumed immediately and entirely, except for innards, feet and jaws, but larger ones take several days to finish.

In the Kalahari heat leopards seek shade by day in trees, beneath dense bushes or in old antbear or porcupine holes. They start to become active towards dusk, which leaves visitors little time to find and watch them before the camp gates close. A better time to seek leopards is in the early mornings when they tend to relax in the sunshine on vantage points after the night's excursions.

They breed at any time of the year and by all accounts leopard mothers are diligent, taking great care of the cubs and staying friendly with them long after they have gone out into the world on their own. One of the quainter sights of the wild is a female leopard leading her cubs through tall grass, tail held straight up above it as a guide for the cubs bumbling through the miniature jungle behind her.

Most naturalists rate the leopard as the most versatile and efficient predator in Africa, a creature exquisitely designed to perpetuate its own species.

The spectacular **cheetah**, scimitar-slender sprinter of the Kalahari, is equally efficient but in a highly specialised way that limits its versatility.

Acinonyx jubatus is in a genus of its own among cats and is designed for speed. It is the fastest animal on earth but precisely how fast is still the subject of argument; some observers claim it can pass 100 kilometres an hour, others that its maximum is about seventy-five kilometres an hour. Whichever is correct (and the cheetah's performance must be influenced by size, age, condition and terrain) it cannot hold that speed for more than a few hundred metres – more than enough, however, for the purpose of catching even a galloping hartebeest.

There are fifty or sixty in the KGNP and they hunt over territories as large as 900 square kilometres, sometimes alone but usually in parties of two to four.

Many naturalists regard the cheetah as the most beautiful of cats with its small head and gentle face marked by long black 'teardrop' lines from eyes to mouth, elegantly spotted body which, in spite of a nose-to-tail-tip length of up to two metres, weighs less than sixty kilograms, and exceptionally long hind legs that give the impression of speed even when it is standing still.

The Kalahari's open terrain is well suited to their swift-running style of hunting. They, too, live largely on the unfortunate springbok, which form nearly ninety per cent of their diet, supplemented by other buck, birds, hares and rodents. With their smaller fangs and claws they do not bite larger prey to death, as do leopards, but strangle them by seizing the throat in their jaws while gripping with their forelegs and dew claws. They do not compete with the nocturnal leopard because they hunt by day.

A cheetah hunt is one of the thrilling dramas of the wild. Sometimes alone, sometimes backed up by partners, a cheetah will move with slow deliberate steps towards its selected victim, its head held low, using cover if there is any, otherwise stopping dead still if the victim looks up. Its flat lean body and facial markings make it difficult to see from head on when it is motionless.

It continues like this for as long as it can, sometimes getting to within less than a hundred metres. When the victim becomes alarmed and starts to run, the cheetah instantaneously bursts into an amazing explosion of speed. No matter how much the prey ducks and jinks and leaps and dives the cheetah matches it dodge for

dodge, kicking up sprays of sand in fast turns while its long tail flails wildly to keep balance, until either the cheetah runs out of steam after several hundred metres, or it catches up.

It does not leap on its prey like the other big cats. At full speed it reaches with its forepaws and smacks the animal off balance. The moment it stumbles, the cheetah is on it, forelegs clutching and jaws clamped on the throat.

If it has cubs it will drag the carcass to them as soon as it gets its breath back or fetch them to it. They will feed immediately. Hasty eating is of the essence for a cheetah because it is easily driven off its prey by other predators. Shy animals, they will attack pestering jackals but put up little more than a token protest for bigger thieves like hyenas, and back off.

'I once watched a brown hyena chase a female cheetah and her three small cubs off a springbok she had just killed,' Dr Mills wrote. 'As the hyena charged, she came out to meet it and slapped at it with her forepaw, but the hyena practically ran through her and then she ran off to her cubs, which had left the scene as soon as the hyena appeared.'

Their blind, helpless cubs, usually three or four but sometimes as many as six, are born in cleverly concealed shelters and are regularly moved by the mother, carrying them by the scruff of the neck, until they can follow her at about two months. At a year they are able to set off on their own.

Athlete of the Kalahari is the cheetah, prince of all it surveys.
Lorna Stanton – ABPL.

The best area to see them, according to Warden le Riche, is along the Auob River because so many springbok congregate in its bed. They may be found relaxing in the shade of a tree watching the ebb and flow of life around them, casually coiled power waiting for release. Or the lucky might see them on the hunt – heads low, eyes fixed ahead, tails drooped, shoulders rippling in the slow motion of stalking, every fibre and sinew taut with tension. And then, for the very lucky, the catapulting acceleration and the immense strides stretching the long body parallel to the ground.

The big cats are not the only large predators. There are also the three hyenas – the spotted with the rhythmic taxonomic name *Crocuta crocuta*, the brown, *Hyaena brunnea*, and the aardwolf, *Proteles cristatus*.

They share the characteristics of occupying old antbear holes, being heavier in the shoulder than in the hindquarters, depositing their droppings in special toilet areas, having close-knit families, and 'pasting' – marking their territories and movements by exuding a special paste from anal glands on the grass, bushes and stones.

In most other respects, especially eating, they are quite different.

Being shy and nocturnal the **aardwolf**, which stands smaller than a jackal, is rarely seen. Elsewhere in South Africa it was habitually treated as vermin because farmers believed it to be a killer of lambs. The belief was reinforced by the presence of gnawed bones at the entrances to their burrows.

This false accusation has now been firmly disproved by researchers and the aardwolf is at last gaining recognition as an animal actually useful to farmers. The bones, it was discovered, were left outside the burrows not by the aardwolf but by porcupines with which it sometimes shares residence, and which gathered them to chew on for their calcium content.

Moreover, the aardwolf lives almost entirely on termites although it will not pass up an occasional meal of ants, spiders, moths or other insects. It particularly favours harvester termites and thus saves farmers incalculable losses of grazing for their livestock. Its molars have almost disappeared from disuse and its single eating tool is its tongue. It uses its incisor teeth to dig and its fangs for self-defence.

A yellowish fellow with a black muzzle and a few vertical black stripes, it is worth seeing for the unusual mane of long hair down its back. When on the defensive it erects the mane to make it look twice its size and barks or roars with surprising loudness.

In the KGNP they inhabit dunes and riverbeds equally, wherever termites can be found, but it will be a very fortunate visitor who sees one, the likeliest times being early morning or late evening.

The big **spotted hyena**, standing nearly a metre high at the shoulder and weighing up to eighty kilograms, is one of Africa's most

familiar animals. It has always been reviled as a foul, cowardly eater of carrion and digger up of the dead – a reputation propped by numerous chilling legends among African peoples, some of whom used to dispose of their dead by leaving them out for the hyenas.

The truth is quite different. Certainly it will eat carrion, as will the regal lion and many other respected predators. But the spotted hyena is second only to the lion as a hunter.

This has been known since the last century but the creature could never shed the millstone of its reputation, especially since in the Kruger and other reserves it was so often seen crowding around lion kills in the company of vultures and other scavengers.

Studies in recent decades in Tanzania's Serengeti Plains revealed that large packs or 'clans' of spotted hyenas live mainly by hunting down buck of all kinds. They do exactly the same in the KGNP where they kill more than two-thirds of their food themselves, though in smaller clans because the desert does not support a high volume of prey animals.

The long-haired **brown hyena**, not much over half the size of the spotted, is indeed a carrion eater, subsisting chiefly on the scraps of other predators' meals plus whatever insects, mice, fruit and eggs it stumbles across. Of the two it is the best adapted to this arid world which is probably why there are roughly twice as many as the eighty or so spotted hyena in the park.

The acknowledged expert on the Kalahari's hyenas, and one of the leading authorities on animal behaviour in the KGNP generally, is Dr Mills, now stationed in the Kruger National Park.

Rarely seen because it is nocturnal and solitary, the aardwolf is a formidable digger of holes in search of the termites it lives on.
Clem Haagner – ABPL.

Sent in June 1972 on a special project to study the brown hyena, he and his wife Margie spent years there, camping out in the desert for long periods to mark, follow, photograph and intimately record the animal's doings.

In an article in the NPB magazine *Custos* Dr Mills said the two species were able to co-exist because of their different diets. Brown hyenas were the proverbial scavengers, crunching up large bones with their powerful teeth to get the marrow and even being able to digest bone. 'An example of their indiscriminate feeding habits was when a large cub ate his mother who had been dead for several days.'

They also eat insects, wild fruits such as the tsamma melon and eggs and occasionally catch a small animal. Dr Mills described how a female that found a nest of twenty-six ostrich eggs spent the whole night carrying eggs to separate hiding places in a one-kilometre radius. It ate seven in two nights – and one ostrich egg contains the equivalent of two dozen fowl eggs.

'Spotted hyenas have a more restricted diet consisting almost exclusively of mammals over ten kilograms,' Dr Mills wrote. They have been known to eat their own kind. Only about a quarter of their food is from scavenging; the rest they kill.

They hunt mainly young gemsbok by cutting them from herds and running them down at speeds of up to fifty kilometres an hour for as far as three kilometres. Their meals, says Dr Mills, come in packages big enough to feed several hyenas whereas the brown hyena, hunting alone, usually finds food in small quantities just sufficient to feed itself.

Because their meals are scattered wide in the desert, both hyenas cover long distances to eat – 'the record for a brown hyena being fifty-five kilometres and for spotted hyenas sixty-nine kilometres. Not surprisingly, their territories are large: 230-240 square kilometres for brown hyenas and 550-775 square kilometres for spotted hyenas.'

A collection of individual brown hyenas, most of them related, occupies each territory, in which they move at will, meet amicably, share food when there is enough and share the chore of ousting intruders.

Spotted hyena clan sizes vary from three to twenty individuals, most close relatives. Their society is closer knit than that of brown hyenas.

Brown hyenas suckle their cubs but also bring food back to the den when they find more than they can eat on the spot. Spotted hyenas suckle only and do not bring food home because they consume everything at a kill. Hence brown hyenas can have bigger litters than the spotted.

The commonest in Africa, spotted hyenas are easily recognisable by their thick-shouldered bodies tapering to incongruously small hindquarters, the speckled pattern of their short-haired coats, bottle-brush tails and heavy heads carrying rounded ears and broad, powerful jaws.

The shoulders and chest have additional strength to give the muscular support the neck and head need for the jaws to slice the toughest hide and crack the largest bone. Clumsy though they may look, spotted hyenas are dynamic hunters as their speed and endurance show. When they catch up with their victim, they bite it on the run until it falls, upon which they eat it in chunks at amazing speed.

An oddity of the spotted hyena is that males and females appear to have the same sex organs, making it very difficult to tell them apart. It is this that gave rise in the time of Aristotle to the fallacy that they are hermaphrodites. For some genetic or hormonal reason, the female organs imitate those of the male which, however, is obviously not fooled.

Another unusual characteristic is that their society is matriarchal: the females are usually bigger than the males and dominate the clans. This too results from the need to supply milk to cubs, Dr Mills

Spotted hyenas are among the dominant predators and scavengers in the Park. They appear most often between dusk and dawn – except when they feel like a bath in a convenient waterhole. Nigel Dennis – ABPL.

The lank-furred brown hyena, smaller than the spotted, carries food from the leftovers of predators back to its den for its young. Clem Haagner – ABPL.

believes: the females are bigger because they have to eat more at kills to produce the milk.

Like the brown, the spotted give birth to their cubs in dens usually dug by that ubiquitous provider of accommodation, the antbear. But these are more than just holes in the ground. The hyenas extend them, tailor them to suit their needs, add extra entrances (or escape exits) and then use them as clubs where the whole clan will gather outside to laze around.

Inside the dens the cubs dig their own additional tunnels just wide enough for them to fit into, and thereby frustrate predators which might try to reach them while their parents are out on the hunt. Not even the parents can enter there and the brown hyena returning with meat for its offspring has to leave it at the entrance to the junior tunnel and growl at them to come and get it.

Brown hyenas are fairly silent because, says Dr Mills, as solitary hunters they have little need for communication. The spotted, in contrast, has a scalp-prickling range of sounds from the familiar rising 'whoo*oop*' of the African night to chuckles, growls, grunts, a lowing noise and the maniacal laughter up and down the scale which has made many a fireside camper shiver in his blankets.

'Each spotted hyena has its own whoop which can be recognised by other hyenas and, with practice, even by humans. Among other things the whoop call serves to inform members of a clan where other hyenas are at any time, so that if need be they can come together quickly.'

All three hyenas also communicate by 'pasting'. By dabbing a thick white paste with a long-lasting smell on boundary points they are not only warning outsiders to stay out but asserting their own right to stay inside as members of the clan occupying that territory.

The brown hyena goes further: it has not one but *two* pastes, rather like those brands of striped toothpaste except that it can alternate them. The other is a thin dark paste whose smell does not last very long. This, zoologists surmise, is to inform other members of its group where it has been foraging so they do not waste time covering the same ground.

Mobbing lions is an occupation of only the spotted, it being too risky for the brown and pointless for the aardwolf. Situations have been recorded where a spotted has located a lion kill from kilometres away with either its extremely sharp senses of smell and hearing or by seeing vultures circling above.

Arriving at the kill alone, the spotted promptly starts whooping and cackling to call up the clan. When the gang gets there they sum up the situation. It the kill has several lions feeding on it, and especially if some are big strong male lions, the hyenas will sit about biding their time until the lions depart and then settle for the leftovers.

If there is only one lion on it, or even two or three lionesses, and the spotted hyena gang is big enough, they will chase the lions off and seize the kill for themselves. This is not an exercise without its hazards; death by lion is one of the main causes of spotted hyena mortality.

Ruthless hunters they might be, but hyenas are very far from being the sinister cowards they are reputed to be and the spotted in particular has a social system more advanced than those of most animals.

They are also said to make good pets, for people who do not mind their furniture being severely chewed. A man who raised a spotted hyena from cubhood elsewhere in South Africa said it was clean, friendly and housebroken and kept away rats, jackals and leopards – and all his friends.

Sometimes, but rarely, those most efficient hunters the **wild dogs** appear in the KGNP, sweeping in silently like pirates in the night and vanishing as mysteriously back into the ocean of Kalahari sand.

Visitors will be lucky to see them, and even luckier in the future because in Botswana, outside the bounds of the KGNP, they are a declared vermin and are assiduously hunted down although they are an endangered species.

Lycaon pictus, also known as the Cape hunting dog and widespread when Southern Africa had more game than people, also carries a millstone of misunderstanding, like the hyena (which, incidentally, is more closely related to mongooses than to dogs).

Their unwarranted reputation of cruelty and wanton destruction stems from their hunting technique of running down an animal and tearing chunks off it until it falls. In fact the technique is swift and no more or less cruel than those of other predators. Nor are wild dogs wanton, except among livestock which do not flee as wild animals do.

And they have possibly the closest knit family system of any of the larger predators. Their cubs always get priority and while they are still in their dens, food is carried back to them and to the adults left to nursemaid them.

Long-legged with very keen eyesight, wild dogs can tirelessly run for long distances at speeds of nearly fifty kilometres an hour with bursts of higher speed for short stretches. Sometimes their prey escapes and sometimes the wild dogs are forced to flee in their turn.

They are easily recognised by their lean bodies of nearly thirty kilograms, bushy white-tipped tails, huge round ears and blotched black and white and yellow coats. The random patterns of their coats are never the same and are as distinctive as fingerprints, greatly facilitating their observation and study by zoologists.

One observer in the KGNP watched four of them, a smaller pack than usual, unsuccessfully chase springbok in the Auob River near

Twee Rivieren, then tree an irate but sensibly cautious leopard, pursue some more springbok out of sight over a dune and suddenly reappear being pursued by a herd of wildebeest, and finally disappear into the dunes.

He noted that they showed no signs of tiring, made no effort to conceal themselves and were silent except when they yapped at the leopard clinging desperately to its tree and snarling at them. All the hallmarks of dedicated hunters.

Wild dogs do in fact have a wide range of sounds from a melodious hooting used to call each other to yelps, barks, growls and a high, bird-like twitter when they are excited. They have also been heard to communicate at night in short, sharp whistles.

Of the smaller hunters in the KGNP, three are cats and the commonest of these is the **African wild cat**, *Felis lybica*, forebear of the European wild cat and therefore of all European domestic cats.

Tamed by the Egyptians 3 000 or more years before the birth of Christ, the African wild cat features prominently in Pharaonic rituals and sculpture, which show it in its distinctive sitting position, almost vertical because of its very long legs, according to the late Professor Reay Smithers.

It is a nocturnal hunter but can be seen sometimes by day and looks very much like an ordinary household cat, if slightly larger than most at about five kilograms. It is a lightly striped tan or fawn colour and shows a clean pair of black heels when running away.

Highly territorial animals, they live on a wide variety of prey including many kinds of rodents, birds, reptiles and some insects and they breed readily with domestic cats.

Slightly less common is that most feline-looking of felines the **caracal** or *Felis caracal* whose common name derives from the Turkish 'garah-gulak' meaning 'black ear'. Also nocturnal, they are not easily seen in the KGNP but are worth looking for. With their red-furred bodies of about twelve to fourteen kilograms and about a metre long to the black tips of their short tails, their tall tufted ears and their sharp-boned faces, they are the epitome of the highly specialised feline family.

Lightning fast and kilo-for-kilo probably the most powerful of the felines, caracal also help to keep down rodent populations but can take much larger animals such as springbok and also, regrettably, sheep and goats when other prey are scarce, which is why they are diminishing in farming areas.

Last of the KGNP felines is the rather rare, beautiful and very seldom seen **small spotted cat**, *Felis nigripes*, whose name has been changed from black-footed cat to avoid confusion with the African wild cat, also black-footed.

Although it is rarer in the deserts than in the rest of Southern Africa, the African wild cat is more easily seen in the Park because the vegetation is so sparse. It looks like a household tabby and is believed to be the ancestor of all domestic cats.
Nigel Dennis – ABPL.

Far Right: The small spotted cat is the smallest in Southern Africa at less than two kilograms. It is nocturnal, extremely shy and virtually untameable.
National Parks Board.

Weighing less than two kilograms, they, too, look similar to domestic cats in shape except for their tails, which are about half as long, and their distinctive mixture of stripes and spots on a light brown or tan background.

Not a great deal is known about them except that they are wholly nocturnal and very shy, eat small rodents and birds and insects, and are absolutely ferocious when cornered.

Unlike the African wild cat and caracal that are found over a large part of Africa, they are known only in Southern Africa. Like the others, they are fast and efficient hunters and make the kill with a single neck bite that severs the spine.

The predator one sees most of along the KGNP roads is the common **black-backed jackal** found all over Southern Africa and East Africa – one of nature's great survivors in spite of determined attempts by stock farmers to eradicate it. Wise animals, they appear to learn fast how to avoid traps, poison and other devices designed specifically to kill them and they multiply against all odds.

Canis mesomelas is the African counterpart of the American coyote and is also known as the saddle-backed jackal because of the black saddle marking on the back of its russet, bushy-tailed body. It is seen so often that after a first flush of interest visitors tend to ignore them, which is unfortunate because the jackal is a most intriguing canine that operates night and day.

They will invariably be found where lions have made a kill, ghosting light-footed just beyond reach of the big cats, dodging swiftly aside if a paw lashes out when they get close, darting in when the lions are absorbed to snatch a snack – a seemingly inordinate risk for so small a reward.

They are hunters as well as scavengers who will readily kill hares, rats, squirrels and other small animals when they get the chance and eat a variety of insects including beetles and termites, gobbling them down in passing. They will also eat such potentially dangerous items as empty biscuit packets and plastic wrappers – good reason for tourists to avoid littering the park with rubbish, as so many do.

At the waterholes in the KGNP one can often see a black-backed jackal slyly approaching flocks of drinking doves or sandgrouse, appearing to look the other way. The birds are seldom fooled and ignore it until it gets too close when they take to the air in a flurry of beating wings. Sometimes the jackal catches the unwary one that stays to sip too long.

Jackals mate for life and defend their territory together, demonstrating a fascinating touch of marital loyalty: if the intruder is a female, the male will stand back and let his wife chase the other female away. If the intruder is male, the husband has to do the chasing.

The black-backed jackal is one of Africa's most successful species. This one is making off with the remnants of a springbok killed by a larger predator.
Lorna Stanton – ABPL.

They too have their young in old antbear holes which they expand inside into sizeable dens. Both bring food to the den for the cubs until they are three or four months old and are able to follow their parents.

They can make the nights hideous with their yaps and long drawn-out yowls that carry for kilometres, especially in the breeding season. By day, however, they are mostly silent.

It is one of the KGNP's more entertaining sights to watch jackals prowling about in full daylight intent on their business, ignoring cars and prudently circling gemsbok and other animals that might object to their presence, trotting with tails draped low and heads down except when they raise their sharp snouts to sniff the air.

It is quite common for not one but several jackals to be within view in the vicinity of waterholes because these are neutral territory open to all. When they meet at the water they will investigate each other and the smaller or weaker will tuck in its tail, hunch down its hindquarters and droop its head, turning it to one side. This is an act of submission and after some ritual sniffing the submitter will straighten up and they will drink, often side by side, and go their ways.

Rather less common in the KGNP is the **Cape fox**, *Vulpes chama*, found only in South Africa, Botswana and Namibia. Contrary to one

The Cape fox is a dainty animal smaller than the average household cat. It eats rodents, insects and fruit by night and hides up in holes by day.
Leigh Voigt.

of its Afrikaans names 'silwerjakkels' or 'silver jackal' it is a true fox, less than a metre long and a third high and weighing two or three kilograms.

Habituees of open country, they move about mainly at night in search of small rodents and insects and rest by day in holes which they, for a change, dig themselves unless they perchance find an old one made by a spring hare or some other small burrower.

Very similar in body shape to the English fox, its colouring is reddish with a silver-grey back, off-white throat and bushy black-flecked tail.

It is a loner except when it mates and little is known about its behaviour – except that it does not deserve the blame it receives in farming areas for harm to livestock. In 1974 a vermin-hunting organisation in the Orange Free State killed 4 000 of them. It is actually too small to do real damage and in fact aids farmers by controlling rodents. Its other problem is that its fur is so fine and thick it is killed for its skin.

The KGNP is the best place to see and photograph this attractive little canine.

Much easier to see and far more appealing are other foxes that strut the desert streets like Parisian ladies of the night – petite black legs twinkling beneath elegant fur coats, large inviting eyes peering from dark-masked faces, small and shapely heads carrying tall, white-fringed hats.

They are *Otocyon megalotis* once known as Delalande's fox but now more descriptively, if less alluringly, called the **bat-eared fox**.

These are the little beauties of the Southern African savannah and nowhere are they as visible as in the KGNP. Because they too are mass victims of farmers who mindlessly equate them with stock-killing jackals, elsewhere they have become extremely shy night-time creatures seen rarely except in car headlights, all too often an instant before they are run over and killed.

Here they are out and about both day and night and are often seen in the bare or grassed flats of the riverbeds, singly or in pairs or in groups usually of two to six but sometimes eight.

There is no mistaking it with those slim legs, plush greyish coat, narrow, dark-masked muzzle, bushy tail and enormous ears fringed with pure white on the inside. The ears alone are distinctive – up to thirteen centimetres long and ten centimetres around the base, larger for the fox's size than those of any other predator.

The only thing that inhibits their daytime activity in the park is heat. Bat-eared foxes have a considerable layer of fat that, with thick undercoats and guard hairs, obliges them to seek the cool of holes or shady trees in the hotter hours.

Diligent diggers that make intricate burrows or extend those of antbears, they too mate for life and treat their offspring preciously until they are able to fend for themselves.

The elegant little bat-eared fox is more visible in this Park than virtually anywhere else. Family groups often appear in full daylight. This one is using its huge ears to listen for the underground movements of insects it is hunting.
Joan Ryder – ABPL.

Their jaws are far too small to cope with the likes of lambs or kids but they are capable hunters in their own small way and do a great deal of good by feeding largely, sometimes almost entirely, on the pasture-destroying harvester termite *Hodotermes mossambicus*. The late Professor Smithers noted that the habitat of the bat-eared fox parallels that of this termite and is actually increasing in Southern Africa probably because of the termite's spread.

They eat many other things, all small: mice, gerbils, moths, beetles, sun spiders, ordinary spiders, berries, lizards and scorpions – stings and all.

Zoologists say the bat-eared fox has good eyesight, an excellent sense of smell and hearing so astonishingly acute it hunts insects by sound. It locates termites by following their small runways in the grass or by listening for the minute bustle of their activity. It cocks the great dishes of its ears close to the ground, almost touching, to pick up the tiny tickings of an underground beetle and then pounces, digging very fast with strong foreclaws.

Professor Smithers raised bat-eared foxes captured at infancy to study them. They were playful and became quite domesticated, he said, and were model parents: they very rarely bit people – only when they believed their cubs or partners were threatened.

Being so small, less than a third of a metre tall, and seldom more than four kilograms in weight, and relatively defenceless except for their speed and agility, bat-eared foxes are often themselves the prey of larger predators including eagles and owls.

Five of the KGNP predators are of the Viverridae family and one of these is among the most popular of all its creatures among tourists, the little **suricate mongoose**, *Suricata suricatta*.

In recent years it has been given more publicity than any other animal, including a book by a French writer/photographer couple.

The suricate or 'stokstertmeerkat' is favoured because it is very common, quite casual about the presence of people, easy to photograph and captivatingly anthropomorphic. People like it because it behaves like people. In the KGNP it entertains as the monkey does in the bushveld.

Averaging about three quarters of a kilogram and half a metre in length, thin dark-tipped tail included, suricates live in colonies in burrows dug in the riverbeds and banks by themselves or by ground squirrels, which sometimes share the holes with them. They are highly sociable animals and it appears that only one or two females breed in each group and the rest help to rear the young.

Daytime operators, they might be found almost anywhere along the park in bands of up to about thirty fossicking for insects or just enjoying the day. If a car stops three or four metres away they will watch it warily for a while and when satisfied there is no threat, ignore it.

They are at their most entertaining in the early morning when the sun rises. They emerge from their burrow, find good places on the mound of excavated earth around it or on some other conveniently exposed position and become pure hedonists.

Most stand erect on their hind legs balancing on their tails and face the sun to warm their chests and stomachs. Their dark-ringed eyes half close, their sharp faces point east and their hands hang loosely in front of them or are held crossed on their tummies, for all the world like people.

They nestle close together – three, six, maybe twelve in a row, exuding blissful satisfaction, here and there an arm draped around a shoulder or a paw touching a neighbour or a mother fondling a dozing child.

Always there are two or three who are far from dozing. Their eyes are open wide and their faces turn to scan sky and horizon and the ground all around. They are the sentinels.

A jackal appears in the distance, or the shadow of an eagle flicks across the ground. A short, sharp bark and in the wink of an eye the colony vanishes underground.

Long seconds later the tip of a nose and a pair of shining dark-

Top right: The suricates are the most familiar of the Park's small animals, commonly seen at roadsides and quite unworried by the presence of human onlookers. From her vast yawn, this mother appears thoroughly bored with feeding her youngster.
Clem Haagner – ABPL.

Top centre: Like commuters waiting for the bus, a group of suricates scan the scene while warming their bellies in the morning sun.
Clem Haagner – ABPL.

Far Right: Easygoing they might seem, but the suricates always have a sentry perched in a nearby bush to bark warning of hawks and other predators.
Anthony Bannister – ABPL.

Sheer cuteness – like this inquisitive fellow's cautious lookabout from the safety of his warren – has made the suricate a favourite of photographers.
Anthony Bannister – ABPL.

ringed eyes appear at the mouth of a burrow. More appear at other holes. In ones, twos and threes the suricates once more clamber out, line up facing the sun and fall into a doze.

When the sun is well up and they have thoroughly warmed themselves they wander off to hunt, digging for larvae and turning stones for other insects, scorpions and the occasional lizard.

Not much less common than the suricates are the slightly smaller **yellow mongooses**, *Cynictis penicillata*, which inhabit all the camps and have become so accustomed to people they come out of their holes to beg food and pick up scraps around the barbecue. They are also colony creatures occupying burrows they generally dig themselves but have none of the cuteness of the suricates and slink fast and silently across the ground like weasels.

Pale yellow-grey with white-tipped tails, their normal diet is also insects, spiders and scorpions though they readily take small birds and frogs.

They will also take the tip of a finger if curiosity and hunger moves them, as a number of incautious visitors have learned when offering them titbits. Like those of all the Viverridae family, their fangs are sharp and readily used.

Much less common are the last three members of this family found in the KGNP. The red-coated **slender mongoose**, *Galerella sanguinea*, with its black-tipped tail is a solitary creature occasionally seen in the riverbed areas moving swiftly across the ground as if on rails. Sometimes it will stop dead for a few seconds to peer at the intruder or, if puzzled, stand erect.

It is about the same size as the yellow mongoose at half to two-thirds of a kilogram and less than two-thirds of a metre in length, and its diet is similar although it also eats small snakes and other reptiles.

Its cousin, the **small-spotted genet**, *Genetta genetta*, is seldom seen, being strictly a night-time operator, which is a pity because it is a very pretty animal with a very long ringed tail, greyish body with even rows of dark spots, large red eyes and big spoonbowl ears – the latter two features equipping it for hunting in the dark.

It does not dig, preferring to live in hollow logs or crevices in the stony banks of the rivers. Its diet is largely of mice, spiders, scorpions and a variety of reptiles. Genets hand-raised from infancy have become tame but in the wild they are very shy.

Scarcest of all is the **banded mongoose**, *Mungos mungo*, which weighs a little over a kilogram and is slightly more than half a metre long. It is distinguishable by bold black bands across the lower half of its grey-coated body. It is gregarious, like the suricate, and moves in groups whose members signal to each other with high-pitched chirps. Although it is active by day it has seldom been seen even by park staff.

Dwarf mongooses are a barrel of fun. Always lively, always gregarious, always playful, once they have become accustomed to an onlooker they provide constant entertainment.
Clem Haagner – ABPL.

The slender mongoose, mainly an insect eater, is ssometimes seen along the Park roads and in the camps.
Clem Haagner – ABPL.

Equally nocturnal and therefore equally difficult to see is a strikingly beautiful animal with a strikingly ugly reputation, the **striped polecat**, *Ictonyx striatus*. It might be seen roaming the bush inside a camp perimeter and while one can watch it by torchlight, it must never be interfered with.

It is hard to believe that so violently offensive a smell can come from so small and lovely a creature clad in wide shining black and white stripes down the length of its furry body. This little African skunk of less than a kilogram and not much more than half a metre can squirt a fluid from stern glands that weighs on the senses like a ton. If the stuff comes into contact with clothes there is nothing for it but to burn them; they cannot be washed clean.

The fluid is the striped polecat's last line of defence and one so successful that it can dare to appear in public so brightly decked it stands out like a flag. Zoologists surmise that its bold markings serve as a warning to other predators not to touch or they will stink for weeks. And yet polecats are killed and eaten by hunters quick enough to avoid their aim, like caracals and leopards.

Polecats, too, are solitary and live under stones or fallen logs or in borrowed burrows, sometimes condescending to dig their own, and eat small rodents, birds, reptiles and insects.

A cousin of the striped polecat because they share the same Musteline family is one of the most fascinating creatures in Africa, the stockily built, thick-skinned, stubborn, single-minded, crusty, powerful, indomitable, courageous **honey badger**, *Mellivora capensis*, or 'ratel' in Afrikaans.

Ounce for ounce one of nature's toughest children, the badger has been described as a numbskull whose dim wits can encompass only one idea at a time which it will follow doggedly to conclusion through hail and shine and flood and drought, unstoppable by anything except death – and it is hard to kill.

A long low animal, it stands about a quarter of a metre high at the shoulder and weighs between ten and fifteen kilograms. Its length is nearly a metre including the short dark-tipped tail that usually stands up like the flag on the stern of a ship. It varies considerably in shading but the entire upper half of the body from eyebrows almost to tail end is lighter coloured than the lower with a clear line of definition between, as if it were draped in a cloak.

Heavy front claws like curved knives enable it to dig easily for food or to make a burrow, or to expand to taste an antbear hole. Large fangs in a strong jaw make it a formidable adversary. It also has two unusual defence systems.One is a skin so thick not even a hound's tooth can penetrate it and so loose that if a hound gets a grip and tries, the badger can revolve inside its own skin to attack

A very rare photograph of one of the best examples of symbiosis in nature, seen only in this Park. Honey badgers rooting in the desert sand for small creatures to eat are often followed by pale chanting goshawks which snap up those that escape. Sometimes jackals join the procession.
Anthony Bannister – ABPL.

The other is the same as the striped polecat's: stern glands which exude a nauseating substance. It rarely seems to use the latter, however, probably because it does not need to.

Stories of badger prowess are legion, such as the occasion one elected to cross a farmhouse lawn and was promptly tackled by three very large and fierce farm dogs. The scene ended with the badger unconcernedly disappearing into the bush on the far side of the lawn at its usual steady gait, leaving on the lawn behind it three bloody, battered dogs bewailing their torn skins and broken bones.

In other parks they have been known to put up furious fights against even lions and to kill large buck – not to eat but out of sheer bad temper when bumped into. Describing how cantankerous they can be, the late Professor Smithers told how one chased a photographer into a vehicle and then tried to get at him inside it, and how another tore the end off a heavily built steel cage to escape, and then attacked and partly crushed the cage. A python that aroused a badger's ire, he said, looked as if it had been run over by a train.

There are not a great many in the KGNP but they are common enough to be suddenly encountered almost anywhere, riverbeds or dunes, night or day. Their shape and motion is unmistakeable: the long sloped body on short legs going at a steady rolling trot like a sailor freshly ashore.

At the Munro waterpoint in the Auob River about twenty-one kilometres from Twee Rivieren, I once watched a badger approach a trough on the opposite side of which an extremely large black-maned lion was already lapping. In the bright daylight of eight a.m. the badger, a big old one with dark grizzled fur, could not have failed to see the lion but it did not hesitate as it came down the river bank at a fast trot. It paused briefly once about thirty metres from the lion then moved forward again and drank from a second watering point about fifteen metres short of the trough. The lion ignored it. Both finished drinking and went their separate ways, honour preserved.

Here, with patience and good luck, one can see a facet of life involving the badger that occurs only in the Kalahari.

An old African legend is of the badger's working relationship with the greater honeyguide; the badger loves honey and the bird likes bee grubs, so the bird finds a hive, leads the badger to it and then feeds on the white larvae in the debris clawed out by its fellow burglar. Actually there is no confirmed record of this happening although the greater honeyguide certainly leads people to hives.

In the KGNP there is a collaboration of a rather different kind that has been observed many times and involves three parties. In fact, one way to find a badger is to look for one or a pair of ambling jackals and see if one or two pale chanting goshawks are staying close to them. If so, then the probability is strong that there is a badger in the vicinity.

Badgers frequently dig for their food, be it scorpions or mice or other of the small creatures that infest the Kalahari sands. In their vigorous digging they send up a small volcano of sand and unearth or scare out all sorts of things, many of which move too quickly for them to catch or which they ignore in their dogged pursuit of one prey.

The jackals have discovered that by hanging about close to the badger they can snap up all sorts of fleeing delectables presented to them on a plate, so to speak. So have the pale chanting goshawks and what escapes from both badger and jackals, they swoop upon. Thus this most fascinating spectacle of a Kalahari foraging expedition – badger in the lead, two jackals a polite distance behind, two goshawks wheeling above. A classic example of sagacious opportunism in nature.

The scientists believe that the badger's very distinctive markings serve the same purpose as the striped polecat's: a warning to others to keep away – for very good reasons.

These cantankerous characters do not seem to like even each other's company very much. They usually live alone but are some-

The shy, nocturnal aardvark is a powerful digger of holes in its constant search for termites, which it harvests with a long sticky tongue, and in making its own den. Its abandoned holes provide accommodation for a host of other animals.
National Parks Board.

times seen in pairs or family groups of three or four. They have the convenient arrangement that males and females each occupy their own territories – which overlap, giving them the best of both relationships.

The Proletariat

The upper levels of the KGNP's wild society, the buck and the hunters, are hugely outnumbered by mostly unseen masses. The dunes and plains and riverbeds dominated by the high-profile aristocrats might appear almost devoid of other animal life apart from the exuberant ground squirrel. But on and beneath the surface, in trees and under shrubs and rocks there is a frenetic, teeming activity of millions, perhaps billions more mammals.

Some are large enough to be obvious were they not so elusive; the rest are small.

One, of course, is that indefatigable creator of accommodation for everybody else, the **antbear** or aardvark, whose appearance is as lugubrious as its scientific name, *Orycteropus afer*, and is so special that it belongs in an order all of its own, the Tubulidentata, which aptly embraces its long tubular ears and long tubular snout.

There is nothing else like it in Africa, a big sad-eyed animal of between forty and sixty kilograms and one and a half to two metres long from blunt, pig-like nose to tip of thick, tapering tail. It has a hunched body and heavy hindquarters supported on short legs and its feet are equipped with massive claws that enable it to burrow underground with amazing speed.

The antbear feeds almost exclusively on termites, hence its tubular snout, long sticky ribbon of tongue and its lack of teeth except for a few molars.

Evidence of their nocturnal activity in the KGNP is common enough and without it many another creatures would be homeless, yet they are very rarely seen because they operate mainly in the dunes, usually alone, and are shy. In pursuit of termites, the antbear snuffles about the sands pausing to dig when it smells a nest, breaking it open just enough to insert its tongue down the many small tunnels and drag out the occupants.

Nothing can match the antbear's digging powers. It bores through the earth so fast that, Professor Smith recorded, a team of men trying to dig one out gave up after thirty-two metres. To shelter by day it tunnels a hole for a few metres just under the surface and it is these that are occupied by so many other creatures from leopards to jackals, snakes and birds. To raise a family it excavates a whole 'apartment block' quite deep underground with several large rooms and passages running for many metres between several entrances.

Many a rider has been thrown in the African veld when his horse stepped into one of these holes, and the antbear is roundly cursed by farmers whose trucks and tractors have had broken springs similarly caused. Otherwise the antbear is harmless and in fact benign in its control of termites.

The other largish member of the masses is the biggest of the rodents, the **porcupine**, *Hystrix africaeaustralis*, also concealed by the night when visitors are confined to the camps.

They are striking animals when seen on the move with their erect crests of long bristly hairs and backs covered with a forest of black and white quills and spines, needle sharp, that rustle and rattle as they move.

Contrary to popular belief, a porcupine cannot 'shoot' or throw its quills and spines. When threatened, however, it will charge sideways or in reverse very quickly to jab them into the threatener.

It, too, is a competent digger and unearths roots and tubers as part of its vegetarian diet. It lives in rocky crevices or more often in old antbear holes and once inside, head down and spiked rear blocking the entrance, it is impossible to extract.

Strangest of the rodents is the **springhare**, *Pedetes capensis*, Southern Africa's mimic-in-miniature of the kangaroo. Not a hare at all, it is an animal in its own category whose ancestral origins are unknown. It has a head rather like a hare's with ears shaped like a horse's, small front legs and huge hind legs like a kangaroo's and a long dark-tipped tail like a cat's, and it stands nearly a metre high and weighs about two to four kilograms.

It does not have the marsupial pouch of its Australian look-alike and raises its young in burrows it makes itself by digging with sharp foreclaws and shovelling the earth out backwards with large, spoon-shaped and razor-sharp hindclaws. The similarity is in its motion: it hops about erect on the hindfeet almost exactly like a kangaroo or wallaby and when alarmed, takes off in long fast bounds, covering distances at an impressive speed.

In the Northern Cape farming areas, it is a common experience at certain times of the year, when springhares are in abundance, to hear them kill themselves by jumping against cars on the roads at night, sometimes in such numbers that a journey is marked by a frequent thump-thump. Whether this is because they are attracted by light, or are blinded and jump wildly, is not known.

They never appear by day but can sometimes be seen in torch-light near the perimeters of camps, eyes glowing bright red in the beam and bobbing as they hop in search of grass, their staple food.

A good look at the desert sand both inside the camps and outside shows it is riddled with fist-sized holes, some of them in large accumulations. Seen from the air it looks as if the entire Kalahari was hit by a blast of shotgun pellets from outer space. All of these holes were made by various rodents and are still occupied by them or by other creatures that have taken possession.

They represent a gigantic population of little animals that fill a vital function in the desert food chain – themselves living on plants and some insects and in turn being eaten by other animals. They also do wonders for the plant and insect life by constantly turning the soil and enriching it with their detritus and droppings.

A very large proportion of these mini-mammals, perhaps most, are of a kind easily studied inside the camp areas by those who have a little patience. Stroll through the scrub near a chalet or tent and soon enough you will hear a short sharp 'Phw*eet*!' rather like someone whistling for a taxi.

This is the alarm signal given by **Brant's whistling rat**, *Parotomys brantsii*, just before diving into its home in its colony, a group of holes each surrounded by small fans of excavated sand.

Squat down a few metres away and stay still for five minutes, maybe ten. A whiskered nose and then a pair of bright black eyes will emerge slowly from the hole, whiskers twitching. Soon the whole animal will come out – a grey body about fourteen centimetres long, big ears, long tail – and sit erect at the edge of the hole. It might lie down for a rest, or nibble on grass or young leaves it has brought to the warren. Raise an arm or click a camera and again … 'Phw*eet*' and it is gone. So are all the others in the colony.

Also easily studied in the camps is a rodent that intrigues because it is the only one to live in trees. It is *Thallomys paedulcus*, called by some a **tree rat**, by others a tree mouse. It makes large untidy nests of twigs in the forks of trees, usually the camelthorn, and emerges at dusk to begin its nightly routine of feeding on leaflets, the fuzzy fur on seed pods and other choice vegetation, scampering about the branches right to the uppermost.

In the camps they have become fairly tame – wary, but unscared by the presence of people only a metre or two away. At Mata Mata one family occupies a fork at about eye level in a scraggly camelthorn right next to a tent site in the caravan park. At Nossob camp there is a nest in a medium-sized camelthorn close to the garden wall of the research officer's house. Nests are easily found: simply examine the ground beneath the trees for a carpet of small black droppings.

Thallomys is an attractive grey rat, or mouse, with white underparts and a dark surround to the eyes as if heavily made up with Indian kohl. Its tail is longer than its body and tipped with black. In the late afternoons the family in a nest can be heard sleepily peeping and groaning as they awaken to face a new night. Then as twilight begins to cloak the sky a face will appear at a hole between the twigs, one will emerge to use the toilet place on the side of the nest, another will dart out and around and back in somewhere else. Well before the dark comes they will be running nimbly through the branches.

Another rodent deserving attention, because it is among the most visible of all the little animals, is the **ground squirrel**, *Xerus inauris*.

It is as common in the camps as outside, becomes very tame and should be treated with circumspection because, like the yellow mongooses which have lost their fear of people, it can mistake a fingertip for a peanut.

It has the classic squirrel looks: slightly plump cuddly-cute body, button-nose face with small ears and big bright eyes, forefeet like tiny delicate hands and a big bushy tail. This one is a pale greyish colour with white underparts and a distinct white stripe down each side. It weighs up to a kilogram.

Prodigious diggers, they live in colonies that inhabit underground warrens up to a metre deep containing grass-padded chambers. These underground homes afford them excellent protection against both heat and cold because, with the insulation of the sand, the temperature inside fluctuates considerably less than in the air outside. Most members of a colony are females and their youngsters; the

A ground squirrel digging for roots and insects is kept company by crows hoping for a snack.
Rudi van Aarde – ABPL.

A ground squirrel grooming its luxurious tail. They are common and quite tame in Twee Rivieren camp but tend to bite the hand that feeds them.
Rudi van Aarde – ABPL.

males are a wandering lot who move from colony to colony breeding as they go.

They are gregarious, lively, happy-looking animals that love playing between the serious business of finding their vegetarian foods and dodging the many predators that make meals of them, particularly hawks and eagles. They are active throughout the daylight hours, shading themselves with their tails when the sun is hot – hence their name of squirrel, derived from the Greek word *skiouros* which means 'shading tail'.

They tease even raptors when they know it is safe, as an incident in the Auob River demonstrated. Some thirty of them were moving about the flat clay floor of the river feeding and occasionally chasing each other when an unidentified raptor too small to take even a squirrel swooped low over them.

Several immediately ran flat out for about twenty metres, bushy tails streaming out behind them, with the small hawk right behind and just above the ground. Suddenly they stopped and whirled about in little clouds of dust, flicking their tails erect and somehow looking twice as big. The raptor was obviously intimidated for it instantly reared up and away.

It circled some distance off for a while and tried again. The charade was repeated several times and not once did the squirrels dive for cover or run for their nearby warren.

At Twee Rivieren camp, against a wire fence between the chalets and the staff residential area, is a warren of about twenty burrows whose residents are so tame they run up to passers-by to beg food and sniff inquisitively at shoes and ankles. This area of about ten paces by ten is what Mrs Doempie le Riche, wife of the Warden, calls her 'garden' and indeed when they are out in the open, scurrying and playing and grooming each other, these pretty little creatures do look like a garden of furry mobile flowers.

The very tameness that so appeals to visitors, however, works against them. One of Mrs le Riche's regular chores is bandaging fingers nibbled by squirrels, having innocently tested them with their sharp incisors. Also, visitors tend to feed them all sorts of delicacies humans enjoy but which are not very good for squirrel digestion, such as chili-flavoured chips and sweets, still in their wrappers. Some have been killed by plastic they have swallowed. Unless people stop feeding them and confine their admiration to watching, the colony might have to be destroyed.

Other small mammals are too numerous to describe in detail and in any case are so scarce or exclusive in behaviour and habitat that they are seen only by the researchers who catch them for study. At least seventeen rodents, of which most live in the dunes and thirteen are nocturnal, have been found so far in the KGNP including the tiny five-gram pygmy mouse, *Mus minutoides*, and various other mice, rats and gerbils.

There is also a variety of animals of different orders such as the scrub hare and commoner Cape hare, the hedgehog, the rare mole, several kinds of shrews and four sorts of bats, some of which flit silently around the outside lamps of chalets on warm evenings plucking insects out of the air.

One last animal warrants special attention simply because it is so strange and so rare that sight of it makes a trip to the KGNP worth while.

If you should perchance see a creature like an oversized artichoke ambling along on two short stubby legs, take careful note, it is a **pangolin**.

Little is known about the distribution, numbers and habits of *Manis temminckii*, the Cape pangolin, one of four species of its kind found in Africa and the only one in Southern Africa. It belongs to the order Pholidota of which fossils more than forty million years old have been found, but whose prehistoric origins are something of a scientific mystery.

The only mammal with scales, it used to be called the 'scaly ant-eater' but this name has been abandoned because it was also used for South America's armadillo, which has the same appearance and habits but belongs to a completely different order. The similarity is put down to parallel evolution – the coincidental emergence in quite separate areas of animals with the same adaptations to the same kind of environmental conditions.

Now it is simply the pangolin, which derives from a Malay word 'peng-guling' meaning 'roller' after the creature's defensive tactic of rolling itself into a hard ball. The origin of its Afrikaans name, 'ieter-mago' is unknown.

The names are as odd as the animal. Reaching more than a metre in length and perhaps twelve kilograms in weight, its entire body from in front of the eyes to the tip of its long, heavy tail is shingled in hard, sharp overlapping scales like artichoke leaves coloured brown with yellowish edges. It walks on its short thick hind legs with its small forelegs tucked close to its chest and its tail extending straight out behind for balance, parallel to the ground like a balcony. From time to time it will lower a forefoot to the ground, touching the sand with the backs of its large claws because they are so curved it cannot put its palm to earth.

It moves slowly and is easily caught but the catcher must beware. When alarmed the pangolin tucks its cone-shaped head into its stomach, folds its arms over it and clamps its tail over everything, presenting to the world a round ball armoured with scales. Grasping the ball is a mistake – using powerful muscles, the pangolin is able to slide the tail from side to side and fingers caught between the scales can be severely cut. It takes the strength of two or three men, preferably wearing gloves, to pull the ball open.

As far as is known the females bear one young a year, using old antbear holes and not, apparently, by digging their own in spite of the strength of their formidable foreclaws. The baby rides around on its mother's back for months clinging to the scales. When danger threatens the mother folds up as usual with the baby inside the ball.

Pangolins live solitary lives and are active mostly at night, seeking their main food, formicid ants, which they detect with their keen senses of smell, taste and hearing. Like the antbear, it digs a large enough opening in an ant nest to push in its nose and then inserts an extraordinarily long sticky tongue, up to thirty centimetres, into the nest's tunnels to extract ants, larvae and eggs.

They have no teeth and apart from the cutting edges of their scales and an ability to exude a foul smell they are quite harmless. Their survival is threatened to some extent, however, because their rather reptilian appearance has gained them an unfortunate place in African lore. Their scales are sought after for ritual and decorative

The strangest mammal in the Park – very rarely seen – is the armour-plated pangolin. It walks mostly on its hind legs balancing with its heavy tail, lives alone, moves by night, opens ant nests with its strong foreclaws, and gathers the ants in with its long sticky tongue. Clem Haagner – ABPL.

use and some tribes burn pangolins in their cattle kraals in the belief that this improves the fertility of the livestock.

In the KGNP they are classified as rare and one ranger, David de Villiers, said he had to wait eleven years to see one – and had left his camera at home. He had to wait nearly three years more before he was able to photograph one.

In the Air

More and more people are visiting the KGNP specifically to see its wealth of bird life, according to Warden le Riche and to J J 'Kotie' Herholdt, ornithologist and former ranger at Nossob camp. The trend does not reflect any decline of interest in its animals (they have their ardent aficionados) or the presence of bird species found nowhere else. Yet again, it is because of the extreme clarity of viewing – the remarkable ease with which birds can be found and observed. And in fact, while the KGNP boasts slightly under one-third of the more than 900 species of birds recorded in Southern Africa, their variety is surprisingly prolific because of the extremes of climate and season.

Precisely how many have been recorded in the KGNP is the subject of some debate. One source says 251, another 264. The list will probably grow because of one group of birds called vagrants – those that do not normally inhabit or regularly visit this kind of country but wander in erratically when conditions happen to suit them or because of pressures elsewhere, or simply because they have got lost.

In his four years in the park, for instance, Kotie Herholdt has identified two African hobby falcons – only the eighth sighting in South Africa and the first in the KGNP.

There are three other categories: the permanent residents, the Kalahari nomads who move in and out from adjacent areas as and when the food supply increases or wanes, and the migrants from elsewhere in Africa and as far afield as Russia, some of which breed here.

Of all the birds forty-two belong to that group that fascinates people as much as do lions, leopards and cheetahs: the raptors – the eagles, hawks, falcons, kites, kestrels, buzzards, vultures and harriers. Perhaps it is their appearance – without exception, large and small, they are striking birds with imperious eyes, formidable beaks and talons, and the mien of aristocrats.

Or perhaps they impress because they are such superbly equipped hunter-killers, each a master of flight in its own specialised way, fast and agile like fighter aircraft, or huge-winged and high-flying like long-range bombers, or swift pouncers like strike planes. Although only about a third of the birds live here permanently, the avian life of the KGNP is a constantly coruscating kaleidoscope of the comings and goings of the migrants, about fifteen per cent of the total, the nomads, about eight per cent, and the vagrants, some forty seven per cent.

The migrants tend to be the most predictable in their movement because it is dictated by the cycle of seasons in their alternate homelands as well as in the KGNP. In the Kalahari the seasons are more elemental – bald winter and summer with no real spring and autumn – and the movement of its nomadic birds throughout the desert is commanded more by the rains, which bring food and water.

The insect and seed-eating sandgrouse and larks, for example, will suddenly appear in numbers after rain when food plants have set seed and even their breeding pattern is governed by this. Resident birds are also susceptible to climatic change: in good times grey-headed sparrows swarm in flocks of up to 600 but in bad times the flocks are down to twenty or less – whether through death or movement is not yet certain.

The vagrants are purely opportunistic, adventurous or aimless. Such extraordinary creatures in this arid environment as fish eagles have been seen – on those rare occasions when the rivers come down in flood, bringing frogs and barbel and other fish from the Namibian hinterland.

Other peculiar strangers include the whitebreasted and reed cormorants and the grey heron, also following the fish, the redbilled teal, bitterns, the black stork, the spurwinged goose and, drifting down from Angola, the palmnut vulture. The great spotted cuckoo has somehow found its way here to join the company of regular migrants like the grey Jacobin and Diederiks cuckoos. How the pinkbacked pelican from Zululand or the Okavango Swamps finds itself in the KGNP is a minor mystery – probably on its way to the fish-rich Namibia coast.

It is impossible to see the park's full spectrum of bird life in less than a number of visits spanning all its seasons, good and bad. Those who know it intimately say the best time is usually in late summer when most of its sparse annual rain is likely to fall, and especially when the flying termites take to the air in hundreds of thousands to pioneer new colonies in the damp ground.

Then just about all the predatory birds come out in force, the smaller raptors, drongos, black swifts and other insect eaters wheeling and dipping to snatch termites in flight while larger birds walk about gulping them as they come out of their holes or when they have landed, or in turn gulping the frogs and lizards that gulp the termites.

The termites' blind genetic strategy is to send forth pioneers in such numbers that the predators will stuff themselves full, the martyrs clearing the way for enough flyers to get through to perpetuate the species. It certainly works – after a while the hunters take to their perches unable to swallow another one and the smokestream of termites rises unhindered.

It is equally impossible to describe all the birds in less than volumes, or really necessary for the average visitor because many are scarce and hard to find and others are very similar in habits and habitat. This account will illuminate the most common, most visible and most interesting.

First is the only one which is not 'in the air' because it cannot fly – that most visible of all birds, the **ostrich**, *Struthio camelus*. In the Kalahari it is still the pure Southern African original, untainted by the North African strain brought south in the heyday of the ostrich feather industry.

One of the memorable KGNP sights is of a line of ostrich males angling in Indian file up the bank of a river or the side of a dune – long erect necks and round black bodies bold against the bright red sand, like ascending notes on a bar of music.

Largest of all birds at up to 157 kilograms, the ostrich in its own way is as well equipped as the gemsbok or eland to cope with the ferocious peaks of heat in the Kalahari. Scorning the shade even when the midsummer sun pushes the temperature of the sand to 70°C, it reduces the impact of the sun's radiation by aligning its body towards or away from the sun to expose the minimum of its body surface – as do springbok. It spreads its wings and feathers to expose its bare legs and skin to the breeze, thus losing heat by convection.

It can go without water as long as it can eat moisture-rich plants and fruits and small creatures like lizards. If there is no fresh water available it will drink salt water and get rid of the salt through special glands in its nose – an ancient characteristic inherited by a number of bird species that is still little understood. And as a further defence the ostrich can safely lose up to a quarter of its weight through dehydration.

A cock ostrich will gather an entourage of up to three hens which will all lay their huge cream-coloured eggs in the same nest, a shallow hollow scraped in the sand. Each lays between three and eight eggs. Only the dominant hen incubates them, taking turns with the male. It is fallacious that the cock sits on the eggs only at night; on very hot days especially he will sometimes relieve the hen while she sheds some of the heat gathered from hours in the broiling sun.

They keep the eggs within a remarkably narrow range of temperature in spite of the ambient heat. They sit on them to warm them when it is cool, shade them when the air temperature is just about right, and sit on them again in high heat to insulate them against it.

Because an ostrich cannot successfully incubate more than about twenty eggs the dominant hen kicks out the surplus ones. Somehow she identifies her own so they are always among those hatched, ensuring survival of the strongest of the species.

Many of their chicks, balls of bristly fluff, are taken by predators but after little more than a month they can run almost as fast as their parents – the ostrich's main defence apart from the raking, tearing forward kick it can deliver with its powerful legs each tipped by two large, sharp claws. Adult ostriches have been timed at sixty kilometres per hour for several kilometres, running with perfect poise in a huge distance-gulping stride. So fast and tireless are they that only the cheetah, even faster over short distances, is able to hunt them with reasonable success.

Infrequently seen elsewhere in South Africa including the Kruger Park, although it is widespread, is the tall and stately **secretary bird**. This KGNP resident is so common at times that after a day or two visitors hardly pay them attention.

They are found virtually anywhere in the riverbeds, singly or in twos and threes, sometimes dozens of them within the span of five kilometres, and tend to gather in dry times at sweetwater drinking places.

Described by some as a walking eagle, *Sagittarius serpentarius* is conspicuous by its height of well over a metre, its grey body with black rump and tail, black upper legs and bare white lower legs as if wearing kneepants, yellow face and, most of all, its 'quill pens'.

These are black crest feathers sticking out behind its head exactly like pens behind a bookkeeper's ear – hence its name of secretary bird. However, the renowned ornithologist Professor Gordon Maclean of the University of Natal says the name's true origin is the Arabic phrase *saqr-et-tair*, meaning 'hunter-bird'.

It paces the earth like a pensive executive with head cocked down at a thoughtful angle as if pondering the woes of the economy, when in fact all it is doing is seeking rodents and lizards and insects and the eggs and chicks of small birds. It either seizes its victims with its beak or stamps on them to immobilise or kill them before swallowing.

Legend has it that the secretary bird is primarily a snake hunter that drops them to their death from great heights before eating them. This is not so; it sometimes eats snakes but simply beats or bites them to death beforehand. It is a dramatic sight when the snake is a large and poisonous one and the bird dances and dodges about it with outspread wings, possibly to divert the snake's attention and harmlessly draw its strike as a toreador deflects a bull's lunge with his cape. It kills the snake with extremely fast strikes of claws and beak.

The secretary bird builds open platform nests of tangled twigs about three or four metres above the ground in smallish and medium-sized trees, usually lays two eggs and is one of the few birds known to carry water as well as food to its chicks in its crop.

A secretary bird mother squats on its haunches to feed water to its chick in their nest in a tree. Clem Haagner – ABPL.

A prize-winning photograph of a pair of secretary birds going through the acrobatic gyrations of courtship. These big raptors are common in the Park. Daphne Crew – ABPL.

Sometimes confused with the secretary bird by novices is another tall and stately strider almost as common as the secretary bird and usually seen in ones and twos but sometimes in dozens.

It is the biggest of all flying birds at up to nineteen kilograms in weight and one and a half metres in height – the **kori bustard** or *Ardeotis kori*, called 'gompou' in Afrikaans because of its predilection for the resinous 'gom' or gum oozed by blackthorn acacia trees.

It looks distinctly different, however, more a *grande dame* stalking with stately tread, plump decolletage outthrust, coiffed head turning slowly from side to side to gaze upon the hoi-polloi.

Its head is large, its eyes yellow and its strong beak is balanced by a short crest projecting stiffly behind the head. The thick neck finely barred in grey descends to a broad body, grey-brown on top and white below with black mottling along the edges of the folded wings and in a collar at the throat.

The kori bustard puts on an impressive mating display. Its crest rises, the tail lifts as a grey fringe along its back, the throat and chest bulge out hugely like a pouter pigeon's and it issues a deep hollow thrumming sound.

It hunts small reptiles, rodents, insects and seeds on the ground and will eat carrion. In turn it is taken by various predators such as the caracal and leopard and, from the evidence of the battlefield, it can put up a tenacious fight. At the scene of one contest its feathers were scattered from a radius of some ten paces around the place of the final kill.

It scorns nest-building and its one or two eggs are laid on bare ground but their coloration is such good camouflage that they are difficult to find.

Two other residents of the same family are the **redcrested korhaan** and **black korhaan**, the former identifiable mainly by the pattern of small massed V markings on the feathers of its back and the latter by the male's conspicuous black neck and face with round white cheek marks and white collar.

The commoner black is often seen and its loud racketing call is one of the familiar sounds of the desert. The redcrested is notorious for its summertime aerobatics. It gallops along for several metres then takes off straight up for as high as thirty metres when suddenly it lets everything go, collapsing in the air in a loose bunch of feathers as if stopped by a charge of birdshot.

It drops like a bundle of rags and just before hitting the dirt its wings flare out to break the fall and it glides for a short distance just above the ground, chuckling.

A great many birds can be discovered with no effort at all, right in camp merely by sitting in a comfortable chair in the shade near chalet, caravan or tent with a good bird book and a pair of binocu-

The kori bustard is the largest flying bird and is found all over the Park, usually stalking with sedate tread in search of insects and the acacia gum which gives it its Afrikaans name – 'gompou'.
Anthony Bannister – ABPL.

lars at hand. The best times are the first few hours of morning and the last few of the afternoon.

Cocky redeyed bulbuls come to investigate the barbecue grids for bits of meat stuck to them after last night's cooking. Slim, graceful swallowtailed bee-eaters in glowing coats of bright green and sky blue and canary yellow perch on nearby branches between darting to catch insects on the wing. Lilacbreasted rollers wheel and whirl through the air after prey like flying advertisements for watercolours.

Tiny pririt batises wearing black burglar masks hop about the sand looking for minute snacks. Extravagantly coloured violet-eared waxbills gather in miniature riots of red and violet and black and cobalt blue and buff and russet. Yellowbilled hornbills land clumsily, teetering in balance between ungainly beaks and flicking tails. Blue-black scimitarbilled woodhoopoes forage in the stunted trees, some-times hanging upside down to probe with their long, curved beaks.

Dripping taps are a favourite small bird hangout and a constant source of entertainment. Cape and house sparrows come in small swarms to peck at the moist earth and cling to the tap to drink from the nozzle. Familiar chats wait patiently to fly up and catch the drops in mid-air as they fall. Sometimes they are chased away by cheeky Karoo chats making small charges with impatient flappings of wings. Squadrons of tiny scalyfeathered finches all wearing neat black bowties ignore the water because they rarely drink and hop briskly about flicking sand aside with their beaks in search of crumbs and seeds. Leave food uncovered on the table at Mata Mata and your back is hardly turned when it is invaded by those avian artful dodgers the Burchells starlings, pecking and plucking and disappear-ing into open pots and bags to steal.

Because they are not threatened, birds have adapted wondrously to the human presence in the camps. At Nossob, for instance, a pair of whitefaced owls, *Otus leucotis*, have their roost almost at eye level in a small pepper tree near the campsite's ablution block. They re-turn there from the night's foray and settle down for the day's sleep, feathers fluffed over feet, heads sunk into necks, golden eyes hidden behind closed lids set in wide circles of black. Not even the whirr of a cine camera from two metres away seems to disturb them.

A Scops owl, *Otus senegalensis*, lives in a large tree next to the same building but is more difficult to find, so cleverly does its grey and black marking camouflage it against the bark and leaves.

Too many birds to list here frequent the camps but some of the more interesting, in addition to those mentioned, are the pied bar-bet, blackthroated canary, ashy tit, yellow canary, rock martin, wil-low warbler, blackchested prinia, ringnecked doves, forktailed drongo, dusky sunbird, whitebrowed sparrow-weaver, greyheaded sparrow, chat flycatcher, rufuseared warbler and Kalahari robin – all

Swallow-tailed bee-eaters cluster close for warmth on a branch in the morning sun.
Leigh Voigt.

The familiar chat lives up to its name and is seen all over the Park.
Roger de la Harpe – ABPL.

of these seen in the space of a few days. Different seasons, of course, will produce different varieties of birds.

Out on the park roads the diversity is greater if not as close by and is filled with colourful glimpses of the restless drama of bird life.

The outermost of the banks of sand at Kijkij, flanking a scraped-out hollow sometimes filled with runoff water, overlooks the water trough a short distance away. It is one of the few 'heights' giving a view in the KGNP and for those with patience, a good place to watch for lions and other big animals.

Thorn trees shade its eastern slope and beneath them the ground sometimes appears to have been churned up by miniature bulldozers. This is the handiwork of sociable weavers flicking away with their beaks to expose fallen seed (for the full story of this unusual bird, see the panel titled 'The Commune Dwellers'. Drongos with long forked tails wait in the branches for unwary insects to pass by. Pretty little Namaqua doves with still longer tails perkily strut the dust. And then, for the fortunate, an unbelievably bright flash of colour will dash from a tree, pausing on branches and the ground.

It is a shrike, the *Laniarius atrococcineus*, virtually identical to the boubou shrikes but with this difference – a chin-to-tail shirtfront of feathers so brilliantly crimson it appears to glow in the shade. In the sunshine it is royal. Few if any other African birds display a colour of such dazzling strength.

The **crimsonbreasted shrike** occurs all over the park and is not shy but because it prefers the cover of trees, it has to be looked for.

In the evenings at Rooiputs and some other waterpoints tall, graceful **blackheaded herons**, *Ardea melanocephala*, reveal an uncharacteristic gawkiness as they find their night perches high in trees. Long legs bending at ungainly angles, they clamber along the thin outer branches struggling to hold their balance, wings extended like a tightrope-walker's pole. They make good photographs silhouetted against the twilight sky. Finally they are satisfied and their legs fold as they settle, safe for the night from predators.

No less clumsy was a **giant eagle owl**, *Bubo lacteus*, that unwisely chose the outer end of a branch in a large acacia tree for its day's sleep. Hardly had its eyes closed and the sun risen than it was detected by a pair of black crows, among the most aggressively arrogant and intelligent members of birddom.

They promptly attacked this unwitting intruder into their domain, swooping down and stabbing with their beaks, making harsh throaty calls. The much bigger owl blinked its dark eyes wide in astonishment and swivelled its head from side to side trying to watch the attackers but made no attempt to fight back. While one crow distracted it from the front the other dived on it from behind. All the owl could do was duck its head into its shoulders as whirring wings skimmed past.

One of the most spectacular birds in the Park is the crimson-breasted shrike, here seen perched beside its nest with an offering for its chick.
Clem Haagner – ABPL.

A giant eagle owl with its prey. It can sometimes be seen by day sleeping in trees or rock crevices hunting at dusk and dawn.
Daphne Carew – ABPL.

Eventually it decided enough was enough. It rose on its short legs and wobbled along the branch deeper into the cover of the tree's foliage. Wings spread out with the feathered tips splayed like fingers, it struggled to hold its balance as it navigated leafy twigs and sharp thorns. At last it reached the fork where the branch met the bole of the tree and the thick canopy baulked the crows' attack. It settled down again and after a final glare at them, closed its eyes.

The crows hovered about raucously for a short time and then apparently decided victory was theirs and flew away.

The **martial eagle** is the epitome of a bird of prey, king of the raptors. Appropriately named *Polemaetus bellicosus*, it is fierce of expression and regal in manner from brown hood and wings down to its ermine-like underparts of white flecked with brown, stands nearly a metre high and has a wingspan of nearly three metres. It is an awesome hunter, stooping from high in the sky in a terrifying dive to take animals as large as a duiker, usually killing with the first blow of massive claws backed by several kilograms of muscle.

Even the martial can be embarrassed. Between Gemsbok Plain and Batulama waterpoints two much smaller but unidentified eagles found a young full-grown martial perched in their territory and swooped to the attack one after the other, veering away just out of reach of its fearsome talons.

The martial was forced to take to precipitous flight and glide to the ground beneath a tall tree where the territorial defenders could not reach it with their low planing strikes. So they continued to circle the tree and pen it in by making an occasional dive to the edge of the overhang.

For some fifteen minutes the martial threw dignity to the winds and stayed under cover, ducking involuntarily every time one of the attackers swooped close to the tree. Eventually , when they landed a short distance away to rest, the martial hastily scrambled on the stump of a dead tree, shook its feathers back into some order and took off fast for safer places.

The **pale chanting goshawk**, *Melierax canorus*, is widespread in Namibia, Botswana and the western half of South Africa and is the commonest raptor in the KGNP, often seen perched on the tops of trees along the roadside and giving passing cars no more than a glance unless they stop too close. Named for its musical voice, it is a medium-sized bird in Louis XV dress of pink stockings, delicately striped white pantaloons and pale grey coat and, as mentioned already, it sometimes shows ingenuity by following badgers to snap up rodents they flush.

There is a host of smaller raptors such as the fast-flying lanner falcon, the rednecked falcon, and several different kinds of kestrels, kites, harriers and hawks – all best identified in the field with the use

Top left: A gabar goshawk swings through the air in masterly flight.
Nigel Dennis – ABPL.

A Western red-footed kestrel cools off its feet and tummy in a pool.
Beverly Joubert – ABPL.

Bottom left: Snakes are part of the diet of probably the Park's best-known raptor, the pale chanting goshawk, named for its colour and its mellifluous call. The prey here is a yellow cobra.
Anthony Bannister – ABPL.

of one of the specialist bird books listed in the bibliography. The smallest of all raptors, the pygmy falcon, is described in the panel on the sociable weaver.

Six different vultures appear in the park, two of them permanent residents and the rest vagrants of which the whiteheaded vulture is the most frequent visitor.

People usually look upon vultures with distaste because of their uncouth (by human standards) eating manners and their general association with death. It is an undeserved anthropomorphic judgement. They carry out an exceptionally important task in the cycle of life by helping to dispose of carcasses, and they are consummate flyers.

They are not exclusively eaters of carrion and to a larger or lesser extent, varying from species to species, vultures will hunt small animals and reptiles.

The lanner falcon is a fast and efficient hunter, sometimes working with others of its kind to flush small birds and strike them in flight.
Lorna Stanton – ABPL.

The lappetfaced vulture is one of the largest and is seen more easily in the Park than perhaps anywhere else in South Africa.
Anthony Bannister – ABPL.

One of the KGNP residents is the biggest of vultures, the **lappet-faced vulture** or *Torgos tracheliotus*, a ponderous bird with bright red bare head and neck and dark body streaked below with black and white. The front half of the massive beak is yellow. Seldom seen outside game reserves and even in them not very often, it is regarded as a threatened species because many of its breeding grounds have been overtaken by civilisation and those left are confined to arid areas.

Because of their size they impose precedence over other vultures at a carcass and tear open the toughest skin with their powerful bills. When they are full they step aside and leave the rest to the others.

Imposing creatures on the ground or in their tree roosts, they are so heavy they have trouble taking off when there is no breeze and in the mornings will wait until the air stirs enough to give their wings lift. If disturbed on the ground they have to run for fifteen or twenty metres with wings spread wide to gather speed for take-off. Like other vultures, they climb far into the sky, almost out of sight of human vision, to scan great areas with their telescopic vision for signs of prey or death.

The commoner **whitebacked,** *Gyps africanus*, is the typical vulture seen in quantity at carcasses and is almost entirely a scavenger. It does not compete with the lappetfaced for food because the lappetfaced eats the outside flesh while it eats the insides.

The best places to see vultures, according to Kotie Herholdt, are the northernmost three waterpoints in the park, Kannaguass, Grootkolk and Union's End, because the water there is sweet.

Eagles are just about everywhere. One of the most beautiful and the easiest to see – and in the view of many bird-watchers the most interesting of all – is the **bateleur**, *Terathopius ecaudatus*. Almost as impressive as the martial, it has a black body and tawny wings highlighted by a bright red face, red rings around the eyes, red legs and usually reddish, sometimes white patch on its back.

Its flight is its hallmark: it seldom flaps its wings and glides straight with a slight side-to-side rocking motion as if balancing on a tightrope. It is this which gives it its name, the French word for a juggler or acrobatic tumbler.

The bateleur is an efficient hunter of other birds, squirrels, mongooses, hares, lizards and insects, will eat carrion when the mood takes it, and sometimes cheekily steals the prey of bigger eagles. It either swoops swiftly on its target or comes down smoothly straight on top of it using its wings like a parachute.

Other resident eagles are the brown snake eagle, *Circaetus cinereus*, and blackbreasted snake eagle, *Circaetus gallicus*, which, as their names suggest, are ardent snake hunters, and the quite

common tawny eagle, *Aquila rapax*. Regular raptor visitors include the steppe eagle that comes all the way from Eastern Europe, booted eagle with its full-feathered legs, and steppe buzzard from Eurasia and North Africa.

A careful examination of trees in the riverbeds will reveal many raptor nests, often with one or both of the mating pair in attendance in the breeding season. The nests appear as solid darker masses in the dark tracery of foliage and are distinguishable from the tree rat nests because the latter are almost always messy heaps in a sharp fork and are more vertical in shape.

Bateleurs like to build their nests inside the tree canopy and the other eagles and vultures on the treetop. They look precariously flimsy, especially when two large birds are standing on them, but are so sturdy they often last for years.

One stretch of riverbed liberally endowed with nests is that between the Nossob camp and the Kameelsleep waterpoint to its south. Every second or third tree seems to have a nest and several of them are close to the road. Some, however, are unused. Many raptors build new nests each year, apparently to escape infestations of mites and other parasites, and some like the bateleur will rotate annually between two or three nests.

Water troughs and seeps from the fibreglass tanks next to the boreholes are fine vantage points for birdwatchers. Avoid those with very brack water, though picking the best ones is a matter of luck – they might be deserted and then within the space of minutes become as busy as an airport at peak hour. Doves and sparrows congregate in large numbers to dip beaks and tilt heads back to swallow, often right beside gemsbok, springbok and other buck and between their feet.

Vultures waddle up to drink at leisure, possibly standing in the trough. An eagle may take a bath, lowering its fluffed-out belly feathers into the water and spraying droplets with a vigorous shake. In the mornings and afternoons flocks of Namaqua and Burchell's sandgrouse come fluttering briskly out of the sky with clockwork daily regularity to drink *en masse* at the water's edge. At the slightest alarm they and the sparrows explode noisily into the sky, the sparrows to fly in a cloud into the nearest tree and the grouse to circle overhead before both land again.

But birds are everywhere, constant surprises around bends, popping unexpectedly out of the roadside scrub. Tiny pygmy falcons flit past displaying black laced wing edges and tails. Yellow canaries bob by – sunflowers in flight. Anteating chats dart perkily along roadside embankments flashing pale wingfeathers. A doublebanded courser with its two black necklaces might be seen streaking across the sand on long legs. Or ostriches taking a sand bath with obvious enjoyment, sitting down and flapping up the dust with their wings. Or a colourful crested hoopoe marching in the shade, poking the ground with its long needle beak. Or any of the many larks, all coloured more or less red or grey to match their red dune or grey calcrete backgrounds.

The variety is great, and endlessly fascinating.

The Abdim's stork is a migrant visitor to the Park, sometimes coming in hundreds.
Clem Haagner – ABPL.

The Commune Dwellers

LIKE people, some birds prefer rural privacy and others the metropolitan huddle. Weavers are the most ardent urbanites and trees and reed beds bedecked with their neat grass nests dangling from slender stems are a familiar sight all over Southern Africa.

Two commune dwellers with singular customs live in the KGNP. One is the whitebrowed sparrow weaver, *Plocepasser mahali,* whose nests look like bunches of tangled hay randomly pitchforked into a tree, for some inexplicable reason usually on the western side. Messy though they are, these large strawballs are well designed with two tunnels in roosting nests and are in breeding nests, a comfortable chamber inside.

The whitebrowed sparrow weavers are clannish creatures generally found in the KGNP in small groups whose members pitch in together to build all their nests. Each pair then occupies its own, but – and herein lies their speciality – only the dominant pair in each group breeds.

All the others are helpers. They dash about all day fetching food for the chicks, usually two, with some assistance from the males who mostly sit about or feed themselves.

This huge mass of grass like a wayward haystack up a tree is a typical communal nest of hundreds and sometimes thousands of sociable weavers. It also provides accommodation for various other birds and reptiles which live on top or inside, like the pygmy falcon.
Anthony Bannister – ABPL.

When danger threatens – a passing kestrel or crow or snake perhaps – the whole group goes into cheeping attack. When the danger has passed they all frantically feed the chicks at the double until they have made up for lost time and then resume their normal pace.

The whitebrowed sparrow weavers have it both ways. There are many groups so they ensure the perpetuation of their species by producing enough chicks to allow for attrition, and although each group produces few chicks they get special attention.

Considerably more complex and better designed for desert conditions is the communal system of the remarkable sociable weaver, *Philetairus socius,* whose fixation on a gregarious life approaches Manhattan proportions.

They are desert birds found only in Namibia, southern Botswana and the north-central parts of South Africa and their nests are an outstanding characteristic of this region – huge shapeless masses of grass hanging on branches like wayward haystacks.

This extraordinary feat of construction is accomplished by birds about the size of a sparrow. A nest might be just large enough for a pair, though not for long before the communal instinct drives others to join them. Or it might be years old, more than seven metres long and several hundred kilograms in weight and accommodate 500 or 600 of them – plus a variety of other tenants.

The sociable weaver nest has been likened to an apartment block and to an African village of grass huts. It is both: a grass apartment block. Simple and fragile it may look with its smooth-thatched top and raggedly holed underside, but it is carefully and ingeniously constructed.

The birds appear to work on the premise that inevitably the nest they are beginning to build will expand to another monster housing project. They begin with the roof, on which everything will depend – literally.

They find a suitable tree branch or fork, preferably large, and fasten to it a platform of strong thorn twigs up to thirty centimetres long – a prodigious effort for so small a bird. Around this they construct the walls of the nest using long stiff grass stalks and, on top of the structure, heavier grass and coarse twigs.

Unlike others of the weaver family they do not weave. The grass stems are pushed into the structure until they bind into a firm mass and once a nest is started, building goes on non-stop for as long as it is used. Every day between feeding, the sociable weavers fly home with fresh grass stalks and thrust these into the growing stack. The roof of the nest weathers to a smooth, firm surface that, like thatch, sheds rain well.

Each separate apartment is a round chamber up to fifteen centimetres in diameter entered from below by a narrow vertical passage some twenty-five centimetres long. The chamber has a lining from floor to ceiling of cottony seed fluff, fur and whatever else soft the tenant can find.

The round entrance to the passage is strengthened with strips of hard green plant like devil's thorn and cattail. For some distance inside the passage the walls are lined with sharp stalks of grass stuck in at an angle to form a barrier against intruders.

And there the sociable weaver lives for the duration of its life or that of the nest – which may collapse from overweight and old age, or in heavy rains, or when its supporting branch dies and falls off as they tend to do in acacias. Then the colony starts rebuilding what is left or starts anew.

The colony functions as a group, setting forth in the cool of mornings and afternoons to feed within a two-kilometre radius of home. They move as a quicksilver cloud of whirring wings to settle on the ground in pursuit of insects, their main diet, and seeds. They expose their prey by brushing the sand aside with flicks of their stubby pink beaks. When they take fright the whole cloud sweeps up into the nearest tree or bush. They rarely drink water, not needing it.

By night and in the middle of the day the colony returns to the nest to rest and sleep in their chambers, where the temperature stays remarkably even within the thick insulation of grass, however hot or cold it is outside. In the freezing Kalahari winters, as many as five birds will share a chamber for added warmth, sleeping on top of each other.

Perhaps the most extraordinary trick they have evolved is their pattern of breeding. Because of the sheltering micro-environment of their nests they can raise young at any time of the year but the rate of breeding stays low in the long dry periods. In these times they concentrate on finding food and

A group of sociable weavers clusters chummily on a branch hanging down from their nest, one with a twig it is about to add to the structure.
Lorna Stanton – ABPL.

A mother pygmy falcon and her chick. These tiny raptors live with the sociable weavers, making themselves at home in their giant communal nests and only occasionally eating one.
Lorna Stanton – ABPL.

keeping the apartment block in good order, often helping each other to build and repair nests. Those that do not breed help the few that do to keep their eggs warm and feed the chicks.

When the rains come and the insect and seed populations multiply, so do the sociable weavers because the abundance of food means they can sustain their chicks. This is a time of frantic maintenance activity – fresh lining is put into chambers, passages are lengthened and their anti-intruder barriers are reinforced.

Then they pair off, one couple to each chamber. Unlike most other birds, the females lay their eggs at spaced out intervals and start the incubation with the first or second egg. In this way they lay up to six with a time gap between each.

There is a clear purpose to this: the older chicks will be bigger and stronger and in the front of the queue to get food brought home by the parents. Therefore should there be a food shortage the older will survive, ensuring that at least some chicks go forth to perpetuate the species, instead of all dying as they would if they were all the same age when the food ran out.

In nature no creature's sanctuary is inviolate and the sociable weaver's is no exception. Tempting as they are to many predators, provided they are well above the ground these huge nests are amazingly secure against all but a very few.

The martial eagle and the giant eagle owl use the nests not as a food source, although they might gobble the odd weaver, but as a convenient base on which to build their own nests.

When it can, the ever-hungry honey badger clambers on top of a nest and breaks it open to reach the chambers and chicks inside.

Pied barbets take over chambers and live in harmony with the builders. So do the smallest of all the raptors, the pygmy falcons, in a very rare example of predator and prey birds living side by side.

Despite its ponderous scientific name *Polihierax semitorquatus,* the pygmy falcon weighs only about sixty grams and is the size of a bulbul, standing smaller than a dove. It is white below and grey above with speckled black and white wings that are clearly identifi-

able in flight. When perched it has a rather budgie look with its short beak tucked into its feathers.

Most sociable weaver nests have at least one pair of pygmy falcons as fellow tenants. The chambers they occupy are easily seen because they are rimmed with white from the falcon's droppings.

Although they live in a virtual larder, the falcons seldom catch the weavers and then usually a youngster, their choice of food being lizards. It is possible that their presence actually assists the weavers by deterring some other predators.

They are fearless raptors that display the aggression so common among little things and are fun to watch. When they fly into a tree with a nest the weavers promptly make a noisy departure or dart up into their own chambers, but do not seem unduly bothered and might loiter about the branches a short distance away. The moment the falcons enter their own chambers or fly away it is back to business.

The falcons have an unusual courting display, the female doing all the work. While the male looks on aloofly from a twig nearby, the female bobs and dips its head forward and raises a ruff of russet feathers on its back. It is not particular – if there are two or three males close it will woo all of them.

Once paired, the female lays two to four eggs at a time and raises a family twice a season. The chicks share the nest with their parents for some time after they can fly so they can stay warm together in cold weather.

One predator the falcons cannot deter is the Cape cobra, *Naja nivea,* which is so long it can anchor itself to the nest while it searches and so thin it easily enters the barriered passages to seize eggs and chicks.

Predation has not endangered the sociable weaver. Outside the park they made a nuisance of themselves by building nests in the crosspieces of telephone poles, which had to be cleaned repeatedly. The problem has been solved by placing special wire brackets lower down on some poles where they can build harmlessly.

Sociable weavers perform one other service: the people of the desert use their droppings gathered beneath their nests as a yeast in their home brew known as 'Nxannetjie-goup'.

The Water Bearers

SANDGROUSE are the fast-flying commuters of the desert – prettily patterned birds uniquely adapted to live in its fierce heat far from the water they cannot do without.

Four species appear in Southern Africa, all similar in size and shape to a dove or small pigeon, and three are found in the KGNP: the Namaqua, *Pterocles namaqua,* the Burchell's or spotted, *Pterocles burchelli,* and the Doublebanded, *Pterocles bicinctus.*

They can be seen only at waterpoints because they inhabit areas out of reach – distant stony calcrete beds of the Kalahari for the Namaqua, red sandveld for the Burchell's and desert hills for the Doublebanded. There they scrape shallow nests in the ground no bigger than the palm of a hand.

It is easy to tell them apart, particularly as they often come to the water together. The Burchell's bodies are red and pink and clearly speckled with white in both cocks and hens. Namaqua males have olive and brown bodies with grey-mottled wings and distinctive white and dark red bands across the chest. The Doublebanded male is similar but has a clear black-and-white forehead pattern. The Namaqua leave a very distinctive, liquidly melodious call when in the air that gives them their Afrikaans name 'kelkiewyn'.

They fly sixty to eighty kilometres to drink water in flocks which can number from a few hundred birds to thousands. Although each bird might drink only once every few days, according to Professor Gordon Maclean's studies, the flocks go every day, arriving at the water with commuter regularity each morning, usually about 10 a.m. in the KGNP. Some prefer to come in the late afternoons, also always at about the same time.

They arrive with a rushing whirr of wings, land a metre or two from the water and walk quickly to it. The habit made them a favourite of hunters because a single load of small bird-shot fired into a descending cloud of these tasty birds brought down scores of them.

Fortunately the practice has come to be regarded as so contemptible that it rarely occurs.

At the water both cocks and hens drink and walk into the shallows for a dip. For the hen it is just a way of keeping cool. For the cock, it is a very special technique that makes sandgrouse so different from other birds.

Doves and some other species like the secretary bird take water back to the nest for their chicks in their crops and regurgitate. Not so the cock sandgrouse. It carries water home in its feathers.

Its lower chest feathers are an evolutionary adaptation. Fringed with fine hairs, they form a network that absorbs and holds water like a sponge. With this load aboard the cock navigates accurately at speeds of sixty kilometres an hour or more back to its nest where the chicks, usually two of them, drink by combing the water out of the feathers with their beaks.

Because the cock does not have to give up its own water for its chicks, it need not drink daily and can live far from water sources. This ability greatly extends the range of sandgrouse and thereby enables them to live where the waterpoints are few and far between.

Sandgrouse are also able to withstand the full blast of the desert sun throughout the day without ill effects in the weeks while the eggs are hatched and the chicks are raised. The hens sit on the eggs by day and the cocks by night.

Just how they beat the heat is still being investigated but it appears they have some insulation in the form of a dense coat of down beneath their feathers. It is also believed that in extreme temperatures a family might huddle together for mutual insulation, exposing as little of their bodies as possible to the sun.

Each sandgrouse is the specialised product of millions of years of evolution.

One of the Kalahari's great
spectacles is the morning and
evening flight to waterholes of
dove-size sandgrouse in flocks
of thousands. Three kinds are
common to the Park. The
Namaqua (above) is sometimes
confused with the Double-
banded (right) and distinguishable only by variations in colour
and pattern. Below right is the
Burchell's, whose markings are
distinctly different.
Nigel Dennis, Anthony
Bannister, Nigel Dennis –
ABPL.

The Five-star Nest

A SHARP eye along the fifty-five-kilometre road through rolling dunes between the Auob and Nossob rivers might spot a luxury nest built by one of the smallest birds in the KGNP.

The little Cape penduline tit – brown and pale yellow with a black and white forehead – likes security as well as comfort. Its nest is the neatest of all, woven as finely as a felt blanket from the softest materials – wild cotton, kapok, wool scraped from sheep and goats by thorns and barbed wire, fine fur from rabbits and hares and any other animal hair it can find.

Similar to the nests weavers make of grass, it is a coconut-sized, roundish bag attached at top or sides to thin twigs at about head height in a small tree, usually a blackthorn because of the protection of its spiked branches.

Just above the middle is a small, round, dark entrance covered by a short roof like the peak of a cap. Therein lies the security: the dark 'entrance' is not – it is false.

The real entrance is in the seam of the cap's peak. It is actually two flaps, upper and lower, opened by the bird with its foot when it enters and leaves. The tight-woven material springs closed behind it and clings together.

There are different theories about the dark false doorway. One is that it is deliberately created to dupe predators, particularly snakes, which futilely butt their noses against it. Another is that it is a landing mark for the tit and coincidentally foils predators.

Inside the nest, whose walls are between half a centimetre and two centimetres thick, is a short tunnel leading to the combined living-room, bedroom and nursery. There, up to six birds might congregate, the females laying up to ten eggs after the rains and all helping to raise the youngsters.

The cunning Cape penduline tit constructs its nest of soft materials like cotton, wool and fur and has a clever way of keeping out snakes. The true opening above the bird's head is shut tight, as if zipped. Just beneath it in shadow is a dark patch on the nest wall which looks like an entrance and deceives predators.
Clem Haagner – ABPL.

The Cold-blooded

Science has recorded fifty-five different kinds of reptiles and several frogs in the KGNP including such incongruous creatures as a purely aquatic frog and a terrapin. Few are permanent residents and most overlap occasionally into the park from adjacent regions, like the black mamba found at Union's End and a python seen just outside the park border.

Most of the frogs and the marsh terrapins are brought in by the flooding rivers. They do not generally survive subsequent long periods of drought and heat although some frogs and the terrapin in particular are able to bury themselves in mud and hibernate for lengthy periods. The hardiest is the little platanna frog, once used by medical science for testing for pregnancies. It never leaves water and zoologists suspect that some may live in some of the park's wells and reservoirs.

So the KGNP does not have a great deal to offer the reptile buff. Its commonest snake is the elegant and very poisonous **Cape cobra**, *Naja nivea,* that hunts just about anything including other snakes. Also quite common are that nemesis of Africa, the ordinary **puffadder** *Bitis arietans,* and the beautifully patterned **horned adder**, *Bitis caudalis,* that lures its lizard prey by waving the black tip of its tail. It sometimes travels by sidewinding in a halfrolling motion like a loosely coiled spring for better traction in soft sand and so that as little of its body as possible touches the stinging hot surface.

For the rest the park boasts a couple of kinds of tortoises and a small selection of skinks, lizards, geckos and small snakes. One of the former is the serrated or **Kalahari tent tortoise**, with the cumbersome taxonomic name *Psammobates oculifer,* much favoured by the Bushmen because its domed shell makes a useful container for herbs.

Few of the latter are worth noting here because they are scarce or seldom encountered by travellers. One is the spectacularly coloured striped **sandveld lizard**, *Nucras tessellata tessellata*, with stripes right down its back, cream-barred sides and a brilliantly red tail. Up to thirty centimetres long and equipped with powerful hindlegs and toes for speed, it lives chiefly on scorpions.

Another is **Sundevall's writhing skink**, *Lygosoma sundevalli sundevalli,* a small, dull, frankfurterish lizard with tiny legs, that emulates snakes by wriggling like them. A local belief is that they are highly poisonous and jump from the ground to strike. It is complete myth but indigenous people still prize the dried and ground body, especially the tail, as a snakebite cure.

Two of the geckos are among the park's more delightful and high-profile characters, the Bibron's and the barking – the first silent and seen, the second noisy and secretive.

The horned adder – seen here with its head withdrawn defensively into the coils of its body – is common and mildly poisonous. The short 'horns' can be seen above the eyes.
Anthony Bannister – ABPL.

Go out in camp of an evening and find an outside light on the wall of a building, especially any of the chalets at Twee Rivieren whose thatch roofs are supported by angled log beams. It is almost certain that on a wall or beam near a light there will be a plump fellow resembling, from a distance, nothing so much as a thick bejewelled bracelet fit for a Cleopatra – a glossy tan, brown or purple object banded with studs of bright white gems.

Move cautiously closer and it becomes a **Bibron's gecko**, *Pachydactylus bibronii,* lurking in ambush for insects drawn by the light, clinging flat to the surface with toes splayed wide at the ends of short fat legs.

Like all geckos it is absolutely harmless and, in fact, it is a boon because it devours mosquitoes and other insects that pester man.

The little **barking gecko** has the most fitting collection of names of any KGNP inhabitant. Its scientific title is *Ptenopus garrulus garru-*

lus and garrulous it certainly is. Its Afrikaans name – 'klipklappertjie' – is more apt because the sound it makes is exactly like clapping two small stones together.

One need not leave a camp to find them – Nossob especially. Just before the sun goes down they start warming up in an unsyncopated succession of sharp, clacking 'barks' that grow after sunset into a continuous chorus. On warm nights it can go on long after dark but usually peters out quite soon when the barkers go forth to catch small insects.

In spite of their racket they are difficult to find because the source of the sound is hard to pinpoint and they are very shy. They stick their blunt heads out of small holes usually dug in the sand heaped around small bushes, bark with bulging throats and duck back down at the slightest sign of anything approaching.

The trick is to spot a hole and wait patiently two or three metres away. When a bark seems to come from the hole, flick a torch. The gecko will stay there, undisturbed by the light, and carry right on barking.

It drives some people distraught. Old KGNP hands say the only thing more irritating on a hot night than the barking gecko is the male of the monotonous lark, which in certain seasons sings right through the night, inviting retribution at dawn.

The Green Life

Under the dangerously extreme conditions of the Kalahari, where everything that can sustain life is used to the limit, every kind of plant plays an important role in the endless cycle of life.

Bleak as it looks, the monotonous terrain contains hundreds of species of flora from tiny ephemeral flowers clinging to the sand to the big camelthorn trees softening the harsh lines of the rivers. Some take root anywhere, others are confined to specific habitats like the edges of pans, the grassy plains or the 'streets' between dunes.

Some have very specialised functions. Two are mundane ground plants without which a great many of the desert inhabitants would certainly die – the annual tsamma melon and the perennial wild or gemsbok cucumber. In dry times they are the prime source of water in vast areas of the Kalahari, and were so in the KGNP before its wells were drilled.

The **tsamma melon**, *Citrullus lanatus,* is a small round melon found in the dunes and plains. Green and ringed with rows of pale mottled patches, it grows copiously after rains on a long ground stem and lasts for most of a year, surviving the sometimes heavy frosts of winter.

These two wild fruits are a key factor in the ecology of the Park. They are the tsamma melon (top) and the wild cucumber (bottom) – major sources of moisture for a great many creatures in dry times, including lions, hyenas, all kinds of buck, jackals and a host of rodents. Without them, the Kalahari could probably sustain far fewer kinds of animals.
Anthony Bannister – ABPL.

And ninety to ninety-five per cent of its content is moisture. In drought it is a staple water source for a huge range of antelope and other animals. Lions, hyenas, jackals, polecats, squirrels, porcupines and many smaller rodents eat them, some for their meagre food value as well as their moisture. Various birds feed on them.

The **gemsbok cucumber**, *Acanthosicyos naudianus,* is a distinctly off-putting object rather like a naked kiwifruit thickly studded with long, soft and fleshy spines. Greenish-yellow in colour, it grows in clusters from a large, thick underground tuber and has about the same water content as the tsamma. It is as sought after as the tsamma and some animals, like the gemsbok, dig up the nourishing tuber, which may reach a metre in length.

Since time immemorial both plants have been a lifeline for the now dwindling population of Kalahari Bushmen, who use them to supplement their buried caches of water in ostrich eggs and to cook or eat raw. The tsamma has often saved the lives of hunters in the desert and still today the hardy womenfolk of the Northern Cape seek out the sweeter gemsbok cucumbers to mix in salads.

The most vivacious of the park's plants, however, are the **camelthorns** scattered along the Auob and Nossob rivers – big, rough-barked, thick-trunked trees with splayed branches carrying lumpish canopies of leaves. Each tree is a micro-environment hosting a fascinating diversity of life.

Its name is a translation of the Afrikaans 'kameeldoring', the 'kameel' being a shortened form of 'kameelperd' or giraffe, which like feeding on this species and once roamed the south-west Kalahari.

Acacia erioloba is the commonest tree in the park, reaching considerable size in the more frequently watered riverbeds and populating the savannah as a smaller, straighter tree. An evergreen although its foliage thins in winter, it produces large grey sickle-shaped or half-disc pods scattered liberally on the ground that make wholesome meals for a host of animals and insects including thirteen species of beetles. When the camelthorn bears many pods, say the old Kalahari hands, there will be drought. It also produces pairs of long thorns strong enough to puncture tyres and shoe soles.

The sociable weavers living in their giant nests draped on branches are the most obvious of the camelthorn's tenants. Martial, tawny and bateleur eagles, vultures, secretary birds, giant eagle owls, goshawks and other raptors make their homes in it and many more birds roost and rest there. The tangled twigs-and-droppings nests of tree rats are bunched in higher forks – ultimately to the tree's detriment because their excretions cause rot. Hollows in the trunk accommodate colonies of Egyptian slit-faced bats.

Lizards, skinks, scorpions and all sorts of beetles inhabit the rough bark. Bees make hives in holes and cracks. In burrows at the tree's

Many living things depend on the ubiquitous camelthorn tree for their survival, feeding on its leaves and velvety grey seed pods. The pods here are sickle-shaped but many are half-round or almost circular.
Clem Haagner – ABPL.

base live more insects and also mice, puffadders and Cape cobras, the last making use of the tree as a personal larder. The sand in the shade is all too often the home of hordes of tampan ticks, soft sinister little bloodsuckers that detect the presence of victims by their movement and carbon dioxide emission, inject them with a neurotoxic local anaesthetic that in large quantity can kill smaller creatures, swiftly bloat themselves with blood and then plop back into the sand.

Lions, cheetahs, hyenas and jackals repose in the camelthorn's shade during the hot hours. Leopards use the higher branches to store their catches, or simply to lie up by day, hindlegs dangling down. African wildcats and caracals also rest there and at night genets prowl the branches for prey.

The camelthorn has many more uses, says Dr P T van der Walt of the National Parks Board. Among them: it makes excellent firewood; being slow-grown, the timber is hard enough for fencing and mine props; the soft, red-brown heartwood is used by Bushmen to make firelighting charcoal and by their womenfolk as a cosmetic. Finally, Bushmen collect the white droppings from the ground under the sociable weaver nests to use as a yeast in making their beer. It is a benign tree, truly a pillar of desert society.

A widespread cousin of the camelthorn that sometimes hybridises with it is the **grey camelthorn,** *Acacia haematoxylon,* seen all over the plains as a shrub and as a few short trees in the riverbeds.

Possibly the most versatile tree for man and beast is *Boscia albitrunca,* the **shepherd's tree** or 'witgatboom'. It is a very ordinary looking evergreen member of the caper family that stands up to seven metres tall and has a rounded shape and thickish white or grey trunk. In the loose sand of the dunes it grows as a many-stemmed shrub. Its name comes from farmers who say its leaves, rich in protein and moisture, are the finest fodder for sheep and goats, and is more than justified by the tree's extraordinary number of uses.

Its best known use is for a coffee substitute the Kalahari's indigenous people brew by boiling its pounded and dried roots. The resultant black-brown liquid takes some getting used to and reputedly has some embarrassing side effects.

The same people make a porridge of flour ground from the tree's soft core, boil the high-protein roots to make a sweet syrup, use dry roots to ferment beer and treat various ailments with the roots and the tree's fruit – sweet-tasting yellowish berries about the size of cherries. The dried buds of its creamy flowers are said to taste as good as ordinary capers.

The tree's oddest characteristic is that its roots, fresh or dry, are an excellent preservative for butter and milk and will keep bread and vegetables free of mould for a considerable time, thanks to a chemical they contain.

In the wild this tree with all-purpose feet grows almost everywhere except along the rivers and around pans and is a main food source for browsers. Lions and other animals lie beneath it in the hot hours because the temperature in its pool of dark shadow can be as much as 20°C lower than outside.

The **blackthorn tree** which hosts the Cape penduline tit has a tale behind its scientific name *Acacia mellifera detinens.* It was given the *detinens,* meaning 'detaining', by the explorer-botanist Burchell after he became entangled in its ferocious mass of hooked thorns.

It is a grey to dark shrub common in the KGNP and can grow into a tree several metres high. In spring its thorny hostility is hidden by an innocent white cloak of sweet-scented puffball flowers. These and its small pods and foliage are also a popular food for browsers, who are undeterred by the spikes.

The blackthorn has a curious association with another bird: the kori bustard is addicted to a thick gummy resin that oozes from its stem. It is this which gives the bird its Afrikaans name 'gompou' or 'gum bustard'.

Its addiction is sometimes the kori bustard's downfall. Bushmen boil the resin into a toffee to satisfy their own sweet tooth – and also to attach a lump to the end of a cord with which they catch the bird.

Other uses of the blackthorn, says Dr van der Walt, are for withies to make baskets and fasten hut poles, for nooses to catch hares, and for a special Bushman artefact – ankle rattles.

They pluck from the tree the large, pale cocoons of a hairy brown caterpillar which lives nowhere else, kill the pupae inside usually by boiling them, and replace them with small stones. They then string the cocoons together side by side on thongs and these, tied around their ankles, give a loud rhythmic rattle as the Bushmen shuffle and stamp in their quaint dances.

A favourite springbok food found just about everywhere in the park including the camps is the **driedoring** or *Rhigozum trichotomum* for which there is no English name. It is a low grey to green shrub whose stiff stems fork into three shorter stems, not thorns despite the name. Bushmen make knobsticks from the roots of the older bushes, use the stems for their arrows and pick long straight ones as mock spears for one of their few games.

'To see who can throw the *X'Harra* the furthest,' says Dr van der Walt, 'the contestants stand on a sand heap called a *X'Heiss* – Hottentot for puffadder – about two metres in length, one metre in breadth and a tenth of a metre high and covered with grass or reeds. They then throw the *X'Harra* onto or through a driedoring tree – a game accompanied by much enthusiastic cheering.'

There are many types of grass in the KGNP when the rains have been good of which the main ones are tall Bushman grass, short Bushman grass, sour Kalahari grass that exudes a dangerous acid secretion, and the very common but not very nutritious sweetgrass. The first two are the mainstay for grazers, especially the rich short Bushman grass covering the veld with a carpet that turns silver in the lowering sunlight.

In those rare years when the rains fall in torrents and the rivers brim with floodwater the KGNP becomes vibrant with life and colour. Grass and shrubs stand waist-high and nature spreads a patchwork quilt of flowery brilliance almost matching that of the famed Namaqualand.

It does not last very long in the ensuing heat and drought and against the appetites of the park's denizens. One kind that does, however, is the **aloe** and two excellent examples of these are right in front of the reception office at Twee Rivieren camp.

They are the very beautiful *Aloe hereroensis* and *Aloe gariepensis,* unusual in that their flowers are almost rose-shaped instead of the typical erect form.

There are only two evils in this paradise, fortunately both still minor ones. They are exotic intruder plants.

The **Mexican poppy** or 'bloudissel', *Argimone subfusiformis,* is a thistle so well established that nothing can be done until a biological method is found to eradicate it. Meanwhile the springbok savour its flowers.

The other is the **mesquite** of the *Prosopis* family from Central and

South America. It has become a pest in Namibia and in the Northern Cape but is fortunately not yet a serious problem in the KGNP, where it was introduced by floodwaters from the north-west. Probably the largest mesquite in the park is the one in the riverbed close to the waterpoint at Gemsbok Plain – a great tree that has half collapsed under its own weight and now provides a shady hideaway for birds and small animals.

The Creeping, Crawling, Flying Horde

A budding entomologist seeking new territory to explore need look no further than the Kalahari's rich store of bugs and beetles, spiders and scorpions and billions of other creatures inhabiting the sand, the vegetation, the water and, of course, other creatures.

Some research in this field has been done in the KGNP and the Kalahari generally and the pace is slowly increasing. But it is barely opening the lid. Many doctoral dissertations must lie under the Kalahari sun waiting for the scientific investigators to pluck them.

'The task of describing the invertebrate species encountered in the KGNP and the relationships among them has hardly been commenced at all,' Dr G de Graaff, leading scientist for the National Parks Board, wrote a few years ago …

With the exception of certain insect orders looked at by entomologists, the rest of the invertebrate fauna has been grossly neglected by visiting and resident scientists to the KGNP in the past.

This is strange, for any desert-like environment allows a far better understanding of ecological processes in operation due to the relative simplicity of the organisation of the arid ecosystem, in contrast to the often bewildering complexity which is usually associated with rain forests or coral reefs.

Dr Rob Toms, head of the Transvaal Museum's Department of General Entomology, was in a collecting party in Botswana that found twenty new species of crickets in two weeks, some of which were discovered only in single places and nowhere else.

He specialises in these busy little predators, which are easy to collect because one simply follows their music to find them, and believes there are probably several species endemic to the KGNP in addition to the ordinary house cricket and others found elsewhere.

Beetles, mainly **tenebrionids,** are abundant in the Kalahari and the subject of much research but it does not appear that any are definitively exclusive to the area. They are also found in adjacent areas.

Right: A pair of Parabuthus scorpions in a mating dance. Common desert dwellers, they reach considerable length and the thickness of their tails reveals they are highly venomous. Their sting causes extreme pain and can be fatal to children.
Anthony Bannister – ABPL.

Ant-lions lurk beneath the desert sand to snatch passing insects with their powerful pincer jaws and suck them dry. Their funnel-like sand traps can be seen everywhere.
Anthony Bannister – ABPL.

One mild oddity among them is a tenebrionid that exhibits rudimentary signs of social behaviour: it appears to congregate in the same living quarters and share the same food store with others of its kind.

This, however, is a typical trap for the novice observer. They sometimes, but not always, gather in the same holes and crevices coincidentally and not from any feelings for their fellows, and they congregate at food stocks coincidentally because they are drawn to the wind-blown organic detritus gathering there.

Unless specifically intent on finding such creatures the visitor to the KGNP is hardly likely to come upon them.

The insects he is most likely to encounter are mosquitoes on the rare occasions it rains enough, flies and perhaps the evil **tampan tick** if he is foolish enough to sit on the sand beneath trees at picnic sites.

He might also cross paths with certain non-insect invertebrates – spiders of assorted kinds and sizes, scorpions large and small and, if lucky, with a quaint character that roars around at high speed with 'arms' extended. It is the **solifuge** or sun-spider, a nocturnal hunter that sometimes emerges by day. It tends to scare the wits out of people by seeming to chase them; all it is doing, actually, is trying to stay in their shadow to evade the harsh sunlight. It is not poisonous and quite harmless in spite of its horrific red hairiness.

Right: It looks like a spider and looks poisonous. But the supremely ugly solifuge or sun-spider is neither – it is a non-venomous creature sometimes called the leopard of the insect world because of its high-speed hunting skill (here a gecko is the victim). Its strong jaws, however, can draw blood from an incautious finger. It appears mostly at dusk.
Anthony Bannister – ABPL.

Most spiders, too, are non-poisonous and there are none in the KGNP so poisonous that they represent any threat even to children.

Scorpions should indeed be avoided if encountered. The sting is not fatal but exceedingly painful.

For the rest, there is nothing in camp or hut that cannot be resolved with a burst of spray from a can of ozone-friendly insecticide.

Left: Scourge of the desert are these tampan ticks which are attracted by the warmth of bodies resting in the shade of trees and emerge in swarms to feed on their blood.
Anthony Bannister – ABPL.

CHAPTER FOUR

Flood and Fire

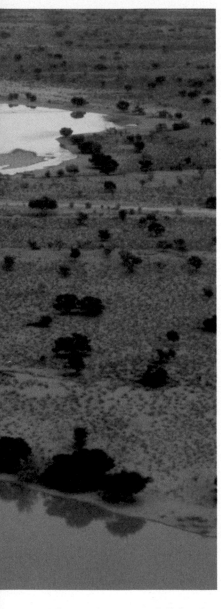

*The Auob River in full flood, a
rare event that brings fish and
terrapins into the Park.*
National Parks Board.

*l*ike a leopard on a leash, the Kalahari Desert is never truly tamed. Sometimes quiescent, sometimes restless, its thin skin of seeming docility scarcely conceals a ferocity pulsating with power. Those who know its temper never relax their guard because it is a killer.

The menace of its heat and drought they can counter, with care, because it is always apparent. But sometimes the desert snaps the leash and catches everyone off guard, lashing out with flood and fire.

The KGNP's ordinary rainfall of about 150 mm a year is a gentle blessing that cools the blast furnace of summer and revivifies plants and animals sufficiently for the precariously balanced cycle of life to turn for another year. But every few decades the sky blackens and dumps water on the desert in torrents that last weeks and even months.

The excess, reaching three or four times the normal rainfall, fills the pans, saturates the sand and brings rivers down in slow, relentless floods, filling burrows, drowning countless small creatures and making the KGNP impassable.

It can kill people too. In January 1934, three years after the park was proclaimed, the heavens grew thick and dark and vomited water for week after week. The bone-dry beds of the Auob and Nossob rivers vanished under advancing masses of muddy rushing water that swelled to sluggish expanses hundreds of metres wide in places. Uprooted trees, dead livestock carried from outside the park, wild animals swept up inside it and other debris bobbed on its surface. Boreholes and waterpoints were buried under tons of silt, causing much hardship when the water, as it always does, vanished later.

At their primitive headquarters next to the Auob at Gemsbok Plain the park's first ranger, Johannes le Riche, and his assistant, Gert Jannewarie, watched this astonishing metamorphosis of the desert in wonder. They never again saw the Kalahari bare its teeth. Both were struck down by the last thing they expected in a desert – malaria – and died within days of each other. In one stroke the entire staff of the KGNP was wiped out.

When the flood was at its height a young man from the Botswana side of the Nossob River gained himself a rare distinction. David Matthys van der Westhuizen went hunting on horseback and shot a gemsbok but did not bring it down. The wounded animal fled to the Nossob and somehow managed to swim the flood to the western bank.

Van der Westhuizen rode into the river in pursuit, apparently believing that if the buck could cross, so could his horse. What exactly happened then is not known but both he and the horse sank, earning him a place in history as the only man on record to have drowned in the desert. His grave is on the river's bank between the Jan se Draai and Kransbrak waterpoints.

When the rain eventually stopped the water dwindled and disappeared except for a few pools. The floods joined at the confluence of the two rivers near the present Twee Rivieren camp and travelled south following the ancient route of the Nossob until stopped by dunes blocking the passage to the Orange River.

The desert was barely dry a few months later when once more clouds curtained the sky and delivered another deluge, again sousing the sands. Finally it cleared and now the harsh terrain became a visual paradise of lush green grass and sparkling trees burgeoning with flowers and vibrant with living things.

The desert calmed to its usual mood of simmering temper. The heat beat down and the air was clammy with humidity until the moisture was sucked away into the atmosphere. The shining green bleached to tan and grey and the grass grew brittle and cracked in the hard clutch of winter. And then in the spring of 1935 the leopard lashed out again.

A thunderstorm raised its anvil head high over the sands. Lightning flashed down east of the Nossob and set the heavy carpet of dry grass alight. The first veld fire in decades ravaged and blackened the land there but was baulked by the barrier of the Nossob from destroying the infant park.

For forty years thereafter the leopard was quiescent. Glazed summers and frosted winters followed in steady succession nourished by about 150 mm of rain each year.

Then it happened again. The leash snapped and for three years running from 1974 the park was drenched, the rivers filled and the vegetation flourished so vigorously that the Kalahari was unrecognisable, akin to the more temperate Western Transvaal. Stunned by the phenomenon, a man who had known the park for decades, Clem Haagner, remarked 'the Kalahari seems to have gone completely crazy'.

For three seasons of super-abundant rain the desert performed like nature's cornucopia. It sprouted vegetation on even the most

A summer storm brings refreshing rain and moody beauty to the Kalahari.
Anthony Bannister – ABPL.

In the heat of the Kalahari day, whirling dust dervishes come suddenly alive, spin across the sand and, as suddenly, die.
Phillip Richardson – ABPL.

Sudden storms drenching the Kalahari turn it into, unbelievably, a desert of pools. The water quickly dries up.
Leigh Voigt.

barren earth. Hordes of birds, some rarely seen in the region, flocked to the feast. Stimulated by the quantity of food, animals bred copiously. In the shade of the large camelthorn trees in the riverbeds grew thick stands of cattail or 'klitsgras', a reddish broad-leafed grass that clings to anything.

Inevitably, the desert struck again.

There were firebreaks in the South African sector of the park but none on the Botswana side. Fire began from the Botswana side. How it started is not known – it could have been lightning or nomadic Kgalagadi people – but it raged there almost continuously for nearly a year and broke out repeatedly for two more.

It roared through great areas of densely grown sour grass, useless to animals, but also destroyed edible grasses, foliage and other plants in an area of about 15 000 square kilometres, nearly half the park, forcing mass migration of animal herds swollen by the good times.

Late in 1976 fire swept into the Nossob River valley on a long front reaching from the Jan se Draai waterpoint in the south to the Kwang Pan north of Nossob camp.

It flared high in the massed cattail under the camelthorns, setting alight the trees and their freight of sociable weaver and tree rat nests, which went up like torches.

About one-third of the camelthorns – home and source of food to so many – were killed outright. Many older, taller trees were burned to ashes. More than half of all trees were damaged, a large number so badly they died later. Blackened stumps still dot the riverbed.

Flood and fire are as naturally parts of the African wilderness as its flora and fauna. In the Kalahari's delicate ecology, however, their impact is disproportionately large and recovery takes longer.

CHAPTER FIVE

The Great Treks

A herd of blue wildebeest climbing a dune gives a hint of what their great migrations of tens of thousands must have looked like before farms and fences stopped them.
Clem Haagner – ABPL.

*t*he KGNP is a vital part of possibly the largest area in the world where great herds of wild animals are still able to move with relative freedom according to the whims of nature – the Kalahari Desert, filling three-quarters of the Republic of Botswana.

Yet this is itself a small remnant of a far larger area in which antelope herds of unimaginable size – literally millions – roamed less than a century ago before they were camped in by the steadily rising barriers of international borders, farm fences and hunting.

It was a huge, crudely triangular tract of the western half of Southern Africa enclosing Namibia, Botswana, the Western Transvaal, the Northern and North-Western Cape and the Great Karoo – an arid plateau reaching west to the Atlantic and the Namib Desert.

This was the homeland of many kinds of buck which wandered from place to place in constant search of grazing or water, or under the pressure of population growth. Yesterday's empty veld would be dotted with grazing herds today, leisurely followed by attendant lions, hyenas, jackals and other predators.

Their only major obstacle was the Orange River and in the main their peregrinations were confined to areas to the north and south of it. But every now and then herds would gather in great numbers and start moving across the veld in a relentless, seemingly aimless tide.

Chief among these were the springbok, whose gigantic migrations were the largest of any recorded mass movements by animals.

Mass migrations still occur sporadically in the KGNP but their numbers of 100 000-plus are a trickle compared to the floods of the late 1800s.

Four typically huge springbok migrations took place between 1887 and 1896 near Prieska on the Orange River, in arid country just beyond the southern extreme of the Kalahari. They were described by a resident of the area, T B Davie:

When the trek was in full move nothing but springbok were to be seen for miles upon miles at a stretch. The whole country seemed to move, not in any hurry or rush, as is generally associated in people's minds with a springbok, but a steady plodding walk march, just like 'voetganger' locusts [hoppers]; no other animal or insect life can afford so apt an illustration. The writer has seen them in one continuous stream, on the road and on both sides of the road, to the skyline, from the town of Prieska to Draghoender, a distance of 47 miles, plodding on, just moving aside far enough to avoid the wheels of the cart.

On this occasion the owners of the farm Witvlei were all sitting in a ring round the top of the well, which at that time was uncovered, the father, son, and son-in-law armed with rifles, firing a shot now and then, and the womenfolk with sticks and stones trying to keep the 'boks' away. This was the family's only water supply left, as the 'boks' had already filled up the dam, thousands being trampled to death in the mud as they pressed on over one another to get to the water.

At last the 'boks' beat the farmers and got to the well and in a few minutes it was full of dead and dying 'boks'. However, the trek passed before evening with the exception of a few stragglers and the Witvlei people soon had their well cleaned out and rendered serviceable.

The springbok melted away in a few days, Davie said. 'They disappeared, nobody knows where...'

Accurately counting herds of that size was patently out of the question but in 1888 Davie and a naturalist, Dr Gibbons, made a calculated estimate.

In the morning as soon as it was daylight we were out, and there we were sure enough in a veritable sea of antelopes. The doctor saw at once, upon being rallied to count them, that it was impossible, but he made a guess after this fashion.

Seeing a kraal, a good large one, he asked [the local farmer] how many sheep could stand in it, and Mr Danth replied 1 500. 'Well,' said the doctor, 'if 1 500 can stand there, then about 10 000 can stand on an acre, and I can see in front of me 10 000 acres covered with "boks"; that means at least 100 000 000; then what about the miles upon miles around on all sides as far as the eye can reach covered with them?'

He gave it up. We left Nels Poortje after breakfast and rode for four and a half hours right straight through them, they never giving more road than was required for us to pass.

The springbok tide was inexorable. They denuded vast areas of grass and water. Another observer, Mr C S Stokes, said they swept along livestock, exhausting sheep and calves and trampling them to death.

He said two black herdboys were killed and the springbok even forced a lion along with them.

Farmers shot them by the thousands in vain attempts to stem or divert the flow. The slaughter was out of desperation with no thought of sport because they were sickened by it. They shot until the barrels of their rifles became too hot or they ran out of ammunition. Then they had no choice but to impotently watch their livelihood being devastated by the seething tide. The stench of rotting carcasses stained the air for weeks afterwards.

The migrations petered out in the emptiness of the savannah as death took its toll. Some were forced to turn west by the Orange River and ended on the desert coast of the Atlantic where the parched springbok drank sea water and died in millions. Their carcasses were heaped along the shore for about fifty kilometres.

Similar sporadic migrations happened south of the Orange River as far as the Karoo and west of the Kalahari in Namibia. One of the last was witnessed by Mr Jack Wakefield.

In 1922, at the age of nine, he and his six-year-old sister and mother were returning to their home in Walvis Bay after holidaying in Southern Rhodesia, now Zimbabwe. It was a long, arduous train journey to De Aar in the Cape where they transferred to another train for Windhoek.

Hampered by floods which cut bridges, the train was diverted west from the main line to the southern Namibian port of Luderitz.

Late one afternoon they were between the Fish River and Luderitz when 'a huge cloud of sand and dust appeared in the distance on our right,' Mr Wakefield said.

'The train stopped again and we were told to close all the windows as a sandstorm was approaching. As the dust cloud got nearer we were amazed to see that it was no sandstorm. It was caused by thousands of springbok racing and leaping across the veld as far as the eye could see.

'When they neared the train, the leaders turned off to the right and the left but the huge herd following could not change course. Hundreds of them tried to leap over the coaches and jumped into the side of the train and slid along the coaches.

'It was all quite frightening for about half an hour until the noise gradually abated. The wild stampede continued on its way, gradually receding into the distance, still covered by the cloud of sand and dust.'

The numbers have dwindled but the natural forces that trigger migrations still exist and they still appear out of nowhere.

Warden Elias le Riche was a small boy in 1938 when a National Parks Board commission led by its vice-president, Mr J F Ludorf, came to look at conditions in the KGNP and he was allowed to travel with the party to the present Nossob camp.

There the astonished commissioners encountered the biggest herd of springbok they had ever seen, about 15 000 of them doggedly on the move.

'We stood still for about an hour and a half until the last buck went past,' Elias remembers. 'Another time we counted a herd of about 8 000. Today a big herd is 1 500 to 2 000.'

His father Joep was patrolling north of Nossob in 1946 when he saw a large cloud of dust north of the Kwang waterpoint. It was a ten-kilometre long herd of springbok travelling south along the Nossob River.

Three years later he found another, bigger herd that took three days to pass. It was moving south-east for a distance later calculated at 300 kilometres.

Other buck also travel but have never been seen in such vast treks as those of the springbok. In 1979 KGNP staff and researchers were making an aerial survey when they saw animals moving towards and into the public section of the park from the northern part of its Botswana section.

They found an estimated 89 286 blue wildebeest, though allowing for error the number might have been as high as 170 000. They were not in the solid, lemming-like phalanx the springbok seem to like but in 269 herds scattered across more than 2 000 square kilometres with the largest containing some 750 animals.

They also counted about 6 000 red hartebeest in 500 square kilometres and more than 5 000 eland spread all over the park, one herd with the unusually high number for them of 105 animals.

The 1984/85 rain season was a disaster in the park. So little fell there were hardly any pans with standing water, the vital wild crop of water-bearing tsamma melons failed, wild cucumber and other moisture-rich plants were extremely scarce, and the grass became dry and brittle.

The KGNP staff and researchers from Pretoria then saw one of the most extraordinary migrations ever recorded.

About 150 000 wildebeest streamed into the park from the northern depths of the dessicated desert as well as about 15 000 eland and thousands of hartebeest, all following ancient instincts telling them there could be fresher food and maybe water in the region of the two rivers.

There was, but nowhere near enough.

The wildebeest and hartebeest streamed south across the Nossob River out of Botswana into the South African or public sector of the park. They drank the water dry at every borehole, immediately jeopardising the lives of the small resident populations of their own species.

So desperate was their thirst that wildebeest jumped on the backs of those already crammed around the drinking places and fought to reach the water. Many of the weaker ones were trampled to death and their carcasses littered the hoof-churned ground. Lions were so full of meat they ignored the abundance of it lying everywhere.

The surviving wildebeest trekked on south, draining all available water, and began swinging east at the park's southern border near Twee Rivieren – back across the Nossob to the Botswana side.

Some continued south into the farming areas and many a citizen enjoyed venison and biltong. Poachers had a heyday: rangers patrolling by air saw one group with about fifty donkeys following in the tracks of the migrating animals. The pilot dived the plane at them, zooming so low the men ducked and the panicked donkeys scattered.

The size of the eland trek was the most surprising. Wildebeest are highly dependent on water and must drink at least every two or three days. Eland, however, are one of the hardiest of antelope and second only to the gemsbok in their ability to survive for long periods without drinking – an indication of how ferocious that season's drought was.

They did not stay with the wildebeest and hartebeest but travelled south-west until they were turned south by the fence right along the KGNP's western border.

The fence helped to keep the animals in the park and away from the farmland of Namibia where they would have faced the additional hazard of men with guns.

At one point, however, a group of lions trapped the trekking buck against the fence – a hunting technique they had developed since it was strung. They killed nine eland and two wildebeest. The rest of the herd pushed the fence flat and ran through.

At the park's southern border the remaining eland too turned eastwards, encouraged by the fence there, and crossed into Botswana.

There food was plentiful but the grass – the wildebeest's staple diet – was bone dry and without water they and the other antelope could not digest it properly. Just how many died in that wilderness will never be known.

They swung north in Botswana in a great circle ... and came back into the park from the north again in a second wave.

The same grim story was repeated. Thousands of wildebeest crowded the drinking places and died in hundreds. This time even the eland came to seek water and were so desperate for it they lost their fear of people. A National Parks Board photographer, Lorna Stanton, held out a plastic jug of water and eland drank from it.

They cleaned out the water so fast that the windpumps at the drinking places could not supply enough. Park staff swung into emergency action, cast concrete slabs next to boreholes and brought in diesel engines to suck enough water from beneath the ground.

Had they not done so then, not only the trekking animals but those which ordinarily reside in the area would have died in considerably larger numbers. The move saved the lives of untold thousands of migrants.

The final toll among the trekkers is difficult to assess. Along the park's roads the rangers counted the jawbones of 1 600 wildebeest. The whitened bones of many more lie scattered all over the dunes and plains.

Shocking as they seem, these huge fatalities are the norm in this and the other harsh environments of the world. To ensure its continuance against extremes of hunger, thirst and predation a species has to breed far more vigorously than it would were it in more congenial surroundings. The excessive population is a buffer against potential elimination, an insurance for the future, and only the toughest live through.

The mechanisms of the mass migrations were long unknown and even today are not fully understood. Shortage of food and water are the prime causes, however, and these can result from various circumstances including drought, excessive rains, fire and the pressure on resources of over-population. The same population peaks generated by heavy breeding in good conditions are a trigger for the killer marches. Nature balancing itself again.

Different animals trek in differing circumstances. Because they are so dependent on water, wildebeest might be forced to move while gemsbok, eland and hartebeest are still quite content. Wildebeest, too, are grazers and furthermore grazers of short grass. The others browse as well as graze. Springbok are the heaviest breeders, thereby destroying their own habitat which obliges them to seek fresh pastures.

Considerable scientific debate is going on about the KGNP's waterpoints dotted along the two rivers and more sparsely among the dunes. Some experts, like Michael Knight, argue that 'stabilising once nomadic populations like wildebeest with waterholes in a fragile environment adapted to *periodic* (as opposed to constant) exploitation could have far-reaching and detrimental effects upon the vegetation and other ungulates'.

This is what makes it imperative that the park remains an international one with free movement of animals between Botswana and South African sides, he says.

While aware of the danger to the environment of permanent concentrations of animals around waterpoints, others, like Warden Elias le Riche, argue that there is no option. Since the huge migration routes extending far to the south and west were shut off by mankind's developments, an artificial water supply has to make good what the animals lost, he states.

The supply of water and the fences in the west and partly in the south are in fact the only sustained wildlife management systems used in the KGNP. There is no culling, no rotational burning of the veld, no translocation of animals.

The only introduction of wildlife is a recent programme to restock the park with giraffe. Visitors will see a large paddock in the Auob riverbed at Craig Lockhart waterpoint near Mata Mata. This is a holding pen for giraffe brought from Namibia and beyond the dunes behind it, hidden from sight, is a camp of many hectares where they roamed free to breed and acclimatise.

Giraffe are not as out of place in the Kalahari as some people might think. They roam the deeper desert in Botswana and in the 1970s a reckless pilot crashed because he flew very low to look at a small herd and the wing of his plane struck one.

These elegant animals vanished from this region probably before it was declared a national park. They diminished under the guns of hunters until their numbers reached the point where they could not regenerate sufficiently to survive ordinary predation.

The last known giraffe in the KGNP died near the Nossob River and its fate is enshrined in the name of the place, Kameelsleep. 'Kameel' is the abbreviation of 'kameelperd', Afrikaans for giraffe, and 'sleep' means 'drag' – where its carcass was dragged across the riverbed into Botswana by the hunter who shot it.

CHAPTER SIX

The Hunters Hunted

*t*he distinction between hunting and poaching is fine. For the unsophisticated people of Africa battered by population explosion and hunger it does not exist.

The KGNP, born of the need to save wild animals from indiscriminate killing, still suffers from both. With his small staff of three rangers and about fourteen game guards, Warden Elias le Riche has to defend an area of just under one million hectares against poachers who kill for sport and profit and indigenous people who hunt to eat.

It is a contest without end, although today its intensity is lower than in the park's early days, because the existence of this giant reservoir of game lures human predators like carrion draws blowflies.

Conservation is a dead concept for poachers who travel from as far afield as the Free State, Western Province and Transvaal to sneak into the park for trophies, meat, biltong and hides for sale, or simply the thrill of illegal hunting. It is a concept beyond the comprehension of the many Third World people struggling to eke out an existence in the forbidding Kalahari, for whom game is a traditional and rightful source of sustenance.

It will take generations of patient education to persuade the latter of the need to conserve. Meanwhile the KGNP personnel cannot for a moment relax their campaign against them or the former, the greedy who should know better.

The park was created in 1931 when some local residents and the government became concerned about the rising rate of slaughter in the south-western Kalahari.

The battle commenced virtually the day the first ranger, Johannes le Riche, and his assistant, Constable Gert Jannewarie, started work. With no more than a donkey-drawn cart and riding horses, they were assigned to patrol more than 650 kilometres through nearly 12 000 square kilometres of wild and trackless desert with few and unreliable waterholes.

Johannes and Gert were hardened products of the arid Northern Cape who would venture into 'die Dorsland', the Thirstland, with no

The ancient bed of the Auob River, now one of the Park's main roads, slices through the endless desert vista.
Anthony Bannister – ABPL.

more hesitation than a fisherman going to sea. But the poachers were just as tough.

Most were so-called farmers along the eastern or Bechuanaland (now Botswana) side of the Nossob River who lived in primitive conditions and whose only regular crop was the game they shot. Others were genuine frontier farmers in the remote reaches of South West Africa, now Namibia, and the Northern Cape. Some came from the Upington area 300 kilometres to the south and elsewhere in the vast, dry Gordonia district of the Northern Cape.

Game reserves were a novelty then. The almost universal belief was that wild animals were there to be shot for sport and the pot. The hunters, now turned into poachers by the imposition of the National Parks Act on their hunting grounds, looked upon the rangers as they did the law: with derision.

They knew this part of the Kalahari like their backyards. Many had better guns than the rangers' ex-army .303 rifles and more horses, carts and donkeys. Those living in Bechuanaland had only to step across the middle of the Nossob River, an international border, to be safe from pursuit.

Some had the remarkable new machines called motor cars and used the Auob and Nossob riverbeds as highways between South West Africa and the Cape. At the park entrances they would openly handle their guns and ammunition (no crime in itself) under the eyes of the frustrated rangers. They knew the rangers could not catch up with them; they had plenty of time to cut the prime meat from what they killed along the road. Some were wanton – they took pot shots at anything they fancied, not bothering to stop if the victim was wounded, and ran away.

That was at the time of the Great Depression. The National Parks Board could not dream of buying Johannes a car. They could barely afford the cart and horses.

It says much for Johannes' and Gert's dogged determination that they did not quit against such odds. Canny men of the desert, they began carefully planned patrols along the Nossob River that caught poachers by surprise and made the KGNP the first reserve in the Cape Province to show a revenue: £20 in fines – a small fortune in those days.

When Johannes le Riche and Gert Jannewarie died of malaria in 1934, brother Joep le Riche was asked to take the reins. He took on Gert Mouton as his constable and the anti-poacher campaign continued with hardly a pause.

They used camels as well as horses but within months got something else that enabled them to step up the campaign by several notches. The Parks Board told Joep he could have a car, on condition he refunded the £200 cost in monthly instalments from his £7 salary ... with interest.

Seeing the beefy four-wheel-drive vehicles the rangers use now, and the number of modern cars which get stuck in the dust and clay of the park's roads, it is baffling that a 1934 car could do better than horses and camels. It was an open Ford 'tjorrie' with narrow tyres and spoked wheels. Its engine boiled without much provocation. It was heavily loaded with extra cans of petrol. Joep used it to move quickly when he had to, saving the camels for routine patrols, and developed a technique of charging at dunes to traverse them without being trapped in the treacherous sand.

In the Ford he and Gert descended on unsuspecting poachers with the impact of a bomb. In those days professional poachers were so contemptuous of the law they set up camps in the park for a week or two, hunting daily and living comfortably in tents and shelters beside their campfires while the venison they strung between bushes and trees dried into highly saleable biltong.

Suddenly a spidery car would come rattling and snorting over a dune and wobble to a stop right among them. There was no escape, no time to pack up everything, saddle horses, inspan donkeys and make a getaway. Even when they tried, the getaway was slow and the tireless machine soon caught up with the tiring men and animals.

Joep and Gert manacled the poachers, loaded skins, biltong and other evidence, seized the guns and led the whole caravan back to base and, eventually, into court at distant Upington.

There a conservationist magistrate imposed fines of £15 for every buck shot – a crippling sum then when a good rifle could be bought for £5. Guns, carts, donkeys and horses were confiscated.

It was the beginning of the end of the easy old hunting days for the poachers. Surprisingly, it seldom led to open hostilities although tension often ran high. On a few occasions infuriated poachers reached for their guns but always one of the rangers had his rifle ready. Once, when Joep had two men with him, the poachers tackled them and tried to grab the rangers' own rifles but were beaten off.

Considerable respect grew between Joep and some of the poachers. They were caught repeatedly, however wily they became, yet always came back. Joep learned respect for them as rawhide-tough men who knew no other way of life. They respected him for his fairness, skill and matching toughness.

As time passed several developments greatly helped to reduce the level of poaching. The first was the decision by the British government in 1938 to expand the park by the addition of a strip of land forty kilometres wide right along the eastern side of the Nossob River border.

The eighty-four poacher-farmer families living there – the biggest bane of Joep le Riche's life – were resettled with their 5 000 head of livestock on new and viable farms south of the KGNP in the Northern Cape, where they and their descendants still farm.

The day after the resettlement was announced, Joep caught a poaching party with the hides of fifty-six ostriches and sixty jackals they had killed over two months.

However, it stopped much of the off-the-cuff hunting and because the park now extended into and was recognised by Bechuanaland, there was no longer easy escape for poachers. The National Parks Board rangers were given jurisdiction over the entire reserve and poachers caught on the Bechuanaland side were taken before a Bechuanaland magistrate at Tsabong – a practice that continues today.

At about the same time a few farms within the park that were still privately owned were bought by the government for as little as a shilling a morgen – but only after Joep in desperation threatened to buy them himself.

The Nossob River was closed as a highway into Namibia. The Auob stayed open (it was closed only on 10 January 1990) and Joep, acting on his hunches, time and again found a dead buck or haunches of venison or some other product of the gun hidden in vehicles he stopped on their way through.

His impartiality became legendary. Such pillars of society as doctors and lawyers fell shamefaced into his net. His biggest fish, perhaps, was a South African commissioner of police.

The policeman ranted and raved when he was caught and threatened to have Joep summarily dismissed. It made no difference. The imperturbable Joep went right ahead and laid a charge, but came up against political pressure he could not deal with.

The then Smuts government did not want the public embarrassment of one of its top upholders of the law appearing in open court on a poaching charge, so it ordered the case to be dropped. Then it satisfied justice by firing the commissioner – a penalty far greater than the magistrate could have imposed.

A poaching problem of a completely opposite kind stemmed from the presence within the KGNP of groups of nomadic Bushmen, the tiny people harassed and hounded out of the rest of Southern Africa over the centuries by the advance of other races. They retreated to the fastnesses of the Kalahari where they evolved such a high degree of skill in desert survival it could be termed a form of civilisation.

Bushmen never killed wantonly, only as much as they needed. They used literally every scrap of every animal they brought down with their poisoned arrows and long, patient pursuit – meat, intestines, bones, horns, hooves, hide.

Minister of Lands, Piet Grobler, father and mentor of the KGNP gave a specific order that any Bushmen found in the park must be given special care and attention and allowed to stay because they needed shelter as a dwindling people.

In 1936 Joep found a group of about twenty comprising several families at Sewe Panne, a cluster of seven flat grey pans, some with water, in the middle of the South African section of the park.

Unfortunately they had been corrupted by professional poachers who had bribed or coerced them into killing for the illegal market. They hunted much more than they needed and made biltong that they traded to the poachers for tobacco and trinkets and sometimes – devastatingly – liquor.

Joep had to stop this. Neither he nor his Nama guards could speak the Bushman language and resorted to gestures and offerings of food and tobacco to lure the Bushmen to their camp. In what must have been a masterful display of sign language, he persuaded them to come with him to Gemsbok Plain, where he had his headquarters at the time.

There the Bushmen settled and were given what they needed. Some became trackers, an art at which they were so skilled they could follow a spoor while riding on the back of Joep's vehicle. Other families drifted back into the Kalahari's emptiness beyond the bounds of the park. Over the ensuing years most were absorbed by intermarriage with the local Nama people.

There are no 'wild' Bushmen left in the park now. Most of the few thousand remaining in Botswana live in the Central Kalahari Game Reserve – a euphemism for a special area set aside by a kindly Botswana government where the Bushmen can continue the way of life they have followed for aeons.

The curse of World War II spun off a blessing for conservation in South Africa. Nervous about the prospect of a pro-German uprising, the government impounded all privately owned firearms in South Africa and South West Africa. All ammunition production was diverted to the Allied forces and the few people who had illegally kept their guns could not hunt.

As a result, poaching decreased dramatically and in the KGNP, as in all reserves, game populations increased. In 1941 a ranger found a herd of a thousand eland at Kameelsleep waterpoint – a number rarely seen these days.

Predator numbers grew too and lions spread outside the park causing havoc in livestock herds and, finding themselves among domesticated animals that did not immediately flee, running amok and killing them with abandon.

Lacking guns, the angry farmers turned to poison and so began an evil practice that some still use. Wild dogs are scarcer in the north of the KGNP because some farmers in Namibia – who are apparently ignorant of the value and rarity of these animals and regard them as vermin – still throw poisoned carcasses over the fence.

Peace in 1945 turned the tables completely. Suddenly there was a flood of firearms. Impounded weapons were returned and surplus army rifles went on sale for fairly low prices. Poaching flowered into virtual massacre.

At first it was mainly by the people living around the park's borders. Then people from all over South Africa and South West Africa climbed into the killing act in a kind of hunting frenzy rarely seen before or since, using modern rifles and vehicles.

Joep and his staff, now equipped with an ex-army Jeep and the advantage of four-wheel drive, swung into action with a vengeance. In a single week in June 1948, he caught forty-two poachers who had shot forty-five large animals and many more smaller ones. Some of his captives were friends and acquaintances; they all received the same treatment.

The Bechuanaland side of the park – large, with no proper roads and no camps or bases – was the worst hit, by poachers darting across the border from South Africa and more so by poachers from inside Bechuanaland. At one camp rangers found the carcasses of more than 100 springbok from which only the choice meat along the backbone had been cut. At another they found what was left of twenty-three eland.

'Peace for man meant war on animals,' Joep wrote in a letter to the district commissioner at Tsabong in Bechuanaland, asking for his help in fighting the onslaught. 'On one occasion I saw 153 springbok carcasses at a poacher camp ... You can imagine how we are fighting with our backs against the wall for the protection and preservation of our game ... The possibility that all our wildlife can be wiped out is greater than we realise ... The time when we could afford our game to be killed for money is long past ... Now is the time to cooperate and conserve what is left.'

Now and then the fight against poachers became grim with no quarter given, like the time Elias le Riche, the present warden, and brother Stoffel, the previous warden until his untimely death, found tracks when they were patrolling at Union's End in the far north of the KGNP.

They and their sharp-eyed game guards spotted the spoor of a light truck and followed it in their own two vehicles until they came upon the carcasses of two lions. The spoor told the tale: a poacher had found a pride of five lions, shot these two and left them to follow the rest.

They kept to his tracks. The poacher, having shot and skinned the rest of the lions, was on his way back to skin the first two when he ran straight into Stoffel and Elias. He immediately spun his truck around and fled.

They charged after him and closed in from both sides while two of his helpers looked on in alarm from the back of his bouncing truck. The poacher was forced to a stop. Stoffel and a game guard jumped from their vehicle and ran up to grab his ignition keys.

The poacher stepped from his truck with two rifles and took aim, clearly ready to shoot his way out. Elias shot first, killing him.

They knew the dead man. He was a young professional poacher from South West Africa and his time had run out. His family still live on a farm there.

One of the Bushmen who settled in the Park years ago, seen here with a Parks Board official. Most have since moved south out of the Park.
National Parks Board.

He had cut his way through the fence stretching along the entire border between the park and South West Africa. While fences will not stop determined poachers, they are a strong deterrent in addition to keeping the wild animals in safety and this one is now charged with an electric current that shocks but is not fatal ...

One of the KGNP's major shortcomings is that so little of its boundary is fenced. The entire Botswana side is open. It is fringed with special hunting areas that give a small measure of protection, but nothing better.

Poaching continues in the KGNP but at a much lower level than during the hectic post-war years. It will never be wiped out as long as there are hungry people and there is money in illegal hunting. Today biltong fetches about fifteen rand a kilogram on the illegal market, antelope and lion skins R700 to R800 apiece and ostrich skins about R300 each. Ostrich poaching is extremely difficult to control because ostriches are farmed on the South African side and there is no way of telling where a skin originated.

Some forms of poaching are peculiar and vicious. Certain people on the park's Namibia side had the sickening method of setting up traps baited with poisoned meat on their side then cutting a hole in the fence. This way they collected the skins of leopards, lions, caracal and other predators. Electrification of the fence has made this difficult because the rangers are immediately alerted if it is cut. So instead they now dig holes under the fence. Often they do not bother to check their traps and the dead animals rot.

Sometimes they simply toss poisoned meat over the fence, apparently in the belief that this protects their precious karakul sheep by reducing the adjacent predator population. In fact, few predators cross the fence because there are fewer prey on the other side.

The penalties for poaching have been pathetic – for example up to R300 or eighteen months' imprisonment, or both, for killing a gemsbok, plus the confiscation of firearms, vehicle and other equipment. In recent years, however, magistrates have been getting tougher. In 1983 Elias caught the owner of a game farm and his two sons with thirty-five live gemsbok, eighteen gemsbok carcasses and also steenbok, duiker and kori bustard.

A regional magistrate fined them a total of R15 000, confiscated their equipment including four trucks and sentenced one son to nine months' imprisonment suspended for five years.

Since then poaching fines and prison terms have been increased dramatically but many conservationists and justice officials believe that the penalties for poaching should be increased still more.

The light on the horizon for this park, like all others in South Africa, is the dawning perception of the value of wildlife, both aesthetically and intrinsically. Conservation is a credo that is spreading rapidly throughout the world and beginning to take hold among even those unsophisticated people who hitherto have regarded all wild animals as meals on the hoof.

Farmers are finding there is profit in keeping game alive, in cultivating it. There is profit in the meat on the local and export markets; there is profit in catering for trophy hunters; there is profit in farming antelope that thrive in areas where cattle struggle.

Not before that credo is firmly rooted will the rangers of the KGNP be able to come off full alert. And even then, it is certain, there will be *someone* who finds the forbidden fruit sweeter.

CHAPTER SEVEN

Kalahari Patrol

The lilac-breasted roller's gorgeous coloration hides a ferocious hunter. This one is swallowing a mouse.
Beverly Joubert – ABPL.

*i*n the charcoal light of early dawn Kotie Herholdt brings the Landcruiser up to the house to load the gear. A long, sun-browned man in thin khaki shirt and shorts and velskoens, he shivers and dons a bush jacket against the morning chill. Izak, the ranger constable, packs the stuff in the open back of the truck with quick lithe movements of his small body – sleeping bags, bedrolls, cold boxes with food and beer, toilet paper, rifle, pots, roasting grids, first-aid kit, research equipment, tools, transceiver in a padded case, bags of clothes. Two forty-four-gallon drums are strapped to the roll bars behind the cab, one full of water, the other of petrol; they are the most important.

We drive out of Nossob camp's gates as early rising campers begin to stir and fill kettles and light gas cookers. Two of us ride with Kotie in the cab and Izak on the back, standing up with the push of air puffing out his grey overalls. Kotie turns north on the road to Union's End.

The Landcruiser grinds noisily through the deep dust of the road flanking the west bank of the Nossob River, here a shallow flat between low, pale red banks. The clean sharp edge of the rising sun's light touches the tops of the trees stippling the dry river bed and slides smoothly down them, peeling the grey gowns of night from their leafy bodies and casting them down as long shadows. The light is immediately warm; in an hour it will be hot.

Kotie constantly scans the trees in the river, most of them camelthorns, some short and scraggly, others large with twisted, spreading branches. After four or five kilometres he slows the Landcruiser and swings it off the road on to the hard flat surface of the river bed patchily covered with pale grass and ridged in the middle with humps of clay deposited by long-past floods.

Near Cubitje Quap he stops near a thin tree about three metres high and climbs out. *Do you see it,* he asks. We see nothing. He points: near the top in the middle of the dense cluster of twigs is a solid dark lump, a nest.

He and Izak cast about until they find a dead branch long enough to prop against the tree. Kotie holds it steady while Izak shinnies up on hands and feet like a monkey. He stretches his arm through the branches, cautious of thorns, and dips his hand into the nest.

It comes out holding a bird the size of a barnyard fowl but far more impressive. Huge dark eyes stare impassively at us from under houri eyelashes in a bright yellow face. New primary feathers fringe the thin, still downy wings and a cluster of black-tipped feathers sticks out spikily behind its brown-capped head. The big black beak is wickedly hooked and large sharp talons tip the long bare legs dangling under Izak's grip.

The bird is astonishingly placid as he hands it down to Kotie. That is the manner of secretary birds, Kotie says, they're very good-natured. This one is about six weeks old. He places it flat on its back on the sand and holds it gently with one hand while with the other he opens a fishing tackle box Izak has fetched from the truck. It lies quite still, making no sound, only its eyes alert.

Kotie Herboldt, bird expert and former ranger at Nossob, comes down from a camelthorn tree with a martial eagle chick borrowed briefly from its nest to be recorded and ringed.

Kotie spreads out one thin and gawky wing and with a sterile needle barely pricks a vein on the inside. From the droplet of blood that appears he takes a smear on a glass slide and stores it in a rack. He selects a numbered aluminium ring from a variety of different sizes in a small drawer and closes it around one of the chick's legs, making sure it fits loosely but not so loosely it might come off. Finally he records on a file card the place, date, time, number of the ring and details of the bird.

Izak clambers up the pole again and Kotie hands him the chick. Izak gently deposits it back in the nest and for a moment the black eye glares at us sorrowfully before the bird settles down and vanishes from view. There is no sign of the parents but they must be around, says Kotie. They'll be back to feed it soon.

The Landcruiser trundles on in the river. The sun is well clear of the horizon now and we shed jackets. The desert fills with life as the daytime animals take over from the nocturnal and go about their unchanging routines.

The passing vehicle does not bother them. Stocky gemsbok trot away a few paces and turn their masked faces and jughandle ears to survey us haughtily. Springbok celebrating the passing of another night without being eaten prance and stride briskly from bush to tussock, breakfasting. Flocks of sparrows fly up from the grass in fluid clouds.

A family of four bat-eared foxes, two half-grown, trots in Indian file across the bows of the oncoming Landcruiser, their small pointed faces and great dish ears turned towards it. Elsewhere they are a rare sight in full daylight, here quite common when the weather is not too hot. Suricates balance erect on hindfeet and tails atop sand humps to soak up the morning warmth, standing in a row like commuters wait-

ing for the bus to work, their heads swivelling in unison to watch us pass. Pale chanting goshawks enthroned on the tops of trees ignore us unless we come too close, when they spread wings and dip away to farther perches.

At Kwang Kotie stops to inspect the borehole that supplies Nossob camp more than twenty kilometres away with water. The diesel engine is thumping away smoothly under its lean-to roof and he and Izak heave and heft a fuel drum to fill its tank. Tracks in the sand beside a water trough show that many animals were here to drink in the night.

The sun is riding the middle of the morning and we are nearing Langklaas, still in the riverbed, when Kotie suddenly brakes the truck to a stop and peers ahead. On a branch in a dead tree in front is a smallish raptor.

Lanner falcon, says Kotie, they fly really fast, lovely to see. He puts the truck into gear and steers to pass slowly about thirty paces from the falcon. As we approach he calls to Izak and reaches his arm out the window. Izak hands him a strange wire contraption, a flat round cage the size of a large dinner plate. A dozen little running nooses of nylon fishline are attached to the top. Inside is a white rat.

When we pass the falcon on our left Kotie spins the cage on to open ground on the right. Some fifty metres beyond he turns the truck to face back and stops.

The falcon's gaze is fixed steadily on the little cage. Through binoculars we can see the rat circling around in it, whiskers busy. The bird is clearly intrigued but for long minutes nothing happens.

Watch for when he ducks his head, says Kotie, then he'll fly down to the cage and his legs will catch in the snares.

The lanner falcon launches into a fast, short dive and lands on the hard sand next to the cage. It walks on top of the cage and right across, seemingly puzzled by this meal so close and yet so far, but without being snared. It is about to step on again when fate takes a hand in the form of several black crows.

The cocky and raucous scavengers come out of nowhere, flying bundles of black rags that instantly see rat and falcon and descend on them. This is too much for the falcon and it flies arrow-swift back to its perch, leaving the rat to the crows.

They clamber on the trap like a coven of witches, poking their big beaks at the agitated rat. That's no good, says Kotie, and we speed to the rescue. The crows wait until we are almost upon them before they flap away. Surprisingly, none is ensnared but fortune favours the cheeky. Kotie leans out of his door to retrieve rat and trap and hands it back to Izak to stow in the rear.

The day becomes a procession of raptor chicks gently plucked from their nests and lowered to the ground to be examined and inducted into 'Kotie's Club' of birds banded for Safring. He always tries to combine bird studies with his routine patrol duties, he tells us, because the park offers such tremendous opportunity for research.

The desert around the Langklaas waterhole yields a good crop. Izak climbs high into a seven-metre camelthorn to extract two pale chanting goshawk chicks (sometimes Kotie climbs but he is nearly twice Izak's weight and the branches are notoriously brittle).

The goshawks are four to five weeks old and aggressive, quite ready to have a go at us – the only raptor chicks that behave like that, says Kotie. Handling them gingerly, Izak ties a thin cord around the legs of each in turn and lowers them to the ground upside down, wings outstretched and eyes sparking indignation. Round-eyed and fluffy, they watch our faces intently while Kotie rings them and takes blood samples and notes. Their hooked beaks stay agape and we keep our fingers at a safe distance.

It takes about five minutes and then Izak, still aloft, hoists them back and replaces them in their home.

Nearer Langklaas Izak goes to a bulky bundle of sticks halfway up a thick old camelthorn. Bateleur eagles always nest in the middle of a tree, secretary birds usually near the top and the others right in or on the crown, Kotie explains.

Izak calls down that with the bateleur chick are black bustard feathers and the remains of a whistling rat and a snake. The parents are feeding it well. The quite large chick, with feathers still emerging through pale down, is six to seven weeks old and is duly ringed and recorded.

At the Langklaas waterhole we find the prize – a martial eagle. Kotie and Izak have been watching it since it was a fresh egg and saw it the day it hatched. It is now thirty-one days old, time to be ringed.

Up goes agile Izak again and from eight metres lowers the martial chick. In complete contrast to its ferocious parents, the leopards of the skies, it is absolutely docile. It comes down inverted on the rope with long narrow wings stretched far out, uttering not a peep. Its entire body is covered in dense woolly down, snow white below, grey on its back, cuddly as a teddy bear.

Only the heavy brows over imperious eyes and the beak designed for ripping flesh indicate the monarch it will become. It lies passively in Kotie's palm while he strokes it with his other hand before sending it up to its home. The nest contains remains of Cape hare, black bustard and suricate, Izak says when he gets down. This chick too is well fed.

Our shadows are shortening fast and Kotie looks at his watch in alarm. It is nearing noon and we have a long way to go and much to do. To make up time he drives out of the riverbed on to the road.

Kotie Herboldt with a secretary bird almost old enough to leave the nest. Young raptors are quite passive when taken from their nest and contrary to common belief, they are not rejected by their parents after being handled.

We check boreholes at Langklaas, Kousant and Grootbrak. All is well; the big fibreglass tanks are full to their rims, the pipes and valves to the water cribs are working and the big galvanised blades of the windpumps turn slowly in the faint breezes.

It is hot now, a dry heat that saps away sweat, and the temptation to climb into a tank clothes and all is strong. Only Izak is cool, revelling in the rush of air on the back.

A few kilometres further Kotie turns right off the road into a great flat pan carpeted in grass and tough grey scrub and thinly fringed with stunted trees. It is dismally empty and silent and the low dunes seen faintly on the other side through heat-rippled air seem far away.

The Nossob is unusually wide and shallow here but the flat expanse is actually a kind of delta where the ancient, long dry Polentswa River enters it from the north, Kotie explains.

We ride across it leaving a scrawny rooster tail of dust. On the far side is a woebegone camelthorn tree. Under it stands a short, crude cross made of two pieces of broken branch lashed together with wire. This is the grave of the geologist Hans Schwabe who died on some mysterious personal mission.

A little past it, rises a yellow dune riddled with whistling rat holes and capped by trees and shrubs. The truck labours up in four-wheel drive, lurching when its wheels crunch through the thin surface into rat warrens. As we climb, a vulture spreads huge wings and lumbers into the air with a thrust of power that makes its treetop perch sway. It is a lappetfaced, fairly rare nowadays, black and white with an enormous beak and a big head shining reddish in the sun. In the tree's crown is a large untidy nest.

It settles on another tree sixty metres away and watches while Izak ascends, reports that there is a single egg, and descends without touching it. Kotie notes the site.

Beyond are two more vultures on trees, the smaller, commoner whitebacks. They flap away as we approach and behind us the lappetfaced flies back to its nest, examines the egg and, apparently satisfied, resumes its sentry post. In the whiteback nests there are one egg and one chick hatching, both of which are recorded but left untouched.

We drive on up the Polentswa, now in Botswana territory. The river narrows between sloping banks of hard white calcrete. Kotie stops next to a wide hole deeper than a man. Its walls slope back inwards. Inside, it is black with shadow and smells dank.

It is an old well dug into the solid limestone by some unknown people – maybe those of Khoi/European descent who vainly tried to settle in the Kalahari, perhaps by others centuries before them. There is no moisture in it; it collects water only when the rains bless this forsaken spot.

It is also a breeding place for barn owls but there are none now, except a long-dead one half mummified by the dry heat.

Back on the main Nossob-Union's End road we feel relief. There is something peculiarly sinister about the wide pan waiting like a silent trap, the sad grave and the lifeless Polentswa River.

We pass Lijersdraai and Koedoebos and at Kannaguass, behind a thicket of straight, thin saplings, a flock of whitebacked, whiteheaded and lappetfaced vultures gathers around the water trough, some drinking, the rest loafing. Some walk or fly away when the Landcruiser rumbles past.

They like this waterpoint and the next two at Grootkolk and Union's End because the water is fresh and unsalty, Kotie explains. They generally drink between about 11 a.m. and 4 p.m. We are lucky to see the whiteheaded vultures because there are only some three pairs in the whole park. They come south from better wooded country in the north, the Caprivi Strip, he says.

At the Grootkolk borehole Kotie stands on tiptoe to look into the brimful reservoir and shakes his head sadly. Reaching in, he gingerly lifts out a very dead and smelly tawny eagle. It must have perched on the rim to drink and fallen in.

A bird seen often at the roadside in the Park is the pert anteating chat.
Clem Haagner – ABPL.

The desert changes here, so subtly we do not notice it in our preoccupation with the heat and the jouncing truck. The long orange dunes fade away. All around us are spread uneven plains glistening with white-gold grass punctuated by thin black trees. We ride in pristine Kalahari, small travellers through an ancient past.

A black dot on the heat-bleached horizon brings us abruptly back to the present. It grows slowly larger until we see it is an old rectangular road sign with faded white lettering saying this is the way to Keetmanshoop and Mariental.

But not any more, not for many years. In front of it the border fence between South Africa and Namibia passes without a break in a straight north-south line.

This is one of the remotest places in South Africa, like Crooks' Corner in the Transvaal or the Makatini Flats in Natal. Lonely, with nothing but fence, road sign, road and a rough picnic site of concrete table and benches to suggest humans have been here. Tourists have to turn back here because there is nowhere else to go, and they usually do so with alacrity, intimidated by the loneliness.

A patrol track closed to visitors continues north along the fence. We turn on to it and travel in a surveyor's oddity, a South African corridor a mere twenty or thirty metres wide that extends north from Union's End for about two kilometres to the point where the South Africa, Botswana and Namibia borders meet. It is flat and featureless.

The sun has begun sliding down the dome of sky. Time is running short, there is a long way to go and Kotie has much to do. He turns

Like a sergeant-major calling the desert to attention, a black korhaan sticks out its chest and opens its mouth wide to issue its raucous cry.
Clem Haagner – ABPL.

the now oven-warm Landcruiser due south following the border fence on a roughly bulldozed road. It is of deep, treacherous, blood red sand studded with little earth mounds pushed up by Damara molerats. The ride is bumpy and the engine roars in four-wheel drive.

Gently rolling savannah slips by and we gradually move back into undulating dune country. The veld bustles with life – yellow canaries, scaly-feathered finches, anteating chats scampering ahead of the truck, chat flycatchers, spikeheeled larks, fawn-coloured larks, Burchell's sandgrouse, occasionally a steenbok jerking up its head to stare at us, gemsbok, springbok. Coming over an orange dune we find an eland bull and six cows. They lope away with stately grace.

We pause at Gharagab and Dankbaar. The windpumps are working and the water is flowing. Kotie sighs with relief. At Dankbaar a twisted tangle of galvanised windpump vanes lies on the sand near the windpump, evidence of the power of the mercurial desert gusts.

Approaching Loffiesdraai Izak bangs on the cabin roof and Kotie slides the truck to a stop. There, Izak says, pointing to the left, over there below that dune.

We stare and see nothing. Kotie spots it immediately: a pale chanting goshawk dipping low and slow over the ground. There, he says, pointing too. A little way ahead of the goshawk two black-backed jackals are coursing through the grass and scrub a few metres apart, pausing frequently with mouths open and tongues hanging.

Look carefully and soon you'll see him, says Kotie. See what? The ratel, he adds enigmatically.

We look. Sure enough, seconds later a honey badger appears over a little ridge of sand, barrelling along with a sailor's gait, head low, body bouncing on short legs and belly fur swinging from side to side. It is some forty or fifty paces in front of the jackals and stops now and then to sniff at the sand and dig experimentally before moving on.

When he finds what he wants, like a nest of rats or beetles, says Kotie, he'll dig so fast to catch them he sends the sand flying. But he also digs out things he doesn't want or just misses and the jackals go for them, and what the jackals miss the goshawk will get. That's why they follow him.

We watch until the mealtime procession passes out of sight over the dunes, this strange symbiotic team of such different creatures.

The shadows are stretching towards dusk as we reach Loffiesdraai, a waterpoint with a campsite for researchers. It is a long oval cement floor surrounded by a thigh-high chicken wire fence and covered by a thatch roof. Inside are stretchers, chairs, freezers and refrigerators run from a generator and other mod cons for scientists to reside for weeks. The kitchen is a small round cement floor in the sand outside with a hole in the middle for a wood fire. Bathing is a shower under the windpump. The toilet is thirty metres away, a long-drop screened on three sides by grass walls leaving a clear view of dunes and approaching wildlife.

Izak is uneasy. We set up stretchers under the thatch roof but he insists on making up his bed behind a small barricade of boxes, trunks and paraphernalia in the back of the truck. Then he wanders off to gather firewood, but not far.

The sun has just slipped behind a dune and we are sitting around the young fire, relishing the evening cool, when we hear the reason for Izak's restlessness. It is a series of deep throaty rumbles, like thunderous grunts in an echo chamber, that seem to come from everywhere. Kotie perks up immediately: lions, he says, but Izak looks depressed and peers suspiciously into the encroaching dark.

Fetch the rifle, Kotie tells him and Izak goes eagerly. Kotie props it against his camp chair and we grill our meat over a bed of coals scraped from the burning logs. Izak keeps the flames going. He picks up another camelthorn branch – and drops it as if it were already alight.

A large black scorpion has fallen from it at his feet and squats flat on the cement, fat tail hoisting its sting high. Izak does nothing. Kotie scoops it up with a shovel and drops it into the fire, where it lands on a blazing piece of wood and sizzles.

Izak is aghast. The people of the Kalahari believe that to burn a scorpion brings bad luck. Now he is gloomier than ever.

The lions continue to roar intermittently in prelude to their night hunt. It is impossible to pinpoint their direction because the sound bounces around the hollows between the dunes, but they seem to be moving away.

We go to bed on our stretchers behind the chicken wire which suddenly seems too flimsy to contain even a chicken. Izak beds down with much grumbling and clattering in the truck. Kotie lays the rifle on the floor next to him.

We are half asleep when there are faint sounds out of the premoon blackness between us and the windpump. Kotie switches on a spotlight. In its brilliance we see four eland drinking at the trough. That means there aren't any lions nearby, Kotie assures everybody, and we all go back to sleep.

At some ungodly hour of the night a new sound wakes us up, all except Izak who is dead to the world. It is a sharp, guttural coughing growl that suddenly chops off into silence. Groggily we listen until we hear it again and this time Kotie feels down to make sure his rifle is there. Again he switches on the spotlight, sweeping the beam slowly over the surrounding dunes and bush and up into the trees.

Nothing. It is a leopard, more feared than lions by many people. Though the most efficient of killing machines, they are elusive – seen only when they do not mind being seen.

We have hardly put our heads down when, it seems, noise wakes us again, this time the pre-dawn chirp and chatter of birds carrying far through the chill, still desert air. There is nothing for it but to get up, splash the face with cold water, dress warmly and kick the fire into being to make coffee.

This is the other beautiful time in the wilderness, matching the entrancing evenings. The air and early light are cool, crisp and shiny, scrubbed clean by the passing darkness. Every grain of sand, every leaf, flower and sound is clear and distinct. Hot black coffee never smelt or tasted better.

We are packed up and back on the road before the sun rises. Hours of hard travel through monotonous dune country lie ahead on the way back to Nossob.

We pass the Dankbaar, Bayip and Haaspan waterpoints, pausing at each to make sure the machinery is working properly, and then reach Sewe Panne. This is another Kalahari freak – seven dead flat, eye-aching white pans between the dunes, a couple of them very big. Why has the sand not covered them as it has everything else?

In one large pan a rectangular trough the size of a couple of tennis courts has been bulldozed to collect rainwater. It is nearly full now between its high banks of piled clay and gravel and various antelope have come to drink, mostly gemsbok and springbok. Jackals trot between them, veering politely aside when they come too close to the buck. A frieze of gemsbok silhouetted against the sun lines the crest of a dune at the pan's edge. Kotie aims the truck straight across and the ride on the flat, crackled surface is blessedly smooth after the sand.

South of Sewe Panne he turns east for Nossob camp and now the ride becomes hectic, a switchback from dune to dune to dune. Rangers take mischievous delight in subjecting unsuspecting visitors to this experience. Foot down hard, Kotie charges the Landcruiser along the double track crossing the sandy 'street' between two dunes, roars up the steep fifteen-metre wall of the next dune and lifts over the crest.

From flying sand and scrub and bushes there is suddenly nothing in front, just thin air and blue sky. For a hair-raising second gravity ceases and the truck seems to hang in the air, engine screaming with the sudden release of tension, and then thumps down hard on the dune's narrow crest.

The relief is brief. In the next couple of seconds the truck roars straight out of a cliff – or so it feels. Its wide, blunt nose blocks the view of the dune's other side until we are plunging down it with

Climbing the seemingly endless sea of dunes in certain areas of the Park is made possible by the new ship of the desert – the muscular four-wheel drive.
National Parks Board

Kotie fighting to hold the wheels straight as the churned track tries to shove them aside.

After three or four dunes the adrenalin level in our bloodstreams returns to normal and we concentrate on finding grips to stop ourselves bouncing between roof and hard seat. A few times, even Kotie is caught unawares when the track inexplicably makes a turn right on top of a dune and there is wild skidding as he slithers through.

We have passed Ratel waterpoint and are nearing Nossob when in a 'street' ahead we see a spick-and-span four-wheel drive parked beside the track. Not poachers, certainly. Tourists wandering illegally?

We stop next to it and four people come strolling out of the scrub, three men and a leggy young blonde in hotpants and T-shirt as if she were on Muizenberg beach.

They are all researchers from a university and have permission to go off the beaten track. They have been waiting for Kotie to return from patrol. He relaxes. What are they studying?

Antlions, they say, and immediately an animated debate begins among this little group of enthusiasts under a blazing desert sun a million miles from anywhere.

Antlions, it appears, come in many types and not all make the little conical pits in the sand into which ants fall to be eaten. Some lurk just under the surface to snatch passing insects in their long jaws like lateral pincers.

The scientists are studying them, they say, to find out what makes them tick, how they survive the desert sand's extreme variations in temperature, among other things. Antlions are very efficient, they explain, they suck from their victims only the digestible juices because they have no waste disposal system.

The leggy lady shows us a collection bottle with a little red sand in it. On it is a fat antlion about three centimetres long, a prehistoric monster in miniature.

Now completely absorbed by this novelty, Kotie invites them all to visit him. We cover the last few kilometres to Nossob camp cheerily; tonight there will be another group of interesting visitors around the campfire – a treasured stimulus out here, so far from the rest of the world.

And for a day or two he can forget about windpumps.

CHAPTER EIGHT

The Alluring Desert

*f*ascinating to visit but a grim place to live, most visitors think as they view the ocean of space all around, thankful they can escape back to their city canyons and ordered homes in well-behaved gardens.

The reaction is understandable among people who come to the KGNP for a few days or a week or even, as some do regularly, for two or three weeks every year. The Kalahari can be a trial for those softened by mild climates and modern comforts, especially for the campers and caravanners.

The summer heat is exhausting – cracking dry except when the rain brings cloying humidity – and the winter's cold cuts to the bone like a scalpel. When the wind rises grit penetrates everything and crunches between the teeth. It is a rude shock in summer to turn on a cold tap and be scalded by sun-cooked water before the pipes cool. The stock in the camp shops is basic and the nearest supermarket is more than 300 kilometres distant. Between forays on the park roads there is nothing to do but eat, sleep, drink or, at Twee Rivieren, swim and (at your own considerable risk) suntan. TV and radio are banned, of course, except for those staff who can receive broadcasts.

Rangers in other national parks are respected and envied for their freedom in the outdoors and their communion with the wilderness. Not here. Here they are certainly respected, but in place of envy they get sympathy.

White-faced owls like this dozing pair can sometimes be seen in broad daylight sleeping on the branches of trees close to the trunks.
Lorna Stanton – ABPL.

It is misplaced. There is not a man among the park's personnel who does not revel in its way of life, who does not want to be there for years if not necessarily for ever. Some of the womenfolk do not perhaps, but disenchantment among them is rare.

It is curious that the enormous emptiness of the desert conceals the enjoyment of living in it as effectively as the bush of Kruger and the forest of Tsitsikamma. The work is just as hard and the stimulus of working with wildlife is the same but there is more challenge because it is spiced by greater risk – the desert is less tolerant of error.

Some KGNP people know no other environment, such as Warden Elias le Riche who grew up in the park, and Ranger-Sergeants

Willem de Waal and Karel 'Vet Piet' Kleinman, all products of the Northern Cape. Others have been drawn to it from very different localities.

Mata Mata Ranger David de Villiers, formerly a policeman with the dog squad, hails from Stanford on the balmy Cape coast between Hermanus and Gansbaai and was captivated by the Kalahari while working for the Cape's nature conservation department in the huge Gordonia district.

'I would have married him even if I had known he would land up here,' says his wife Alta.

Johannes Jacobus 'Kotie' Herholdt, former ranger at Nossob, is a product of the Karoo and Orange Free State whose studies and work took him to the Addo and Bontebok parks and Bloemfontein's university before he took the job. His wife Hanlie cried. Then she became hooked on the Kalahari.

What is it that grips them so? What makes life so special when the hours are long, the pay poor and the work hard and sweaty and often dangerous? It is the wild and the beautiful and the unexpected.

No one knows what is about to happen when going out through the camp's gate. Every trip, every chore, is a voyage of discovery. Even within the camps each day is unpredictable.

Elias is seated at his desk shuffling papers in triplicate when the grizzled Sergeant Willem enters, stands at attention and announces that lions from the park have turned up on a farm just outside to the south-east, in Botswana north of Bokspits. They have killed a couple of goats. Will he come and shoot them, the farmer says.

Elias sighs, I suspect with relief, and tells the sergeant to fetch the Landcruiser, the rifle and the dart gun and the immobilising drugs. He dumps the papers in a tray and puts on his hat.

Several hours later he returns without having fired a shot. The lions scampered back into the park before he reached them. They often do that when they hear a vehicle coming; there is no doubt they know where they are safe.

It is not always so easy. On another occasion four or five lions were darted south of the park and it was decided that they should be taken far back inside, well away from the border. The comatose cats were loaded like sacks of hay on a flat trailer hitched to a tractor and Sergeant Vet Piet was told to drive them right up to the Nossob camp region and offload them there to recover.

He set off confidently on the long journey but what nobody had taken into account was that a tractor travels rather slower than a truck. Sergeant Vet Piet was almost there, near Kaspersdraai, when he heard curious noises above the rumble of the engine.

He turned in his seat and discovered that the immobilising drug was wearing off. The lions were waking up – still very dopey but

The light of a campfire in the Park – often the ideal time to reflect on the day's encounters, although also, according to Elias le Riche, an effective way of attracting the Kalahari lion.
Andrew St. Pierre White.

most certainly awake. A couple were sitting woozily on their haunches two metres away and eyeing him with speculation.

The sergeant wasted no time checking their condition or intentions. He unhitched the trailer in record time and drove off at the tractor's fastest speed.

'It is not pleasant when they sit like that looking at you from behind,' he said afterwards when he was able to laugh about it. 'They were very close. If they had jumped they would have jumped right on top of me.'

Lions figure in a great many of the funny and frantic experiences of the park's people. There are no more than 150 to 200 lions in the South African side of the KGNP because in the desert their territorial areas are necessarily large, but for the same reason they travel far and fast and encounters are common.

They are also arrogantly fearless of humans and blessed with overwhelming curiosity. By day when the rangers are alert and armed, whether on foot or in vehicles, this is no great problem. By night it makes them a downright nuisance – and dangerous.

The best part of the desert patrol is the overnight camp – relaxing over a drink with one's companions at the fireside while the meat grills and the potatoes bake. Elias is a fastidious camper whose party always sleeps on a tarpaulin stretched on the sand, using stretchers in summer to avoid the attentions of scorpions, and whose razor, toothbrush and other gear are neatly laid out for him in the mornings.

Bush tradition has it that the best deterrent to lions at night is to keep the campfire burning all night but he lets it die down to a bed of coals.

'If you want to attract a Kalahari lion, you light a fire,' says Elias.

He has had more night meetings with lions than he cares to count. Typically, he was woken in the middle of the night at Jan se Draai by a clatter of pots and peered in irritation from his bed to see a lion standing right at his feet with his companions hurling kitchenware at it.

His rifle was beside him but he dared not shoot because his men were in the dark beyond. He yelled at one to throw the heavy fireside spade at the lion, which the man did. Far from taking fright, it promptly savaged the spade. They finally managed to drive it off by pelting it with hot brands dragged from the embers of the fire.

'Many times we get up in the morning to find lion spoor all around our beds,' says Sergeant Willem, who is more philosophical about them. 'They are just curious. One time they plucked the blankets off some sleeping people but they were just showing who's boss.'

Another night he was awakened by lion cubs tugging his bedclothes. He lay very still because their mother was close by and nothing triggers a lioness' temper as fast as perceived danger to her cubs. Eventually she gave a low growl and they abandoned the bedclothes to go to her side.

The Loffiesdraai waterpoint in the dunes has a special campsite for researchers with a concrete floor surrounded by a metre-high chicken wire fence under a thatch roof and a long-drop toilet some thirty metres away. Several times saucer-eyed scientists have been trapped in the doorless loo by passing lions looking at them as they themselves would look at a lion in a zoo, or have come scuttling back to the campfire clutching their trousers.

Kotie Herholdt slept at Loffiesdraai the night a bold young lion leaned heavily against the chicken wire and stretched its head right over to nuzzle the feet of a sleeping man. The man woke up with a yell that lifted everybody off their stretchers and sent the lion scampering.

David de Villiers was awakened from deep sleep under the stars by an odd sound. He raised his head to see a lion sniffing him and other lions sniffing at all the others in his group as if savouring the entrée. He lay still, trusting they would leave when their curiosity was satisfied.

One of the other men, however, was also awake and could not stand the tension. He suddenly screamed and hurled his blanket over the lion. It got such a fright it took off in a huge leap, landed on top of David's truck blanket and all, and fled. In the commotion the others vanished into the night.

David regards this as a mild experience compared to the night he was awakened by odd scratchy sounds on the groundsheet under his bedroll.

'I switched on my torch and all I could see around me was pure scorpion,' he said, shuddering at the memory. 'I never slept on the ground again in summer.'

Even the puffadder discovered under his blankets when they were rolled up at another camp was preferable.

Sometimes the lions come to him. The Mata Mata waterpoint is close to the camp and hunting lions have driven eland right inside, once making their kill there. The ordinary farm-type fence around Mata Mata is an easy hurdle for either eland or lions but when a gemsbok is chased, he says, it tends to go straight through the fence, leaving a convenient gap for the pursuing lion.

Doempie le Riche, Elias' wife, is accustomed to similar visitors. Having grown up in the Eastern Transvaal Lowveld where wild animals are a part of current affairs, albeit not quite so intimately, she attuned quickly when they set up home at Nossob in 1965.

Elias caught a number of young springbok to be sent to the Golden Gate National Park and put them in a wire enclosure about

Gemsbok can live indefinitely without drinking water but when they get the chance, they seize it, like this one helping himself at the pipe from a reservoir.
Nigel Dennis – ABPL.

A yellow mongoose yawning in the morning sunshine. They have become so accustomed to people in the camps they frequently forage for scraps around campfires.
Anthony Bannister – ABPL.

fifteen metres from their house. Lions broke into it so silently nobody heard and ate the lot, leaving only heads and hooves.

On other occasions they attacked camels in a nearby kraal until Elias shot one to drive them off, left their large tracks inside a fence around the house that was supposed to keep them out, scratched the rump of the Le Riche dog for barking at them, and peered into the house, forepaws resting on the windowsill.

Elias went out to meet a stranger on his stoep one evening and the stranger was a lion. He went smartly back inside. In the morning it was still in the yard. He had to chase it away in his truck.

None of these close encounters bothered Doempie particularly. What did was the time she went out the back door and a Cape cobra rose up right in front of her, face to face.

'I don't know what I did,' she says. 'I must have jumped right over him, but he got just as big a fright as I did.'

When Elias and Doempie lived at Nossob technicians were hired from outside the park to fix a windpump and borehole at Kwang twenty-three kilometres to the north, which supplies the camp's water.

The technicians were hauling up the pipe section by section from the borehole with a power winch. Its racket filled the air and they were concentrating on the job because they were in a hurry to get it done.

They did not notice the group of several lions emerge from the dunes to see what all the noise was about, inquisitive as always. Nobody saw them until one of the men glanced up and there was a lion, right next to them, watching the activity with great interest. He yelled.

Everybody suddenly saw lions everywhere. Before they could think about it the men were right up in the windpump's derrick, clinging desperately to the lattice steel frame not meant to carry this much weight. Their tools lay where they had fallen, the suspended pipe section was forgotten and the engine thumped on.

The lions apparently thought this was highly entertaining. Ignoring the shouts they lay down on the sun-warmed sand and made themselves comfortable to watch the further proceedings.

The men might have been stuck there indefinitely had Elias not decided to see how the work was going. By the time he arrived in his truck the workers had been clinging like monkeys for three hours. They looked so woebegone and the scene was so hilarious, he chuckled later, that he was almost reluctant to interfere.

The lions grumblingly picked themselves up when he drove his truck close and slouched off into the desert. With the strong incentive of lions, the technicians finished their job with rare celerity.

Meetings between man and lion have not always gone so smoothly, however. In his book on the Le Riche family, author

Hannes Kloppers tells of the time Joep went with Gert Mouton and Ranger-Constable Andries du Pont to chase back three lions that had killed three donkeys outside the park.

With the other two on the back of his vehicle, Joep drove towards the lions until they were forced to give way and ran in the general direction of the park border, always for a short distance and never in a direct line.

This went on for more than an hour with the lions' tempers rising with the sun. Every time the vehicle approached they growled louder, their tails whipped the grass and they stood fast until Joep was almost on top of them. Whenever one lion or another veered off too far to the side Gert and Andries jumped down from the truck and shouted and waved their arms to turn it towards the border.

A powerful young male decided it had had enough of this herding and made its stand in a tangle of branches. Andries and Gert clambered down and Andries looked for a stick to throw at it. And then Joep saw that this lion was enraged and dangerous.

Several things happened at once. He shouted at the men to get into the cab with him and gunned the engine to place the truck between them and the lion. Its wheels sank into a warren of rat holes and stuck fast. The lion charged from about fifteen metres. The two men took off as if on wings and landed on the exposed back of the truck, not in the cab. Joep stepped out with his rifle.

The lion's first charge was a mock one – a bounding, sand-spraying display with tail erect. Now the lion aimed at him and charged for real. He stepped quickly away from the truck to give himself space to shoot. The first fast shot killed the lion and the force of the heavy bullet hurled it back. He fired a second to make sure.

Andries was peering with huge eyes over the roof of the truck. Gert saw nothing – he was crouched with his head buried in sandbags.

Once when Joep took his two young sons Stoffel and Elias with him, they camped for the night at Jan se Draai. There were no big pug marks or other signs of lion around the waterpoint.

In the early dark Stoffel challenged Elias to come with him to fetch a stick he had left in the veld beyond reach of the firelight. Elias was about to take up the challenge when Joep told them not to be silly and to stay put.

They were cooking supper, including a whole steenbok head the rangers favoured, when one of the rangers went to fetch more firewood about six metres away. An unearthly roar split the silence. The ranger was back at the fireside in a split second in two huge bounds, yelling in fright. Beside the firewood stood a large lioness that had charged out of the dark.

It stood menacingly, grunting. If anybody ran for a gun, or just ran, it would charge again.

Joep plucked the steenbok head from the fire and threw it hard. It bounched off the lioness' face spraying ash and sparks. A ranger hurled a burning branch. The lioness retreated a few strides.

In the light from the branch they saw three more lions … right where Stoffel and Elias would have gone to fetch their stick.

Joep bundled everyone into his truck, counter-charged the lions with it until they fled, and then sought a safer campsite nearby. The place where this happened, says Hannes Kloppers, was thereafter named Steenbok Head.

Sergeant Willem probably owes his life to fast thinking by Joep. On one of their many expeditions to chivvy truant lions back into the park from farming areas, they found a lioness lying under a tree.

The sergeant, by now blasé about this business, stepped from the truck and hurled a stick at it. It did not move. He bent to pick up another stick – and then it charged.

Joep instantly plucked off his bush hat and spun it between Sergeant Willem and the lioness. It stopped dead in its tracks in surprise. The sergeant was already moving too fast: 'I jumped into the truck right across my seat and on to Baas Joep's lap.'

Darting lions for research or translocation is ordinarily without risk because it can be done from the safety of a vehicle thirty to forty metres distant. The immobilising drug takes effect in about fifteen minutes and for the next three hours or so the doped lion can be manhandled like a sack of mealies. But nothing is predictable, as Sergeant Willem has learned.

Joep darted a lioness with a crossbow, a popular method before darting rifles became more efficient, and it fell on its side with the dart underneath. They waited a full quarter hour before the sergeant strolled over to the prone cat and grabbed its tail to heave it over on its other side and retrieve the dart.

The lioness was far from asleep. Having its tail pulled galvanised it into action. It flashed on to its feet and went for Sergeant Willem. He fled for the truck and yanked the door open – right into the lioness' face. It stopped the half-doped animal just long enough for him to clamber in.

Being a careful man, David de Villiers never had narrow escapes of this kind although he darted more than thirty lions and twenty leopards. His Landcruiser bore the brunt of the attacks, leaving it scarred by scratches and dented in a few places by teeth.

'The lions of the Kalahari don't tolerate much and they attack. The leopards too, they always give you the most difficult targets and then get fed up and attack.'

The only wounds he received were inflicted when he caught a very young lion by throwing a blanket over it and wrapping his arms around it. The cub was more or less immobilised but not its claws;

they came through the blankets and his thin clothing like a bunch of sail needles. The cub repeatedly extended and retracted its claws and one went in and out of his forearm every time.

He says he has learned the trick now: 'You grab them very carefully, avoiding the sharp bits.'

In spite of all of these confrontations, lions have never killed or even bitten a human in the KGNP.

Of all the animals in the park Sergeant Willem has most respect for the gemsbok because of its amazing dexterity with its horns and the great physical strength with which it wields them. Lions commonly kill young gemsbok but are wary of the full-grown adults – with good reason, for dead or dying lions have been found occasionally with horn wounds and once or twice with broken pieces of gemsbok horn still in them.

And yet, in the days before darting, gemsbok were caught by chasing them in the desert until they were so tired several men could jump off the vehicle and hold them by the horns and heels. The chase usually lasted a few kilometres.

The eland is much easier to catch in the sergeant's opinion: 'He kicks a bit but that's all. He tires more easily, his speed is slow and he runs in a straight line whereas the gemsbok dodges. When you catch him he just gives up and he is easily led and transported.'

His closest brush with death came when catching hartebeest by running them down with a vehicle. They are hard to catch, he says, because they are very fast, jink and swerve and kick hard.

He was trying to grab an injured hartebeest when it lunged at him. The hooked horns ripped open his shirt and scraped across his stomach. A centimetre closer and he would have been gutted.

Life in the KGNP is not made up entirely of unnerving confrontations with animals. For the rangers it is mostly long days of checking and repairing windpumps and reservoirs, patrolling for poachers, and a seemingly endless round of camp maintenance, fixing vehicles and – with the help of their wives – paperwork, running the camp shop and looking after tourists.

Between these many chores they somehow find the time to devote to their pet interests. David de Villiers, a keen observer of desert life, particularly of predators, wrote occasional articles for the NPB magazine *Custos*.

'You don't come here to see only lions or leopards,' he says. 'You come here to see the small as well as the big, the birds as well as the animals.'

He helped Kotie Herholdt with bird observations. Kotie, who completed a three-year national diploma course in nature conservation and worked more than three years with the University of the Free State ornithological department, is an avid avianist.

He has a permit from Safring, the South African Bird Ringing Unit of the University of Cape Town, and from 1985 has ringed many thousands of birds and personally observed over half of the more than 900 bird species in Southern Africa.

Just about every second starling, sparrow, finch, roller and other bird in Nossob camp had a ring around one leg to certify its membership of 'Kotie's Club', such is his enthusiasm for this international bird monitoring system.

His speciality, however, is raptors and he has had numerous scientific articles published on bird life from his research.

No raptor within striking distance of Nossob could evade Kotie's attentions. After joining the KGNP in May 1988, he ringed hundreds there and more than 1 000 elsewhere.

'To live there one has to be a nature lover,' he says. 'Just looking after windpumps would drive a person to his death. There is tremendous opportunity if one is interested in nature – I'm also involved in collecting butterflies and other insects.

'Once every two months we went to Upington to church and to see the doctor and the dentist and do everything else.'

Because it is so remote the park attracts genuine nature-lovers and most of these are bird-watchers, he says. They come to enjoy its special wildness: the feeling of being in a great, savage desert, its special sounds – the night chorus of barking geckos, the 'whooop' of button quail after rain, the endless call of the monotonous lark.

Nossob is a simple camp without air-conditioning or any kind of recreation yet it is a favourite. People from Europe in particular love it; only some South Africans complain about the lack of facilities.

Nor is there any sort of recreation for the ranger and his wife except their children and books. No TV reception, bad radio reception, no sports facilities. So tourists and visiting researchers become an important part of their life – a stimulus and link with the outside world.

Being the main entrance camp and slightly closer to civilisation, Twee Rivieren has a fuller life and more amenities including its restaurant and little swimming pool and does receive TV and radio broadcasts. But there, too, the desert is very close, just outside the wire security fence.

Doempie le Riche's transition to the Kalahari from sub-tropical Magoebaskloof was dramatic. 'I grew up amid plentiful fruit and flowers, and here we battle to get avocadoes. From being used to a whole lettuce for a lunchtime salad I have learned to use one leaf at a time.

'At first everything looked grey and dry here but I soon found there was plenty of life. After rain there are beautiful veld flowers, as if they had been sown, even on the dunes. This is where I learned to value the smallest flower. So one's life changes completely. You begin to develop all sorts of other interests. I started collecting butterflies.'

Now she is completely familiar with such desert delicacies as wild cucumbers, raisinbush and the delicious desert truffles, *nabbas.*

When she and Elias began married life at Nossob camp she planted mesquite and pepper trees for shade but the ground squirrels dug up the seed and ate whatever seedlings emerged. The first three of their two sons and two daughters were born there and the Le Riches covertly kept a cow to provide fresh milk for the youngsters, hiding it whenever somebody from the NPB arrived.

There are special problems attached to raising children in the KGNP, Doempie explains. There are few if any other children and no group activities so they have to learn to keep themselves busy and, later, to associate with their peers.

That means sending them far away to school and long, painful separations between parents and children, who can come home for weekends at best.

Doempie had nobody to turn to for advice when she was raising babies at Nossob except by radio – and power for that was limited to a few hours a day.

Their oldest son Joseph was about three years old when he drank paraffin accidentally and went white in the face and blue around the mouth. Doempie radioed the NPB headquarters in Pretoria and they gave her emergency first-aid advice, then she and Elias set off in the night to drive Joseph to the Upington hospital.

They were not far from Nossob when Elias saw that the boy's colour and breathing were back to normal – the emergency treatment had worked. They turned back home. They were lucky.

Housekeeping is much as it would be on a remote Kalahari farm: long, costly travel to shop and ferry children, expensive meat, few vegetables, brackish water. Initially she and other wives in the park missed the theatre and other cultural activities but to some extent this is compensated by the interesting people they meet in the flow of visitors and by the demands of work.

As her husband's administrative assistant, Doempie is kept busy in the Twee Rivieren office. She is also the camp's medic, having been fully trained in first-aid following young Joseph's paraffin experience.

Mainly she has to patch up the fingers of people foolish enough to feed the ground squirrels, which quite innocently tend to bite whatever looks tasty. Another frequent chore is treating painful scorpion stings among the children of the camp's staff who persist in playing barefoot in the sand and woodpiles. She keeps anti-venom serum handy for both snake and scorpion bites – Cape cobras being the commonest snakes in the park.

In real emergencies Elias flies people to hospital at Upington but this has happened only twice, with a woman who broke her hip and a man who had a heart attack.

He is himself a bit of a bundu doctor and on patrol always carries with him rudimentary dental tools in his first-aid kit because there is nothing worse than an agonising toothache far out in the desert.

He and his ranger companions were relaxing at a campfire one night when a Bushman materialised out of the dark and squatted silently nearby. A little later more Bushmen appeared and sat around the fire. The first one spoke.

A ranger interpreted. The Bushman had a toothache, could Elias do something to help? Elias had no anaesthetic or pain-killer. He flourished his formidable dental pliers. The Bushman showed no fear.

Elias extracted the bad tooth as gently as he could. It must have hurt but the Bushman was stoic and gave not a whimper. In admiration Elias presented him with a disposable cigarette lighter. The Bushman flicked it alight in wonder – this would dispense with much rubbing of sticks to start cooking fires. The other Bushmen watched him in envy.

Another Bushman spoke up. The ranger looked at Elias and said 'Now this one also has a toothache ...'

At Twee Rivieren camp a ranger who knew of Elias' tooth-pulling prowess came to him for help. The tooth was bad but Elias was reluctant to extract it because it would be very painful. By coincidence an anaesthetist friend was staying in the camp but the Le Riches had no anaesthetic, only the drug used in darts to catch animals – not meant for humans.

That will do, the anaesthetist said, and administered it himself with delicate precision that put the ranger into a semi-conscious condition. Elias painlessly whipped out the offending tooth.

That ranger is probably the only one in history to have had an operation under an immobilising drug.

One of the commoner chores for rangers is rescuing stuck or lost tourists. Most visitors are people with a special interest in wildlife who are well-behaved and careful not to pollute, says David de Villiers, and the other rangers agree. However, there are always a foolish few who will insist on driving off the road for a closer look at some animal or who will drive on patrol roads closed to them.

Often they become stuck. It is easy enough to stick in deep sand or mud on the main road, which can happen to anyone, and far easier off the road.

When they have not reported back in camp by gate closing time, which is obligatory in the KGNP, the office informs the ranger. If they have not returned by 10 p.m., a search is started.

The cracked surface of a drying pan records the tracks of a predator on the hunt.
Anthony Bannister – ABPL.

Usually the missing party is found shamefacedly awaiting rescue, sometimes way off the main road. Occasionally an empty vehicle is found when the occupants have very foolishly tried to walk home, a formula for getting totally lost – or for a dangerous encounter.

Such silliness, however, is nothing beside the stupidity of people who leave their cars to walk closer to lions.

The Kalahari has claimed only one victim in the KGNP, and that is the mysterious case of Hans Schwabe ...

The Forlorn Cross

In the north of the KGNP between the Grootbrak and Koedoebos waterpoints a long, flat, featureless pan mingles with and loses itself in the wide bed of the Nossob River. This is the end of the Polentswa, a barren watercourse which might have justified the title of river hundreds or thousands of years ago but today is hardly discernible.

Its dry, sand-fringed bed not much deeper than the valleys between the dunes meanders northwards into the infinite grey nothingness of the Kalahari. The view up it is utterly depressing, its gloom deepened by the vultures nesting in scraggly thorn trees on one low bank. Why anyone would want to come here is beyond understanding.

Why Hans Schwabe came here is one of the mysteries of the Kalahari. What he found was an unpleasant death and his final resting place.

Schwabe was a geologist from Germany who lived in an apartment in Johannesburg. KGNP Warden Joep le Riche and his family knew him because his business had several times brought him through the park to and from South West Africa along the Auob River road.

In October 1958, he turned up again at Twee Rivieren and visited Joep and Cillie for coffee and a chat. They talked as usual about the Kalahari and Schwabe raised the subject of diamonds – could there be any in the desert? Diamonds were a popular subject at that time because their value was high and new pipes were being found by imaginative prospectors in hitherto unsuspected places.

The Kalahari was regarded as unlikely then because of its frustrating blanket of sand. Not many years later some of the richest diamond finds in the world were made in this desert.

Schwabe said he was heading for South West Africa through Mata Mata as usual, finished his coffee and left. What happened after that has been reconstructed from accounts by Elias le Riche, Senior Sergeant Willem de Waal and the late Joep, as he told it to author Hannes Kloppers.

Schwabe travelled the few kilometres from Twee Rivieren to the confluence of the Auob and Nossob and there drove off the road to hide his Pontiac car in a clump of the blue bush widespread in this area. He waited an hour or two, presumably to see if anyone was following him, and then drove on – not up the Auob towards Mata Mata but up the Nossob.

Two or three days later (there is uncertainty about the time) the Bechuanaland Protectorate police telephoned Joep to say they had found an abandoned car at Kwang but had not had time to investigate or search the area. Could he look into it?

Joep was puzzled. He knew of no car going that way and there was nothing except animals along the almost 250 kilometres of the Nossob – no camp yet, no entry to South West Africa because Union's End was closed, very little water.

He set off with a couple of rangers including Sergeant Willem, son Stoffel who had recently joined the park staff, and son Elias. At the confluence Joep saw the tracks where Schwabe had left the road and immediately recognised them as those of his car. He guessed what they would find at Kwang.

He was right. Schwabe had parked the car and left an enigmatic note that read: 'No water for car, no water for myself, no food, follow this road. Monday 8 a.m. H. Schwabe' – enigmatic because the car's radiator was full.

The geologist's trail led north. They followed it with difficulty because wind had partially erased it. They found several places where Schwabe had stopped to dig with a geologist's pick into the hard calcrete where it was not covered by sand. Whether he sought evidence of diamonds or something else will never be known; geologists use a pick as habitually as a pipe-smoker uses matches.

The searchers followed the trackers all afternoon in blistering heat for nearly fifty kilometres and reached the bleak pan where the Polentswa joins the Nossob. As they crossed it the shape of a low dune emerged to the north above the shimmering haze and just beneath that, a dark dot that became a small camelthorn tree.

A vulture perched on top of the tree.

Schwabe lay under it, or what was left of him. Hyenas, jackals, vultures and other waste removers of the wild had been at him and there was little more than head and feet and a few pieces between, all decomposing.

Joep sent an urgent call for police and a doctor and while they waited they tried to piece together what had happened, why Schwabe, who should have known better, had done this strange thing and died.

Near the tattered corpse lay an empty one-gallon tin in which he had carried water – and he must have known he could get more at

The lonely grave of Hans Schwabe, the geologist who inexplicably wandered off into the desert and died under this tree, where rangers found what scavengers had left of him.
Wilf Nussey.

When the remains of the lost wanderer Hans Schwabe were buried, an oil can was placed at the foot of the crude cross. It has since disappeared.
National Parks Board.

boreholes he had passed shortly before he parked his car. They also found a packet of biscuits, anti-sunburn gel, a half bottle of sleeping tablets and his geologist's pick.

He had also carried fireworks, says Elias. They found the remnants of a quantity of firecrackers and sparklers he had used, apparently to chase off predators. The memory is vivid in Elias' mind; he had to spend the night watching over the fragments of the corpse.

When the police arrived the doctor with them estimated that Schwabe had been dead about three days and was probably killed by thirst, though there was little enough of him left to guess from.

Then they had to decide what to do with him. He was on Bechuanaland territory and to take him back across the border for burial would entail all sorts of international paperwork for which there was no time – the desert heat was not improving him.

They decided to bury him then and there. A hole was dug in the sand beneath the camelthorn and Schwabe was packaged and lowered into it with a few words of prayer.

A short stump of camelthorn branch was anchored at the end of the grave and another piece wired to it in the form of a cross. Someone scratched with a knife on the gallon can: 'Here lies H Schwabe. Buried 23/10/58/' and placed it against the cross.

On his grave they placed other relics, an old bottle and a few blackened, battered tins, cigarettes, the biscuits, the pick. Some tins and a bottle are still there, now stuffed into a hollow in the tree, but the other things have vanished.

His fate was announced but nobody ever came forward to claim him, give him a full burial or erect a proper headstone. He is forgotten now except as a reminder of what can so easily happen to the incautious in the Kalahari.

The desolation of the Polentswa makes an apt setting for his forlorn grave.

Headquarters of and entrance to the Park is Twee Rivieren, the largest and southernmost camp with comfortable thatched chalets, restaurant and pool.
Anthony Bannister – ABPL.

CHAPTER NINE

Visitors' Guide

When to Go

For dedicated wildlife enthusiasts and the lover of outdoor life the KGNP is a constant delight. Although tough at times, its rewards outweigh its discomforts. It is not always suitable for holidaymakers who seek only a place to loaf, sleep and eat, like Skukuza. For much of the year the park can be quite uncomfortable.

In August and September alternating chill winds from the south and oven-dry berg winds from the north accentuate the desert's monotony by blanketing it in fine dust that penetrates everything except unopened tins.

Seasonal temperatures swing from one wild extreme to the other.

The average maximum and minimum in January are 35.7°C and 19.5°C, and in July they are 22.2°C and 1.2°C.

Such radical change does not tell the whole story because these are *average* temperatures. Between November and January the mercury sometimes soars to 49° C and conversely in June and July it frequently drops below freezing point and has plunged to a bitter -11.3°C.

The cold notwithstanding, winter is a peak season for the park because school holidays occur then and because the phenomenal temperature fluctuation makes the sunlight hours tolerable and even hot.

Summer can be an ordeal for many people, especially children, for whom there is little distraction in the camps during the blazing hours except the swimming pool at Twee Rivieren.

In spite of this, the summer flow of visitors is also rising steadily, due largely to the proliferation of air-conditioners in vehicles and their installation in the huts at Twee Rivieren – though not yet at Nossob or Mata Mata.

Warden Eias le Riche says the best times to visit are in autumn, from March to May, or in spring between August and October, particularly if there have been good rains in the autumn.

Rain and the spectacular changes it brings about are very much chance here but records over ten years show that on average 77.8 per cent falls between January and April, 18.6 per cent from

September to December and a meagre three and a half per cent in the cooler months of May to August.

It is not the sort of reserve whose panorama of life can be seen in one visit because it changes so markedly from month to month, from season to season, sometimes quite unpredictably.

In short: if your priority is comfort and relaxation, visit in spring or autumn; if it is to see the living desert, come any time.

Where to Stay

The huge area of the KGNP contains only three camps at present although several more of different kinds are envisaged among various other developments.

They are Twee Rivieren in the far south at the park's only gateway, Nossob camp about half way along the stretch of the Nossob River within the park, and Mata Mata on the border where the Auob River enters from Namibia.

Game viewing is the smallest variable in making a choice between them because most of the park can be easily reached from any camp in a day and there is little difference between their local wildlife. The KGNP has nothing like the changes in terrain and species one finds, for instance, between Skukuza, Letaba and Shingwedzi in the Kruger National Park.

Choice is governed more by comfort, time, distance and the distinctive character of each camp.

If comfort is the priority then Twee Rivieren comes first with its air-conditioning, swimming pool and restaurant – none of which the others have. If it is privacy, then it is small and distant Mata Mata where royalty could find solitude. If real Kalahari remoteness and a taste of Beau Geste, then it is Nossob.

But why not all of them – a couple of days in each for a week if reservations are made early?

Twee Rivieren

One comes upon it quite suddenly at the end of kilometres of dusty white road in the Nossob River from its meeting with the Molopo, a big barred gate between bulbous posts of water-smoothed river pebbles set in concrete.

A wizened Bushman in uniform opens the gate and beware ... if you are a minute late he will not open that gate until precisely the proper moment next morning.

To the right on the east bank of the river beyond a fence is a rather untidy collection of buildings, one quite large. They comprise a Botswana government post on the side that is sometimes noisy at night.

Twee Rivieren lies spread up the shallow-sloped west bank. Low down, near the gate, is the site for twenty-five caravans thinly shaded by a few sparse trees.

At the top is the largest building, the park's headquarters and shop at the centre of a long arc of chalets with the restaurant and pool behind them.

The whole camp was refurbished in 1981 and now all the buildings have walls cobbled with smooth river stones and thatched roofs supported by angled log beams bedded into the flagstoned patios outside – traps to trip the unwary wandering in the dark. The architecture is far from typically Kalahari but attractive.

Twee Rivieren grew steadily from its small beginnings and for a number of years stayed at twenty-six chalets or cottages, called 'huts', until these were increased to thirty-one units.

Most chalets are semi-detached units which can be booked separately or together.

They offer the National Parks Board's usual, slightly confusing, range: chalets of two rooms with three beds in each, or of one room with two beds and a double bunk, or of a room with four single beds, or of lesser combinations – all planned with flexibility in mind to accommodate anything from singles to families of all sizes.

All have shower, toilet, bedding, towels, extra blankets, small carpet and the usual comforts of a good country hotel plus an excellent supply of cutlery and crockery and a refrigerator and hotplate stove in the kitchen.

Each has its own very practical outdoor barbecue area with concrete table and benches and garden table and chairs on the flagged stoep.

One of the pleasanter Kalahari experiences is evening on a stoep in any of the three camps when the sun draws its curtains of brilliant blue and gold and fiery red. This is when another set of life emerges – the Cape serotine and Egyptian free-tailed bats dipping and swooping to scoop insects near outside lamps, the fat shiny geckos lurking on the walls to stuff themselves with bugs.

One of the daytime characteristics of Twee Rivieren is the call of the Brant's whistling rats. These plump little rodents like to sit at the entrances to their burrows in the dune sand and whistle at any sign of danger – a short sharp *fweeet* like someone hailing a passing cab – before diving underground. Sit and wait and within minutes they will slowly reappear nose first and twitching.

A feature much favoured by children lies at the northern end of the camp just beyond the arc of chalets: a sizeable dune of bright red sand, speckled with blue bush and other shrubs, whose steep sides are good for toboganning down on the seat of the pants.

It is also part of a useful walk around the camp's perimeter for people who feel the need of exercise after hours of sitting in a vehicle.

Twee Rivieren has the only shop of any size in the KGNP where a reasonable range of canned food and drink, frozen meat and vegetables, sometimes fresh bread, clothing and souvenirs, toiletries and guide books can be bought.

Nossob

The remotest of any camp in any national park in South Africa, it probably has more champions than either of the others.

Coming from the south, you are almost upon it when you see it – a couple of off-white buildings against the off-white sand before the road suddenly turns into the gate.

It is a small camp of only twenty huts and caravan and camp sites plus a couple of houses for staff and researchers and a large ablution block beside a fine caravan park shaded by several big trees.

Whitewashed stones mark the driveway to the office and rudimentary shop just inside the gate, beneath the cool shade of a large tree, and to the chalets.

These are plain, square, smooth-plastered buildings looking more like barracks than resort accommodation and give the camp its faintly Foreign Legion atmosphere. It would be unsurprising to see a train of camels sway over the horizon.

But they are quite old, thus thick-walled, fairly cool and comfortable, contain the same amenities as Twee Rivieren's – minus air-conditioning – and also take two, three or four people per room. They are being refurbished but without changing their character.

Adding to the Foreign Legion ambience is the early morning sight, heralded by a light swishing sound, of camp workers strolling about dragging wide sweeps across the sand to smooth away the tracked record of the previous day. Nossob begins the new day immaculately groomed.

Some people like this camp so much they seldom move out of it. There is much to see there. Starlings and flocks of sparrows have cheekily made themselves at home among the caravanners and campers, living on crumbs and scraps and crowding at dripping taps.

For years two white-faced owls slept their days away in a low pepper tree next to the ablution block, becoming so accustomed to people that the whirr of a cine camera from a metre away would not disturb them. A scops owl lived in a tall tree on another side of the block.

The Nossob camp on the Nossob River seen from the air. It is probably the most popular because of its remoteness and wildness.
National Parks Board.

Black-tailed tree rats (or mice, some call them) occupy a stunted tree behind the researcher's house near the office, giving their display of agility every evening at dusk.

At about the same time, during much of the year, begins the clacking chorus of the barking geckos – a stone-against-stone sound that continues well into the night. But try seeing one of these elusive fellows ...

And quite often in the afternoons and evenings lions can be seen close by without being forced into the confines of a car.

They like to drink at waterpoints less than a hundred metres from the camp gate in the bed of the Nossob River and come slouching down the river or its bank without paying the slightest attention to onlookers.

Yet another attraction at Nossob – and an important one for serious students of the Kalahari – is its garden.

It is an area of undisturbed bush lying between the campsite and the top of the shallow rise on which the ranger's house stands.

Several interleading paths wind through and the various indigenous plants, almost all low shrubs, are labelled. Pamphlets available at the office or shop give details about them.

Here the vegetation that seems so uniform and monotonous while one travels the roads takes on new meaning. One can see the difference between grasses and identify such shrubs as the driedoring

(*Rhigozum trichotomum*) whose three-spiked branches are not, in fact, thorny at all.

Finally, Nossob camp does give closer access to slightly more varied scenery than the other camps, being closer to the dune road and the stepping-off point for the trip to Union's End which is rather distant from the other camps.

Mata Mata

It, too, has its adherents and they champion it fiercely.

Born as a border post in the rough old days when the Auob was a main road between South Africa and German South West Africa, now Namibia, Mata Mata stayed small. When South Africa took over the administration of South West Africa as a League of Nations mandate after World War I, the border restrictions ended and most travellers preferred to drive straight through instead of overnighting here.

In January 1990 this route into newly independent Namibia was closed because the logistics and costs of maintaining a full border post were not justified by the trickle of traffic.

Mata Mata has a delightful character all of its own. It is a small camp – with only five chalets and ten caravan and camp sites. The

huts are part of the much-loved character of the camp, each with its punkah fan and the same equipment as the other camps.

As far as possible solar energy will be used for heating and lighting to reduce or eliminate the nightly rumble of diesel generators.

Its caravan camp will not change. This pleasant tree-shaded oasis with twelve sites right at the foot of the Auob's high bank, giving a wide view across its bed and to a nearby waterhole among trees, is the best camping area in the park.

Because of its small size, its position at the end of the line against a border and its distinctive character, the National Parks Board intends to use Mata Mata more as a wilderness camp than a base camp like Twee Rivieren and Nossob.

It certainly lends itself to this function. No more than an ordinary farm fence separates it from the rest of the Kalahari and the desert's inhabitants have often found themselves inside.

Buck being chased by lion have crashed through the fence. Leopards sometimes steal through. There is always something small and interesting to see inside – the starlings and drongos stealing from campers careless enough to leave food about, the black-tailed tree rats, the squirrels ...

Mata Mata also has a small shop, rather better stocked than Nossob's, attached to its office and, like the others, a filling station.

Where to Look

Because the KGNP is so uniform – flattish terrain about 870 metres above sea level comprising dunes, pans, plains and riverbeds – the distribution of its fauna and flora is similarly uniform. It is not possible to say with certainty, as in some other parks: lion shall be found here, eagles there, and eland over there.

Almost all birds and animals and trees and grasses and flowers can be found anywhere, within their specific habitats, though some species are more *likely* to be found in some regions than in others.

Thus eland and cheetah are commoner in the north than in the south. The rare wild dogs are more often found in the far north and far south. Starlings are rare at Twee Rivieren but common at Nossob and both starlings and drongos are notorious thieves and scavengers at Mata Mata.

Union's End at the far northern tip is the only place to see rosy-faced lovebirds because they are visiting vagrants, not everyday residents – green, red-headed birds the size of Namaqua doves that breed in holes in trees and antheaps and in sociable weaver nests.

Union's End and the two waterpoints before it, Grootkolk and Kannaguass, are good places to see sizeable groups of several kinds

The little Mata Mata camp on the Auob River where it crosses from Namibia into South Africa. The border post has been closed.
National Parks Board.

of vultures because they favour the sweet water there. But vultures can be seen wherever other creatures are living, or dying.

Lions are ubiquitous. So are springbok, wildebeest, gemsbok, squirrels, eagles, badgers, jackals, sandgrouse, bat-eared foxes, secretary birds, leopards, steenbok, duiker, kori bustards ... Their appearance and numbers fluctuate more by season than by region.

Within this uniformity there is subtle variation – a side road into unexpectedly lovely riverbed, a personally favoured waterpoint, trees full of raptor nests, or simply a pleasant place in the shade where animals sometimes pass in entrancing parade on their way to who knows where.

The following account is intended to help people enjoy the park. Most of it is within easy reach: with the exception of the remoter 128-kilometre road north of Nossob to Union's End, visitors can travel the other roads from any camp to another and back in a day. That, however, is not the best way to see wildlife; trips from camp should be planned with plenty of long pauses.

Precisely how much road the KGNP has is still a matter of some conjecture. The total is almost 500 kilometres depending on loop roads taken, tyre slip in the thick sand and similar imponderables.

There are no guarantees in this guide of what the visitor will see ... a tree might have toppled, a waterpoint might have dried up, or for some unfathomable reason animals may have opted to go somewhere else.

The Auob Road

The Auob River is reputed to be the best area of the park for seeing cheetah.

From the barred wooden gate out of Twee Rivieren camp into the park, the road follows the west bank of the Nossob River with Botswana on the other side. The riverbed is flat, edged with dull, fleshy bluebush and early on most mornings is full of lazing, cud-chewing springbok, which sometimes present a problem as this is also an airfield. Pilots have to buzz the strip to chase off the buck before landing.

The road forks four and a half kilometres from Twee Rivieren's perimeter fence near the confluence of the Auob and Nossob rivers, the right prong going to Nossob camp and Union's End, the left to Mata Mata.

The left follows the west bank of the Auob, whose bed is narrower, and banks higher than the Nossob's. It winds and backtracks considerably, following the curves and contours of the riverbank, often through puddles of dust fine as face powder. Study this dust: it bears record of the creatures that have crossed it. •

Just past the windpump and water tank at the first waterpoint, Houmoed, a side road angles across the Auob and climbs rather steeply up the far bank. It goes no further than a rocky viewpoint giving a bleak outlook over the desert.

The Auob's west bank is more rounded and gentle than the east bank, which is sharp and ridged and lined with miniature calcrete cliffs penetrated by small caves. Parts of both are capped by smooth red dunes.

Early one morning near Munro, 5,3 kilometres past Houmoed, while parked under one of several large grey camelthorn trees that cast welcome shade over the road, we had the unusual experience of watching a huge black-maned lion using the road like a jogger in the morning.

Its dense mane bounced and its massive forepaws flopped loosely forward with each step as it loped towards the car with jaws slightly open and eyes fixed ahead. Wherever a bush grew next to the road the lion diverted briefly up the sandy bank to hoist its tail and spray on the foliage.

It passed a metre from the car unconcernedly, giving only a side-long glance.

Reaching Munro, the lion jogged to the low water trough in the middle of the riverbed and sank to its belly to drink. While it was lapping, a badger trotted down the far bank making for the same waterhole with determination written in every line of its chunky body.

The badger was a matter of metres from the trough when it saw the lion and paused. The lion continued drinking, seemingly oblivious of the badger's presence.

Confrontation loomed: neither badgers nor lions are apt to give way. After long tense seconds the badger chose discretion and drank from a puddle in a seep before returning up the bank.

When it had had its fill, the lion stood and roared like the thunder of bass drums in a cathedral before loping off in the direction of answering roars beyond the dunes.

In the hour or so that this episode endured not a single other tourist or vehicle appeared. It was exclusively ours. This is one of the great delights of the KGNP – its uncrowdedness.

Continuing north-west towards Mata Mata, the Auob retains the same character for much of its distance. From Munro old stone ruins appear on the crest of the east bank.

These are remnants of simple houses and sheep kraals built just before World War I by men sent to drill boreholes in the Auob bed so the South African forces would have water should they choose to invade German South West Africa by this route.

Borehole guards stayed on long after the wells were drilled, building a few more homes as far upstream as Urikaruus, and ran livestock to supplement their tiny incomes. The shells of one or two houses are still standing but most have crumbled to low stone walls.

A first list of sightings up to Gemsbok Plain, the sixth waterpoint, reads 'springbok, wildebeest, red hartebeest, ground squirrel, many kori bustards, secretary birds, jackal, western red-footed kestrel, many sociable weaver nests, large flocks of sparrows, sandgrouse at Auchterlonie, gemsbok, spotted eagle owl ...'

At Gemsbok Plain another short road crosses the Auob to climb to the top of the opposite bank. Just past mid-river it passes the living wreck of a large tree that appears to have collapsed at some time, dropping branches that now grow flat.

It is an example of an exotic species introduced as a shade tree to Namibia many years ago which has spread south via rivers and is becoming a pest in the Northern Cape, the Mexican mesquite, *Prosopis chilensis*. This particular one is a landmark and a haven for many birds.

Atop the viewpoint at Gemsbok Plain stands a small stone cairn bearing a plaque marking the park's 50th birthday on 26 March 1981.

Just four and a half kilometres beyond Batulama, the next waterpoint, the great naked trunk of a dead camelthorn tree rises from the middle of the riverbed like an abstract sculpted column, impressively gaunt and textured.

Enfolding its top is a fine example of one of the Kalahari's most fascinating creations – the huge, haystack-like communal nest of the sociable weaver or colony bird.

A loop road encircles the tree and the nest is one of the more visible and photogenic in the park but certainly not the largest.

A couple of metres from the edge of the road six and a half kilometres south of Mata Mata is a tree carrying a giant communal nest with the debris of a fallen one on the ground beneath.

It is an ideal place to watch the sociable weavers in the middle of the day when the heat makes them quit foraging to return to the cool of the tree and their insulated nests.

They swarm like bees around a hive, chattering non-stop while they busy themselves with repairs to their nest, flying vertically into the entrances.

This is also the best time to see pygmy falcons, the tiny raptors that seize apartments for themselves in the giant nests. When they suddenly fly in, the sociable weavers withdraw a respectful metre or so but carry on their hectic activity. The little falcons ignore the masses and sometimes indulge in courtship, bobbing and bowing at each other.

There are similar, easily viewed colonies at many places on the park roads. Three other particularly good nests are in trees at one-kilometre intervals beyond Leeuwdril on the Nossob road.

Beyond Batulama are the Montrose and Rooibrak waterpoints and 2,8 kilometres past Rooibrak another road crosses the Auob to a viewpoint on the far bank. A further 1,4 kilometres on is one of the park's rather rare leg-stretching places, a shaded picnic site with concrete tables and chairs.

Be cautious when driving under the trees: fallen thorns can puncture tyres. Be equally cautious when stretching the legs: tampan ticks could be lurking in the sand.

Past the picnic site is the Kamqua waterpoint and 0,7 kilometres beyond that, a wide road crossing the Auob and vanishing into the distance. This is the fifty-five kilometre road linking the Auob and Nossob routes, a roller-coaster ride over dunes and 'streets'.

Continue along the Auob past the unremarkable Kamqua and Urikaruus waterpoints and six and a half kilometres beyond the latter a loop road turns off into the riverbed for two kilometres, circling around the Kleinskrij waterpoint.

It is the first of a succession of three attractive loops off this stretch of main road – all well worth taking because they wind through copious trees (for the desert) in the centre of the dry river.

The second of six kilometres meanders around the Grootskrij waterpoint and the third of 3,3 kilometres around Dalkeith.

Sightings recorded here include a leopard in a tree right next to the Grootskrij loop with its young springbok kill, a black-backed jackal following a trail in the Kleinskrij loop undeterred by a car following a few paces behind it, gemsbok, springbok and doves all drinking together at the Dalkeith crib and numerous other birds including the crimson-breasted shrike and pale chanting goshawk.

Next after Dalkeith is Craig Lockhart where man's activity disrupts the scene: in the sandy river bed stands a large, high corral of poles walled in plastic sheeting. A track runs past it and vanishes across the far bank.

This is a holding pen used for giraffes reintroduced to the KGNP, after hunters had wiped them out decades ago. Beyond the pen and out of sight over the crest of the Auob's east bank is a fenced paddock of many hectares in the duneveld where they were kept until they acclimatised enough to be allowed to roam free.

After Craig Lockhart is Sitzas and then the red sand and red walls of Mata Mata, the smallest camp in this park, right up against the Namibia border.

The Nossob Road

This route is said to be the best for finding spotted hyenas and, with a bit of luck, wild dogs at its southern and northern extremities.

From the confluence of the rivers the Nossob road veers north-

north-east, swings north some fifty kilometres further and then gradually turns westwards past Nossob camp to Union's End 245 kilometres distant.

It begins in the riverbed and wanders back and forth between the white concrete beacons marking the Botswana-South Africa border, sometimes on the east bank, sometimes in the middle, mostly on the west.

The middle stretches make it an exceedingly lively road to travel in wet weather. The Nossob's banks, like the Auob's become ensnaring mud but the clay surface in the bed turns into a vehicular skating rink. Many are the visitors the rangers have had to tow out with their four-wheel-drive trucks.

For the first fifteen kilometres from Twee Rivieren to the Leeuwdril waterpoint the Nossob road follows a wide stretch of river with a high west bank and an east bank so shallow it nearly disappears in places.

There are few trees, mostly scattered on the east side, including a large one beside the road 7,9 kilometres from Twee Rivieren where scaffolding has been erected for close-up study of sociable weavers.

Leeuwdril, as the name implies, is popular with lions and a good place to find them. Exasperatingly, they are probably there more often than they are seen because they laze in the shade of bushes just over the crests of the river banks.

Past Leeuwdril the river narrows and there are more trees. At the end of each of the next three kilometres there is a grey camelthorn tree nearby containing a large sociable weaver nest.

Rooiputs, 8,6 kilometres on, is notable because it has the usual fibreglass water tank but no windpump. Water is drawn from the borehole here by a solar-powered pump – low-profile devices that will eventually replace all the unsightly windpump derricks.

On the Botswana bank of the river, just before Rooiputs, the ruins of a stone house can be seen. It was occupied by desert 'farmers' – mainly poachers – until they were resettled when the Botswana side of the park was proclaimed.

One of the prettier places in the park is Kijkij, thirteen and a half kilometres beyond Rooiputs. There the river narrows and the upstream is a view of a green glade of trees, refreshing after the bleak vista of the sand and calcrete.

Just past the Kijkij windpump and tank on the road's west side are two large hillocks of sand bulldozed from a pit between them. A short side road twists around and over them and from its dizzy height of about three metres there are attractive views upstream and down.

Behind the sand hump furthest from the road is a row of thorn trees. Once parked there, it is possible to see a wide variety of birds

Top right: Patience will reveal this plump little rodent right in the camps. The Brant's whistling rat signals its presence with a short, sharp wolf whistle and dives into its hole when approached, but is soon overcome by curiosity.
Clem Haagner – ABPL.

Centre: For much of the year and especially in summer, Kalahari evenings are enlivened by a chorus of sharp clicks like small stones being struck together. These are the territorial calls of the barking gecko, appropriately named Ptenopus garrulus. Hundreds live in holes in the sands of the camps but they are shy and difficult to see, except by waiting patiently with a torch.
Anthony Bannister – ABPL.

Bottom left: A red-crested korhaan displaying its decolletage. These birds have the odd habit of rocketing into the sky then falling as if shot.
Lorna Stanton – ABPL.

Bottom right: Not easy to see except at night by torchlight is the very common springhare, a big rodent which moves like a kangaroo on its large hind legs. Its eyes reflect a bright red.
Anthony Bannister – ABPL.

foraging for food in the trees and in the sand and 'klitsgras', *Setaria verticullata*, under them, while at the same time keeping an eye on all points around. A considerable variety of animals seems to favour the water about a hundred metres away including bat-eared fox, porcupine, gemsbok, wildebeest, springbok and lion.

From Kijkij north to Dikbaardskolk there are the Melkvlei, Gunong, Kransbrak, Jan se Draai and Kameelsleep waterpoints with little to choose between them but all worth pausing at briefly to study the scene.

At Dikbaardskolk there is the usual camelthorn-shaded picnic site with concrete furniture and here the dune road from the Auob River comes sweeping down into the Nossob over a high sandy bank.

From there on past Cheleka to Kaspersdraai is a repetition of scenery but at Kaspersdraai begins a feature of interest to bird enthusiasts: raptor nests.

They are found all over the park but for some reason there is a profusion of them in this stretch of the Nossob River to north of Nossob camp – large, dark, untidy bundles of twigs and branches about the size of the average laundry basket.

Some cling precariously on the thin branches right on top of big camelthorn trees, others just inside the tree canopies, some to forks in the middle of the trees. These latter are the nests of bateleur eagles, those right on top usually of vultures or martial eagles and the others might be the homes of any of several of the larger raptors.

Not all of these residences are in use. Raptors tend to have two or more nests and switch between them from year to year – probably to allow the annual build-up of lice and other parasites in them to die off for a season.

It is well worth parking in a shady spot at the roadside, (*not* off it – it is too easy to get stuck) to watch these nests for a while and see what comes and goes. Vulture nests are easier to identify - the occupant is often perched right upon or close to it, projecting from the treetop like a gargoyle.

Fifteen kilometres north of Kaspersdraai a fork to the right leads into a road rather more interesting than the main road. It is Marie's Loop and follows the river closely for eleven kilometres, passing Marie se Gat waterpoint and Rooikop, a thick red dune topped by a surveyor's beacon.

It runs through uncharacteristically non-desert country, an almost temperate zone with copious trees and bush and attractive scenery, until it rejoins the main road.

From there it is a few minutes' drive past the Haagner borehole to the Nossob camp sprawled on a long sandy slope rising west of the riverbank.

The large Steppe eagle gets its name from the steppes of Russia. It migrates from there and eastern Europe. In spite of its size and fierce appearance, its favourite food is flying ants – the alates of termites.
Clem Haagner – ABPL.

The 130-kilometre trip from Nossob camp to Union's End is necessarily rather tedious because it must be done there and back in a day at the forty kilometres per hour speed limit. There is no camp at Union's End, nothing except one of the remotest picnic places in the world.

From Nossob camp north, the park undergoes a significant change of personality. The red and orange dunes steadily give way to long sandy plains spreading far and wide. They are thinly speckled with scrub and solitary trees stand sentry.

Horizons seem very distant. There is a sense of great emptiness, of great loneliness, and when the sun's heat drenches down in the middle of the day, of nowhere to escape to.

This is a quite different country – in fact most of the Kalahari is like this, scrub savannah and bush, all of it dry.

The plains spread wider and flatter on the way north past Lekkerwater, Cubitje Quap, Kwang, Bedinkt and Langklaas and all the way there are trees in the riverbed with the dark bulk of raptor nests in many of them.

The same animals are here but they seem fewer and occasionally a herd of eland glides like royalty across the sand.

Past Kousant the Nossob's bed spreads so wide between its banks it almost becomes part of the desert plains, hardly discernible as a river.

A handsome if rather unkempt bird sometimes confused with the Steppe eagle, the tawny eagle will as readily scavenge at carcasses, rob other birds and eat flying termites as hunt for itself. Here it is preening.
Phillip Richardson – ABPL.

A red-necked falcon makes a meal of a laughing dove.
Clem Haagner – ABPL.

Next stop is the rather desolate picnic place at Grootbrak about half way between Nossob camp and Union's End. Anyone using the toilets there might notice that the polythene plastic thrones are scratched and scarred. This was the handiwork (or fangwork) of some bored lions that ripped them out, chewed them and played ball with them in the sand. No visitors were about at the time.

Between Grootbrak and Koedoebos the opposite bank all but disappears in the distance across a broad and dead flat plain. Its surface of dry and cracked mud carries a stubble of brittle bushes.

It is the fossil delta where the Polentswa River flowed from the east into the Nossob many centuries ago, perhaps thousands of years. Some distance up its course in Botswana, beyond reach of visitors, is the dismal grave of an adventurer who challenged the Kalahari and lost, Hans Schwabe.

Past Koedoebos and Lijersdraai there are the sweetwater boreholes at Kannaguass and Grootkolk so favoured by vultures. Steadily increasing bush softens the harsh bareness of the plains here.

The bush is fairly prolific for the Kalahari at Union's End, where a very old road sign to towns in Namibia indicates that this was once a through route. Now the way is barred by an international border fence.

Between Kamqua on the Auob and Dikbaardskolk on the Nossob are fifty-five kilometres of up and down monotony of dune after dune after orange dune, or so it seems.

Built specifically to give people a view of the dune country barely visible from the riverbed roads, it is indeed monotonous if travelled non-stop at the speed limit.

The scenery is repetitively uniform: up one side of a dune, down the next, across a shallow valley, up the next dune ... to the point of making delicate stomachs seasick.

Every dune, valley, patch of scrub and blade of grass looks like the last one. Here and there a tree or maybe a little cluster of trees appears suddenly with all the impact of finding a skyscraper. There are three waterpoints, at Eland in the east, Vaalpan in the west and in the middle, Moravet. Boring? Definitely not for people with patience and sharp eyes.

If the road is travelled slowly with frequent stops it can be exceptionally rewarding, especially in the mornings before the day's heat peaks and from mid-afternoon (which unfortunately leaves little time to return to camp).

This is the best territory for seeing eland and here steenbok are likeliest to be found. Here too is the best chance of spotting a badger on the prowl with its attendant train of a jackal or two and a couple of pale chanting goshawks. Only in this environment can one find the soft, exquisitely woven nest of the Cape penduline tit, probably on a blackthorn tree.

Almost all the creatures found in the riverbeds appear here, according to the season, grazing and other variables, though not in the concentrations generated by the riverbed waterpoints: gemsbok, wildebeest, hartebeest, springbok, jackal, hyena, lion, cheetah, wildcat and more.

Perhaps most striking about the dune country is its sense of absolute solitude when the breeze stills and the silence is total. Then the world is simplified to two stark elements, the red-orange sand all around and the cobalt-blue sky above.

For people who fear loneliness or open spaces it can be quite frightening. For others it is beauty consummated. In everybody it generates awed respect for those hardy characters who opened up this country and still live in it, though they can never tame it.

Things you Need to Know

The KGNP keeps a close eye on its guests – for their own good. Nobody is allowed to leave camp without having their destination recorded. Gatekeepers will not let people through without seeing their KGNP permits, which must be handed to camp offices for safe-keeping between trips.

This is not petty red tape. The park staff must at all times know where all visitors are.

When the gates close every evening the staff at each camp tally the permits handed in against the lists of who should be where. If someone has not arrived the rangers are alerted and if the person or persons are still missing by 10 p.m., a search is mounted.

Unless there is a valid reason such as mechanical failure, the late-comer risks being heavily fined.

Opening and closing times at both camps and the main entry gate change seasonally and are displayed at all camp offices. These are the times:

	Open	Close
January	06.00	19.30
February	06.30	19.30
March	06.30	19.00
April	07.00	18.30
May	07.00	18.00
June	07.30	18.00
July	07.30	18.00
August	07.00	18.30
September	06.30	18.30
October	06.00	19.00
November	05.30	19.30
December	05.30	19.30

Accommodation rates at the KGNP are revised on 1 April every year. Their range is being expanded upwards as the national parks expand their choice of accommodation to five-star level to cater for wealthy foreign tourists. It is not possible to give precise figures here.

However, as in all national parks the fees compare with hotels offering accommodation of similar calibre and camping is relatively cheap.

There are also a twenty-five per cent discount from 1 November to the end of February and special discounts for people over sixty-five.

CHAPTER TEN

Tips For Tourists

A family of ostriches out for a sedate afternoon stroll on the Auob road.
Anthony Bannister – ABPL.

Clothes

Except in winter – May to August – it can be taken for granted that the park will be hot by day and quite warm at night too, especially in mid-summer. But temperature fluctuations can be so extreme that, even in summer, nights may be unexpectedly cool.

Winter nights are often freezing and days are usually cool to warm although they can occasionally become hot.

The trick, therefore, is in summer to bring loose, lightweight, cool clothing. To protect you from sunburn you should wear long sleeves and collars that can be turned up. Choose pale colours to reflect the sunlight. And take along a jersey or jacket for the evenings.

In winter take the same kind of clothing plus plenty of warm things to wear over it – jerseys, warm jackets, woolly track suits, scarves, even gloves and long johns for the bitter nights – particularly if you are camping or caravanning and have to cook outdoors. The chill winds make it wise for women to wear slacks.

Take a hat – desert sun burns throughout the year. The floppy cloth kind is best.

Sandals are cool if you don't mind sand constantly filtering in. Casual footwear like running shoes or velskoens is more practical.

Laundry

Twee Rivieren and Nossob, but not Mata Mata, have laundry rooms and ironing areas with ironing boards in their ablution blocks. Electric irons are not available so if you insist on looking immaculate in the wild, bring your own iron.

The simplest solution is to make a deal with the helpful maids who houseclean the accommodation. They earn extra by doing laundry in their off-duty hours.

Health

First-aid care, including treatment for snakebite and scorpion stings, is available in all three camps but if full medical attention is needed, the nearest doctor is at Upington. In emergencies patients can be flown there.

For the treatment of ordinary cuts, bruises and headaches bring your own kit of sticking plasters, antiseptic ointment, anti-allergy pills and creams, aspirin and so on.

Make sure it includes enough effective sun-blocking cream. Even inside a car, faces can be burned by reflection from the bright sand.

Bring moisturising cream because the desert air is very dry.

More sensitive stomachs may be upset by the drinking water in the camps, which has to be processed to varying degrees because it contains a variety of minerals. One answer is to bring the appropriate pills; another is to stick to soft drinks, soda water or beer.

Sunglasses are a boon – even essential for people with sensitive eyes – because the glare from sand and sky is fierce.

Photography

The Kalahari Gemsbok National Park is a photographer's feast. So brilliant is its light, so open is its scenery, so varied are its moods, so available are birds and animals hard to find elsewhere, that many of the people whose photographs appear in this book return to the park year after year. It attracts amateurs and professionals from all over the world.

That does not mean, however, that taking pictures is easy. It requires the proper equipment and materials and, in particular, taking great care of the equipment because the conditions for cameras are harsh.

The casual photographers using cameras with fixed lenses or the more usual variety of medium-focus lenses up to about 200 mm will be frustrated by the tantalising long-range opportunities missed.

But there is more than enough within range to keep their shutters clicking. In the camps there is a host of creatures well inside the reach of such lenses: birds so tame they perch on taps or are attracted by crumbs, the jewel-like Bibron's geckos on chalet walls, ground squirrels, tree rats, yellow mongooses, scorpions ...

Along the roads most species can be found at some time or another, with patience, close enough for a 200 mm lens. Springbok, wildebeest, gemsbok and suricates are almost always available, as are the large and thus easily captured kori bustards and secretary birds.

Many waterpoints are so near the roads that an hour or two beside one in the morning or late afternoon can yield excellent shots of jackals, sandgrouse and many other smaller birds and, with luck, badgers, lions and hyenas as well as all kinds of buck.

For the really intent photographer, however, a 500 mm or, better still, 600 mm lens is a window to breathtaking opportunities. A 1 000 mm lens opens the window that much wider but aggravates the problems of quick handling, light factors and the heat distortion of images.

The KGNP is truly the place of the telescopic lens because of its uncluttered views that make accessible pictures at much longer distances than one generally finds in other parks.

For instance, in the bed of the Nossob River in particular, south and north of the Nossob camp, are many free-standing camelthorn trees with the nests of vultures, bateleur, martial and other eagles, and secretary birds. All but a few of the trees are beyond effective range of a 200 mm or 300 mm lens – a Big Bertha is needed to catch those intimate shots of a mother feeding its chick.

This holds true even at closer ranges when capturing small life like the sociable weavers and their uninvited tenants, the pygmy falcons (though a wide-angle might be needed to photograph the gigantic nest), the fork-tailed drongo with a cuckoo in its nest, and the mongoose with a snake.

Long telephoto lenses can lead to camera-shake. In the park one cannot get out of the car and mount camera and lens on a tripod, so the shooting has to be done through the car window.

One trick is to buy a bracket that clips on the edge of the windowglass and serves as a rest for the barrel of the big lens or is a screw-on mount. Simpler still is to make a small sandbag and drape this over the window edge as a lens rest. Then all you have to do to adjust the lens elevation is wind the window up or down.

Another suggestion: buy a couple of those wrist sweat-bands tennis players use and put them around the barrels of your lenses to prevent scratching and denting in use.

To get successful pictures you must plan ahead. Make sure you have the right film: so powerful is the light it need not be very high speed and you must be back in camp by dusk anyway, but bring some fast film for dark conditions. Check the batteries in the camera and light meter and take spares.

Make sure the camera body is thoroughly clean inside and out and clean your lenses at both ends. If you have gradation filters and know how to use them, bring them – they can make a significant difference to the tonality of pictures in these stark lighting conditions.

In summer bring a cold-bag big enough to store a six-pack and a freeze block which you can re-freeze every night – not for your beer but in which to keep your film safe from heat. Store film in a refrigerator by night – all chalets have them.

Be certain to bring a dust-blower – one of those little rubber squeeze bulbs with a nozzle for puffing dust off equipment – or a can of the compressed air which camera shops supply for the same purpose. Bring a camelhair brush, too, for getting into awkward corners after using the blower – but remember that brushing causes static electricity in the desert dryness which simply attracts more dust, so a final light touch with a damp brush tip will be necessary.

By all means bring the popular chamois leather – but do *NOT use it except to wipe off the camera or lens body!* Wiping lenses, viewfinder glass or mirrors with a chamois or cloth, however soft it might seem to you, is the surest way to scratch the surface. Keep the chamois or cloth slightly damp to avoid creating static electricity.

The dust is so powder fine that even if your lens looks clean, it almost certainly is not.

Dust is a major problem. It hangs in the air long after a vehicle has passed. The slightest breeze lifts and carries it. It necessitates extra special care of equipment.

Attach an ultra-violet or optically clear filter permanently to every lens. It is much cheaper than having to replace a dust-scratched lens.

It is easy enough to keep a fixed-lens camera, and some with zoom lenses, in closed cases when not taking pictures but this becomes limiting for those with a variety of interchangeable lenses and maybe more than one camera body.

For them the simplest solution is to keep the equipment covered with white and well-washed towels (preferably not cotton which tends to give off lint) when out of its cases. Put it on the car seat beside you. If this entails relegating your wife to the back seat, then store the equipment on the back seat and have her hand you the pieces as you need them.

Do not keep your gear on the car floor: apart from the higher dust hazard, it can be damaged by bumps and vibration.

Keep your equipment out of direct sunlight, even in cool weather. The sting of the sun from a clear desert sky is dangerous. It can turn the inside of a camera body into a mini-oven that curdles the emulsion on a film and it can warp the mounts of elements in lenses, especially in items with a black finish.

For the same reason *never* leave camera gear in a closed car or in the trunk.

Equipment should be carefully cleaned at the end of every day's use and stored in its cases until you are ready to use it again.

Finally, the art of taking good photographs is a highly individual talent. But all talents have two ingredients in common: one is such complete familiarity with equipment that using it is second nature;

The Park's western border is marked by a long, straight fence with an inspection track beside it. Here a young eland wanders along it seeking a way through during a time of bad drought. National Parks Board.

the other is the patience to anticipate and catch that animal or bird doing something extraordinary, not just standing there like a stuffed dummy in a museum.

Looking at Animals

Binoculars are an absolute must for visitors to the KGNP – and everything that is said about camera care applies equally to binoculars. A good pair is expensive and all too often they are treated as casually as a pair of gloves.

The kind of binoculars you take depends to a degree on what you wish to see; many people visit this park primarily to look at birds and everything else takes second place. But the long viewing distances mean that bird-watchers cannot depend entirely on the most popular size used in birding, about 8 X 50 (which means a magnification of eight with a front lens element 50 mm wide).

Ideally, visitors should bring two pairs of binoculars, one for viewing at close to medium range and the other for long range – be it looking at birds or animals.

Mine were a 7 X 35 Bushnell Birder and a 8-24 X 50 Bushnell zoom and they served well. The problem with the zoom, however, was that when hand-held and above 12 X magnification the slightest movement made the animal I looked at wobble, and at 24 X the mere throb of my wrist pulse made the entire scene heave wildly.

If you use binoculars of magnification greater than 12 X then use a rest, as with a telefoto lens.

One enthusiast in the KGNP was seen using a brass naval telescope about a metre long with a window-mounted support – surely the ideal for studying feather details at two hundred metres.

Acknowledgements

a book of this nature is never the exclusive product of one person; it is necessarily an amalgam by the author of the knowledge, skills and enthusiasm of many people. Much of the knowledge comes from the writings of authorities in their fields who are accredited in the bibliography, but the book would not have seen the light of day without additional support from many quarters.

Foremost among them is Doreen, my wife, an unflagging supporter who helped to gather the information, then used her expertise to assemble it into logical working order, thus making its committal to paper an easy and pleasant task.

The unstinting generosity of the Warden of the Kalahari Gemsbok National Park, Elias le Riche, and his charming wife, 'Doempie', was the watershed for success. The facts and stories in the book reflect his unmatched experience of the park and the Kalahari, and also the willing co-operation of his personnel.

The staff of the National Parks Board in Pretoria were most gracious, in particular Susan van der Merwe, Editor of the Board's *Custos* magazine, and Trevor Dearlove of the Board's Southern Parks division.

The book would not exist but for the unselfishness of Anthony Bannister and the many hours of work by Lesley Hay of the Anthony Bannister Photo Library (ABPL). His brilliant photographs and those of other outstanding contributors to his library made it come alive.

I am indebted to Wulf Haacke of the Transvaal Museum for the fascinating details he supplied about the German pursuit of the rebel, Simon Koper, into South Africa and Bechuanaland in 1908.

Far from least, thanks for her encouragement and photographs to that most extraordinary artist and outdoors enthusiast, Leigh Voigt.

Schagen
June, 1993

231

Bibliography

- *Mammals and Birds of the Kalahari National Gemsbok Park* – undated pamphlet issued by the National Parks Board.
- *Plants of the Kalahari,* by Dr P T van der Walt – undated pamphlet issued by the National Parks Board.
- *Kuruman Moffat Mission, A Historical Survey,* by Alan Butler. Kuruman Moffat Mission Trust, 1987.
- *Gee My 'n Man,* by Hannes Kloppers. Afrikaanse Pers Boekhandel, 1970.
- *Field Guide to the Snakes and Other Reptiles of Southern Africa,* by Bill Branch. Struik, 1988.
- *The Mammals of the Southern African Subregion,* by J D Skinner and R H N Smithers. University of Pretoria, 1990.
- *Birds of Southern Africa,* by Kenneth Newman. Macmillan SA (Pty) Ltd, 1983.
- *Robert's Birds of Southern Africa,* by Gordon Lindsay Maclean. John Voelcker Bird Book Fund, 1985.
- *Kalahari,* by Michael Main. Southern Book Publishers (Pty) Ltd, 1987.
- *Guide to the Kalahari Gemsbok National Park* by Gus Mills and Clem Haagner. Southern Book Publishers (Pty) Ltd, 1989.
- *The Land and Wildlife of Africa,* by Archie Carr. Time-Life International, 1968.
- *Trees of Southern Africa,* by Keith Coates Palgrave. Struik, 1984.
- *Custos,* Journal of the National Parks Board — Vol I Nos 3, 7, 8; Vol 2 Nos 2, 4, 5, 6, 8, 10, 11, 13; Vol 3 Nos 1, 3, 4, 7, 8, 9; Vol 4 Nos 4, 6, 9; Vol 5 Nos 3, 5, 6, 8; Vol 6 Nos 1, 5, 9; Vol 7 Nos 2, 6, 7, 8, 11, 12; Vol 8 Nos 4, 5, 6, 7; Vol 9 Nos 1, 4, 6, 12, 14; Vol 10 Nos 3, 4, 7; Vol 11 Nos 7, 8; Vol 12 Nos 3, 4, 8, 10; Vol 13 Nos 2, 3, 4; Vol 14 Nos 6, 8, 10; Vol 15 Nos 3, 6, 8.

Index